CRITICAL CHOICES!
Ethics, Science, and Technology

Just one world, let us not blow it
Just one planet, let us not pollute
Just one humanity, let us not starve it
Just one race, let us not discriminate

Chaitanya Kalevar

CRITICAL CHOICES!
Ethics, Science, and Technology

Edited by:
Henry Wiseman
Jokelee Vanderkop
Jorge Nef
The University of Guelph

THOMPSON EDUCATIONAL PUBLISHING, INC.
Toronto

Additional copies of this publication may be obtained from:
        Thompson Educational Publishing, Inc.
        11 Briarcroft Road, Toronto
        Ontario, Canada M6S 1H3
        Telephone (416) 766-2763 Fax (416) 766-0398
Please write for a full catalogue of publications.

Canadian Cataloguing in Publication Data

Critical choices! : ethics, science, and technology

(Ethics and technology)
Papers presented at a conference held at the University of Guelph, Oct. 1989.
ISBN 1-55077-001-2

1. Technology - Moral and ethical aspects - Congresses. 2. Science - Moral and ethical aspects - Congresses. I. Wiseman, Henry. II. Nef, J. (Jorge). III. Vanderkop, J. (Jokelee). IV. Series.

BJ59.C74 1990   170   C90-094917-1

ISBN 1-55077-001-2
Printed in Canada.
1 2 3 4 5 6   95 94 93 92 91

Table of Contents

Acknowledgements

The issues discussed in this volume speak of the substance and critical relevance of the debate. But they cannot adequately reflect the intellectual and political vibrancy of the conference itself. The more than 800 participants from many parts of the world confirmed in active dialogue and argument the timeliness and importance of the issues. To all, therefore, we owe a great debt for their individual and collective knowledge and enthusiasm. Our deepest appreciation is also extended to the University School of Continuing Education of the University of Guelph and particularly to Virginia Grey, Chair, Education Division and Rick Nigol, Assistant Chair, Education Division for their exemplary patience, devotion and organization, so critical to the success of the conference.

Henry Wiseman
Conference Chair

About the Editors

Henry Wiseman is Professor of Political Studies at the University of Guelph and was Chair of the Conference, "Ethical Choices in the Age of Pervasive Technology," at the University of Guelph, October 25–29, 1989. He was one of the editors of the pre-conference publication, *Ethics and Technology: Ethical Choices in the Age of Pervasive Technology*. (Toronto: Thompson Educational Publishing, Inc., 1989). Dr. Wiseman was also co-chairman of the conference on "International Peace and Security" in 1983 held at the University of Guelph in cooperation with Prime Minister Trudeau's Peace Initiative Task Force. He is a Visiting Scholar at the Ontario Institute for Studies in Education, Toronto and was Special Advisor on Disarmament, Canadian Mission to the United Nations in 1983. Dr. Wiseman has written and edited books and articles on peace-keeping and conflict resolution, including *Peacekeeping: Appraisals and Proposals* (ed.) (New York: Pergamon, 1983); *From Rhodesia to Zimbabwe: the Politics of Transition* (New York: Pergamon, 1982) (with A.M. Taylor). He was director of special conferences on peacekeeping and conflict resolution and a lectures and symposia participant from 1970 to 1984 in various centres in Canada, the United States, Mexico, Venezuela, Nigeria, Cameroun, Rhodesia, England and continental Europe.

Jokelee Vanderkop received her M.A. degree from the Department of Political Studies at the University of Guelph in 1986 in part on the basis of a thesis entitled: "The State of Canadian Foreign Aid." She played a key role in the organization of the "Ethics and Technology" conference at Guelph and edited the pre-conference publication, *Ethics and Technology: Ethical Choices in the Age of Pervasive Technology* along with Jorge Nef and Henry Wiseman. She has published articles in *Konflicternes Verden*, the *Canadian Journal of Development Studies*, *North/South*, and in *The World Food Crisis: Food Security in Comparative Perspective*, (ed.) J.I.Hans Bakker (Toronto: Canadian Scholars' Press Inc., 1990). She has worked as an editor and translator. She works as editor/producer of *Worldscape*, an International Development periodical put out by the Centre for International Programs, University of Guelph, and is currently an instructor at a secondary school in Wellington County, Ontario.

Jorge Nef is Professor of Political Studies at the University of Guelph. He has taught at the University of Chile and the University of Santa Barbara, and has been a Visiting Professor at various Canadian universities. His research is concentrated on the Latin American region with interests in development issues, food security, terrorism, comparative public administration and authoritarian regimes. Between 1981 and 1983 he was President of the Canadian Association of Latin American and Caribbean Studies. His articles have appeared in *Latin American Perspectives, Interamerican Review, North/South, The Canadian Journal of Development Studies, Latin American Research Review, The Indian Journal of Public Administration, Public Administration and Development, Etudes Internationales, Relaciones Internacionales, Revista Centroamerican de Administracion Publica, The Indian Journal of Political Science, International Perspectives* and others. In addition, Dr. Nef has worked as a consultant with the Pan-American Health Organization and the International Development Research Centre.

The Editors

Ethics and Technology: Across the Great Divide

It is almost a truism that a world divided into antagonistic compartments cannot resolve the foremost problems of our time. It cannot cope with ecological degradation, the maintenance of peace and the abysmal disparities between rich and poor. Historically, antagonism has been depicted in Western civilization as the foundation of competition and the motivation for innovation, in the last analysis bringing about the development of society. The cost of this competitive process, rooted in the ethos of what C.B. MacPherson has called "possessive individualism" has been perceived as one which the strongest and the fittest—the industrial countries, the entrepreneur or the pioneer—could either bear or transfer somewhere else. Today, however, this antagonistic style of development, while still able to unleash creative forces, has become the agent of ever increasing, unbearable human and ecological burdens.

Competitors are driven by various motives such as ambition, knowledge, technique and power, and also, in theory at least, by a system of ethical principles which are made compatible with these motives. Some competitors "succeed," thus contributing to what is referred to as "progress;" their accomplishments accrue to development over time. Others "fail" and are cast into the dustbin of history. What survives is knowledge, techniques, and—in the case of literate societies—inscribed records. Over the long-run, however, the most ostensible element which seems to stand the winds of time is the technical. As in an archaeological excavation, what strikes us first are the artifacts—products of craft and technology. The most powerful perception is the artistry, the technique and the utility of the artifact, while the image of the society, which produced the artifact as such, is often clouded in mystery. The most difficult aspects to determine in an archaeological dig are the patterns of life, the feelings and thoughts, which can reveal to us the guiding ethical principles of the culture whose artifacts we uncover. Thus, our image of history tends to be that of an archaeological museum: lifeless and static and presided over by physical objects, similar to those of the natural world.

This metaphor is quite applicable to our own time, one in which the artifact predominates without memory; it stands alone as the most evident display of "reality," overshadowing life itself. Technology clearly becomes the symbol of, and synonymous with, "progress," "evolution" or "development" while ethical principles are relegated to the world of abstractions. From this optic we often perceive the world as divided between two poles, or as two distinct cultures. One is "real," practical and concrete—the "real world" of technology. This is the realm of "objective" scientists, engineers, technologists, industrialists and financiers: those who produce and use the technique—and who are, therefore, the instruments of progress. The other world is "subjective," theoretical and abstract—the "ethereal world" of ethical principles. In terms of social actors, this is the realm of those who contemplate "lofty" ethical principles: theologians, philosophers, or academics. The chasm between these two worlds has widened through political alignments of policy-makers, political parties, interest groups, non-governmental organizations, and the public at large. This seemingly unbridgeable chasm has become a cultural crisis.

In the face of the gravity of ecological degradation, the threat of annihilation through war, and the destructive disparity between rich and poor, we are compelled to seriously reassess the meaning of progress. We must attempt to rediscover and refine the essential link between ethics and technology. It can no longer be left to chance and the competitive process alone. The process needs a purpose. This linkage is not just an intellectual exercise. On the contrary, it is central to the most pressing and practical issues of our times: global survival, sustainability of resources, economic efficiency and productivity, social equity, justice and well-being, political liberty and order, intellectual enlightenment and the accessibility of knowledge.

Definitional Interpretation

Before entering into a description and elaboration about the rationale, structure, and content of this book, we think it necessary to discuss our interpretation of the terms "ethics" and "technology." Needless to say, this is not an easy task, since these are terms pregnant with ambiguities which reflect cultural biases or the rationalization of individual interests. Nevertheless, our description will, at least, offer guidance to the historical and philosophical understanding of the dynamic and ever-changing relationships between these concepts.

By "ethics" we mean the series of basic processes and principles whereby social systems devise common base values and grounds for individual and collective behaviour. It is, in a certain way, the fundamental code, or a society's compendium, of "prime directives." It involves as well "overriding commands" (both "do's" and "don'ts"), which make up the foundational "software package" of that society. Such "directives" and "commands" make up the inner and outer limits of what is socially acceptable and desirable. Some of these are grounded on religious belief and tradition, others on a calculation of interests, reason, and logic, while still others are rooted in personal loyalty and leadership appeal. More often than not, however, they are a combination or an uneasy amalgam of all of the above. No ethical system is, or could be, completely rational, though it can be subject to rational and systematic study. Nor is such a system truly universal, except in the most abstract sense. On the contrary, the closer the internal homogeneity and interaction within a group, the greater the propensity to develop distinct sets of values, often discordant with those of exogenous groups. Conversely, the greater the external interaction and diffusion of ideas, the greater the likelihood that what were once internal values and norms become "universalized." In this sense, it is not uncommon that the very term "ethical principles" could be used as a cloak for the inner contradiction between values and behaviour, or as a plausible mask for sheer hypocrisy. This inner contradiction between ethical principles and actual behaviour (mores) is similar to the chasm that has evolved between social ethical "norms" and technological "reality." Unfortunately, ethical norms have been for too long ex-post facto rationalizations, or worse, corrupted and ignored. As Henry Margenau argued:

> Ethics is a matter of concern to us largely because of its failures; science is the object of admiration because of its successes. But ethics, too, has a working methodology which is arresting in view of its successes and deserves the same sort of painstaking positive analysis science has been getting ... [Most] accounts of ethics dwell upon its *unsolved* problems, upon the reasons why it is not and cannot be as authoritative,

as cogent in its appeals to men as is science; upon its lack of uniformity, its so-called relativity; upon the conflicts it is unable to resolve; upon its helplessness without religion. Rarely is there an acknowledgment today of the patent fact that human societies would be impossible except for the order and uniformities ethics has indeed achieved, or of the usefulness of ethics as that singular accomplishment which elevates man above nature and thereby enables him to develop such disciplines as science.

Social organizations, however, are—and will always be—purposeful and bound together by norms, rules and values; even when these are implicit, contradictory and perhaps dysfunctional. Human agency exists on the coalescence provided by its ethical "glue." These ethical bonds which maintain the cohesion of smaller human societies are even more dramatically needed in the complex global village. Global interdependence will surely make the world more dangerous and unstable without the commensurate development of an explicit global code of ethics. This code entails a real, valid and effective consensus on fundamental "do's" and "don'ts," not just the creation of formal legal norms. Trans-cultural commonalities do exist and are evolving, though often distorted by apparently different labels. They are increasingly, albeit embryonically, found in various emerging international regimes in trade, finance, labour, human rights and in the storage and transmission of information, to mention just a few. Even in the conduct of inter-state relations—once considered the absolute purview of the "national interest"—global codes of ethics and conventions are beginning to emerge. As our world shrinks and—whether we like or not—we move towards a form of global citizenship, the necessities of common existence will equally require the development of a common ethical base.

Conceptual Framework

For the sake of systematization, we could distinguish three analytically different levels of ethical directives in a culture.

A) The first and most foundational is the *axiology* or the more general and abstract value system itself. It is composed by the basic value algorithm—or value scale—both at the individual and at the modal or aggregate level. If we use, for example Lasswell's eight-value categories (wealth, knowledge, power, skill, well-being, affection, respect and rectitude), and include religion and spirituality, an individual or a society will possess a fundamental axiological profile which, while subject to change over time, defines what people perceive to be the most desirable combination of core values.

B) The second level is that of *teleologies*, or the desired state of future social organization structured around those values which people want to arrive at. The notion of future—or ideal point of arrival or objective—is central to the notion of a teleology. It involves a more concrete "model" of a social order to be achieved, no matter how narrowly defined. Teleologies, as visions of the future, are more "graphic" or "pictorial" than the underlying axiologies, yet they are fundamentally ideological. Taking an example from Lasswell's analysis mentioned above, we could find a correspondence of a value system which puts a premium on well-being and a teleology defined as "health" (i.e. the Alma Alta declaration of the WHO, "Health for everybody in the year 2000").

C) The third level is that of *deontologies*: the means, processes, techniques or instruments which carry with them the ways of accomplishing and/or maximizing both a value and a particular vision or teleology. Teleologies often carry an implicit, piecemeal and fragmentary set of ethical (or more specifically, moral) principles. These involve an "ought to be" component inserted in a social practice and a commitment to accomplish certain goals which are assumed to be socially desirable. Professions, technologies and techniques are eminently deontological, as could be observed of Medicine, Engineering, Pedagogy, Management, Law, Social Work, and certainly of the complex group of activities which encompass development practices. It is at the level of deontologies that an ethical system practically penetrates, intersects and overlaps with the realm of technologies and practices.

As for technology, the term refers to a society's matrix of know-how for problem-solving. It includes: a) "material" artifacts, tools and instruments; b) the social organization of labour for the operation of such material objects and, c) more "intangible" components such as knowledge, skills, experiences and practices for the reproduction and innovation of techniques. For instance, a television set is a material or "gadget" technology while the organization, membership and programming are a social technology. From this perspective, a technology is much more than the material aspects of civilization. It involves as well the latter's "cultural software"—the knowledge, codes and institutional structures which are used to manage, manipulate or transform people or things, including here the social practices, mores, and ethical codes extant in the culture. Although there is a common tendency for most of us to separate technology from the realm of culture and treat it as if it were in the domain of natural phenomena subject to "objective" laws and devoid of normative connotation, technology is a human phenomenon. It is a human creation, having effects on humans—as well as on the physical world—and therefore is subject to human scrutiny and valuation.

It is only in the cultural milieu of the XIXth and XXth centuries that the aesthetic, economic, and social principles of modernism—fuelled by the astonishing velocity of change—provided a construction of reality separating "technology" from "culture" and "facts" from "values." Nowhere is this tendency more patent than in Scientific Management and its claim to social engineering. While in the so-called "primitive" (and mistakenly characterized as "simple") societies there was a practical fusion between the instrumental and the teleological, in the so-called "modern" societies these are separated. "Objective," scientific, and technological positivism have gained preeminence over "subjectivity," metaphysics and intuition.

Thus came the creation of the great divide. It was enlarged by institutionalization, growing specialization, professionalization and atomization of the process of learning. In this exponential expansion of segmented "know-how" and "know-why," most ethical questions were soon relegated to the level of the unimportant. From there, under the inexorable logic of positivism, they increasingly moved to the realm of unmeasurable epiphenomena, nuisance, or worse, the twilight zone of the unquestionable.

The great divide can be bridged. This bridge, however, will require a great deal of soul searching—a reflection on the meaning and substance of reality, and a liberation from myopic beliefs about singular or exclusive factors of historical development. Above all, it will require an understanding of the processes of social change to enable the world to manage the fundamental transformations taking place today. There is too much ground to cover, much more than can be encompassed in a single volume. Yet everyone who has thought about these issues in an interested and concerned manner will have a particular point of view, perhaps compatible or perhaps in contradiction with the views of others. Yet, as we have argued, constructive approaches and possible solutions to the problems which face us require not only a common appreciation of the interaction between culture and technology, but also an honest willingness coupled with a modicum of humility to search out, discover, re-discover, or invent the cardinal principles that could be universally applied to the problems of the human ecological and resource problems of the global village.

Though necessary, that will be a very difficult course to chart, and an equally difficult course to navigate. The initial steps, we believe, are an understanding of the issues, and a corresponding relationship or schism between ethics and technology in the fundamental areas of global concern.

This is the challenge to which our endeavours have been directed; it is a challenge, recognized in one way or another, in most parts of the world. But how to proceed is the difficult question. We have brought together the often contradictory perceptions of various groups in society as well as experts on a broad range (practitioner, professional, scientific and philosophical) of endeavours related to technology. Our aim has been to provide an intellectual space to allow them to express and explore their own actually-existing teleologies, knowledge, techniques and competing interests in search of ethical principles which can provide guidelines for the resolution of some of the most pressing issues of our times. The conference, "Ethical Choices in an Age of Pervasive Technology" was the forum to initiate a dialogue. It was also a vehicle to set general parameters and start examining the overall relations between ethics and technology.

The panorama of areas covered, as related to specific workshops, were agriculture and food, animal husbandry, arts media and culture, communications and computers, development, economics, education, energy, environment, health, industry, labour, law, peace and security, and research administration.

In order not to isolate the very important issues of women and youth, these matters were treated within the existing workshops. In fact, each workshop, irrespective of its title, format, or schedule was forced to examine related issues discussed in the other workshops and this indeed was the intent of the conference organizers. This was a very ambitious undertaking; yet how else to prepare the ground for a universal dialogue for the future of our global village?

What follows therefore, are the articles which examine the basic tenets of fourteen areas covered in the workshops. The first sector begins with an examination of the increasingly complex interaction of a multitude of factors affecting the globe, such as population, food, resources, environment, ecology and consequences of exponential growth by Alexander King. There follows an historical appreciation of the relationship or separation of ethics and technology by William MacNeill who states that modern bureaucracy promotes technological revolution; a culturally oriented philosophical analysis of these matters by Paul Durbin who lists twelve major problem areas that society must contend with today as a result of our technological society; a scientific perspective by Geraldine Kenney-Wallace on the interface between technologies and human response; an economist's perspective by John Kenneth Galbraith who points out that pragmatic thinking needs to replace ideological attitudes to capitalism and socialism; an examination of the developmental, environmental, and ecological factors by Jim MacNeill and Digby McLaren with both arguing for the necessity to slow down growth and live in balance with the environment in order for development to be sustainable; the impact of technology on the ethics of war and peace by Richard Falk requiring a fundamental shift in our outlook from one of conflict based on fear and greed to a hope/need axis based on participation and cooperation; how the Third World views these issues, and the related burden of cost and consequences of development in relation to the environment by Shimwaayi Muntemba; the critical industrial perspective by James Stewart who doesn't deny that profitability largely determines business decisions but counters that business fills those demands set forth by the public; the related responses of labour by Shirley Carr; a philosophical values perspective by Archie Graham outlining the need for a techno-ecological realism, and finally, a call for everyone in society to bring ethics into the practical realm of daily existence by Carol Anne Letheren.

All the writers are well recognized for their knowledge and proficiency in their various fields. But even so, we cannot be sure whether significant areas were treated too lightly or perhaps ignored. For that reason, the edited proceedings of a diverse panel of experts and participants' responses are also included.

The second major section of the volume contains the analysis of fourteen workshops. Allan Thomas, the head rapporteur, follows with his own commentary on the workshop reports. The workshops addressed some of the most significant issues dealing with the impact of technologies on ethics and social behaviour. Original papers were presented in the workshops. The rapporteurs provided frequent updates of the material and have written summary reports. The editors have attributed authorship as appropriate, but have in some cases taken liberties in the interest of clarity and consistency, and have themselves authored some reports.

What comes out strongly in these workshops, despite differences and antagonisms, is the overall recognition that ethical considerations must become an integrated part of the decision-making process as it affects society as a whole. To do this, participation, cooperation, dissemination of information and education between specialized interest groups, the public, government and non-governmental organizations, both nationally and internationally, are a must. There was also consensus on the fact that technologies are value-laden. The need to consider new technologies in a socio-cultural and ecological context is not in dispute either. Where the problem arises is in how to proceed. There tends to be a polarization between those who favour reform and technological development within the existing socio-political framework and those who call for a radical rethinking and restructuring of the very scientific, technological system. This includes a reassessment of the "us" and "them" and a new definition of "we" entailing a willingness to sacrifice. In either case, the axiology, or the more abstract value system referred to earlier, and "who gets what, when and how," must be attuned to a new global environment, where growth is no longer the optimal value, if we are to endure as a species. We have the means and techniques yet we have not delved into the types of new technologies that could assist us in this endeavour. It is the application of these new technologies and ethical considerations which will create a future wherein the cultural axiologies, teleologies and deontologies will balance with the constraints and opportunities of the physical world.

The Editors

Top: **Ben Johnson**, Olympic Sprinter; **Carol Anne Letheren**, (Canadian) Chef de Mission, Seoul Korea Olympics; **Henry Wiseman**, Conference Chair.
Bottom: **John Kenneth Galbraith**, Paul M. Warburg Professor of Economics Emeritus, Harvard University.

Right: **Geraldine Kenney-Wallace**, Former Chair, Science Council of Canada; **Digby McLaren**, Former President of the Royal Society of Canada.

Below: **Ursula Franklin**, University Professor Emeritus, University of Toronto; **The Honourable William Winegard**, Minister of State, Science and Technology; **Alan Thomas**, Professor of Adult Education, Ontario Institute for Studies in Education; **Henry Wiseman**, Conference Chair.

Left: **Alexander King**, President, Club of Rome.
Right: **Jokelee Vanderkop**, Executive Assistant to Conference Chair; **Henry Wiseman**, University of Guelph and Conference Chair; **Daphne Taylor**, Executive Assistant to Conference Chair.

SETTING THE STAGE

Alexander King

Matching Social Values with Changing Technologies

To give the opening address at a meeting of this kind, covering so very many subjects, is a difficult task. On the one hand, I must not be overly general or superficial, and on the other, I dare not be too specific, considering the multitude of topics we have agreed to discuss. So I have decided to talk about the situation of the world as it is at the moment, and in particular speak on the question of the morality and immorality of our present behaviours both personal and certainly collective. I take as a cue for my speech, a quotation from Betaine's essays:

> He who does not provide new wisdom and new remedies for new problems, must expect new evils, for time is the great innovator.

The actual title of my talk is going to be the *Three Environments of Man*. It seems to me that all of us live our lives in three separate but linked environments. The first of these is the *outer environment*. We have talked about the outer limits for some years: the environment of the world, the physical milieu in which the air, the water and the land are a subject of great concern because of what man has done to them. The second environment I call the *inner environment*. This is the social milieu: the places where people interact, the situation of marriage and the family, of relations within the community, within the nation and internationally. Finally, there is what I call the *innermost environment* which is the internal, secret life within each one of us. It is from here that stem our motivations of which we are aware spasmodically and in some cases only subconsciously. And it seems to me that there is a projected similarity between this environment and the way in which the world and nations are governed. We are dealing today with technology and ethics which comprises the outer world although, as I will try to indicate later, the connection between it and the other two environments is very close.

For many decades, we have essentially regarded the outer environment or nature as something to exploit. The bounties of nature—the air, water, land and other natural resources—the externalities or pre-goods of the economists, seemed infinite and were there for us to use. The purpose of science was originally to explore the secrets of nature, while technology has tended to develop an applicable order without any ill thought to exploit nature to human benefit or to the benefit of those who develop the technology. But we have come to a period where we are very unsure whether the bounty of nature is indefinite.

Economic growth remains a major consideration for all governments. Economic growth of course requires human ability, skill and cleverness, but also materials and energy which nature has to provide. But although governments expect to have economic growth increases all the time, it is clear that this exponential situation, like other exponential curves, has got to flatten out sometime. If global economic growth of five per cent per annum were to continue for a hundred years, it would require about 500 times the present use of resources and energy—not to mention wastes. That is clearly not possible. But how it will change? At this point in time, we are quite uncertain whether a qualitative change can be made and this makes most of us quite restless and somewhat uncomfortable about the situation.

One of the main causes of our concern about nature arises essentially from the greatly increased human activity that has taken place this century and continues. The totality of such human activity comes from two separate factors compounded. The first of these is the increase in the world population. Today, there are over 5 billion people. There will be six billion by the turn of the century, and ten to twelve billion by the middle of the next century at which time it is expected that the curve will flatten out. More important, however, than the population growth is the component of human consumption. The amount of goods and services we require have grown enormously since the beginning of the Industrial Revolution. Then, the standard of living of the average European country was much the same as that of an average developing country today. The disparities today in consumption between the average industrialized countries and the average underdeveloped countries is about 40: 1. In the extreme disparity of the rich and poor it is probably about 200: 1 while in some cases even very much more. The combined effects of population growth and consumption factors mean that we are placing great strains on nature, both in exploiting her resources and in getting rid of the wastes which come from our activities.

The situation concerning environmental problems has changed rather fundamentally in public and political appreciation in the last decade. Until recently, most of the environmental concerns were relatively local. They could be dealt with by individual countries, and in some cases regions, or even cities in isolation, at a cost of course but one that could be borne. But we are faced now with what could be termed *mega-pollutions* which are world-wide, global in character and cannot be solved by individual countries in isolation. They threaten the continuation of our societies on the planet by the very irreversibility of some of the damage. The four obvious ones are, of course, the spreading of toxic wastes throughout the world, acid rain, the ozone layer depletion and the greenhouse effect. The latter comes from carbon dioxide, this invisible pollutant which has always seemed in the past to be benevolent.

Although predictions are fraught with uncertainties, there is general consensus among meteorologists and climatologists that global warming results in more rain and snow thus producing possible increases in sea levels and its inevitable consequences. The chief contributor is the burning of fossil fuels, petroleum, natural gas and (non-fossil fuel) fire wood which is used as the domestic energy source of a very large population of this world. The Toronto Conference of 1988 put forward the idea that in order to prevent this heating up from taking place, it would be to necessary to reduce carbon dioxide emissions by about 20 per cent by the year 2005—a very radical action, and one that is probably impossible without a great deal of disruption of industry.

This raises the question whether or not economic growth, in the purely material sense, can continue much longer. A related question is the extent to which an economy driven by conspicuous consumption can continue with its wastes and other dysfunctions. A third fundamental question constitutes a problem of enormous proportions for those countries in the South plagued with hunger, in many cases overpopulation, disease, unemployment and poverty; how can their development, which is vitally necessary for a harmonious world, be continued? For instance, if we must decrease our burning of fossil fuels with a corresponding industrial impact, what then happens in relation to the industrialization of a country such as China which has enormous coal reserves? Here we have a nation with the biggest population in the world basing its industrial future on coal. Considering our own patterns of industrial development, have we in the West the right to say to China or any developing country that this is not ecologically sound? To do so would be politically disastrous, morally wrong unless we altered our path of development, and practically impossible. There are plenty of contradictions in the ecological equation which raise issues and very difficult dilemmas of human morality and human solidarity in relation to the future of life on this small planet.

Technology has been the driving force for economic growth. When I went to the OECD first about thirty years ago, the economists were not yet ready to accept that idea. Technology was regarded as something which was generated by the interaction of economic forces. This was true in part. But more and more, technology came to be regarded as an autonomous subject, one which was a major factor in industrial, agricultural and economic growth. Denis Gabor, one of the early members of the Club of Rome, the Nobel prize winner discoverer of holography, stated the situation very well. He said that our present civilization is built materially on an extraordinarily successful technology but is spiritually built on practically nothing. And this I think is behind many of our concerns at the moment.

When the industrial revolution came it gave, of course, great power to the human being, so much greater than the muscular power of men and animals. We are now through the micro electronics revolution, and are seeing this power being extended through machines that can remember and can think. Technology such as this, whether directly or indirectly, has altered the nature of society and changed the quality of life. Even more changes are likely to come about as we drift consciously, deliberately and accidentally into the post-industrial society.

Now that technology has begun to display its miracles and lead the North to its present prosperity and way of life, unwanted side effects have also begun to appear. In the late 1960s we had the student riots starting in Paris which spread to most of the industrialized countries. We had the first serious public reaction to the environmental deterioration, with many people beginning to feel alienated and wanting to leave behind the present kind of society. Even those with more conventional views felt that the quality of life was being affected. There was a period of disillusionment with science and technology which was of course greatly reinforced by fears of the nuclear holocaust and annihilation. But as a few more years passed, people became somewhat passive about these issues and more concerned with the general rise of unemployment in the world. Materialism and accumulation of capital became the natural strategy of survival. It was during this period that the Club of Rome was founded. It was actually established within the OECD which was the altar of economic growth. Some of us, however, including the Secretary General of the organization, felt that in pressing for more and more economic growth, governments were unable because of the short-time horizons to concern themselves with the socio-economic consequences of rapid growth. The result is a kind of "lopsided" society—a society driven by technology with excessive reliance on the fruits of technology, hell-bent on material gain, in which the spiritual or finer values are being lost or neglected.

If the present metamorphosis of society is to produce a truly human environment with equity and dignity for all people, it would seem necessary to complement the material success by giving greater attention to enriching and developing the non-material aspects of humanity. This entails the employment of the marvellous qualities of the human mind in gaining knowledge and insights on the nature of man and his behaviour, and in *creating* wisdom beyond the material civilization in which we live. I mention the creation of wisdom because there are very few signs that wisdom has increased very much at all over the last 5000 to 6000 years—information yes, knowledge yes, wisdom no. The notion that man does not live by bread alone ceases to be an oft-repeated sermon to become a present reality. A common concern today is that this growth-oriented lopsidedness should in fact be compensated by correspond-ing growth in the human spirit. Nearly all technology, from the first primitive tools, have added to man's physical capacity. The automobile gives us legs, the airplane gives us wings while the ICBM is an extended fist. But what about an extended heart or an extended mind?

This brings us to the difficult and relatively taboo questions of the innermost environment of both the individual and society. While knowledge and political action omit taking into consideration the innermost environment, we are essentially dealing with symptoms of a disease rather than understanding the disease itself.

Going back to the human aspect, I wanted just to mention that there are many unresolved areas of dichotomy relevant to the world scene which are manifested in many ways in different societies, different religious groups, and so forth. These are enduring questions. Their ethical importance varies enormously as does their value significance. I mentioned first the disparity between the rich and the poor. There is also discrimination against minorities, the absence or unequal dispensation of social justice and exaggerated, destructive and self-seeking rivalry between political parties. There are conflicts between religions, at times erupting into violence, despite the commonality in the search for the eternal verities and the similarities of concerns expressed in the sacred texts of the Vedas, the Ghita, the Bible and the Koran. There is the balancing of rights and duties, privilege and responsibility, discipline and license and the unresolved ambiguity between economic growth and quality of life. Other contradictions involve the difference between the caring community versus the impersonal, faceless welfare state; material needs and spiritual needs; lack of under-standing between the elites and the masses, between those who know and those who do not know; the separation between science and culture; the conflict between rationality and intuition. All these matters are relevant to the inner limits of society and have great impact upon, as well as being affected by, the inner most limits.

We ought here to say a little bit about social values. The word *value* is very ambiguous. The good, the true and the beautiful are absolute values although they may be interpreted differently in different regions so as to be hardly recognizable from one to the other as being the same. As frequently suggested in the West, the traditional system of values in societies is corroded even more by a devotion for material gain. This might be partly so but I am quite convinced that the values from the past have been contained within most of us. The problem is that we tend only to pay lip service to these inherent values rather than live up to them. This is exemplified by the double standards in the behaviour of many individuals, not to mention governments profess-ing their belief in peace and disarmament while profiting greatly from the sale of arms. Collectively, long-term national and global benefits are sacrificed for immediate gain. Individually, it expresses itself in personal behaviour such as credibility gaps between young and older generations, a lessening of faith in religion, and a generalized erosion in public trust and confidence.

Our value system requires a great deal of reconsideration in both individual and collective terms. I believe that human egoism is at the root of all our problems. This was the life force of the Victorians. It is something possessed by all organisms which strive to survive, to reproduce and to prosper. Indeed, it is the driving force of innovation, progress, prosperity, and ambition. But it is also the cradle of selfishness which in today's civilization translates into greed, antisocial behaviour, brutality, a lust for power, exploitation and dominance. Society strives to reconcile these aspects of egoism and strike a balance between individual enterprise and social behaviour. This is not an easy task and requires constant effort. In many ways this situation seems to be biological. The negative properties of the human, such as those mentioned above, were in fact positive qualities in the early stages of evolution. They led to man becoming the conqueror of nature and the less strong, though not necessarily less wise, of the human race. In the process, these latter properties pitted individual against individual, nation against nation. However, there is no place for them in the next stage of human development in which we need to build a wisdom which not only ensures the sustainability of the entire species but also promotes a higher order of values at the level of societies and entire states.

To do this, we must look for a new approach. Could it be based perhaps on an enlightened common self interest? Could we establish a sense of global solidarity centred on the recognition that we are all destined to live and die on this one small planet? Can we extend our ego to care for intergenerational problems—the future of our children and grandchildren perhaps even a little longer? Could these things help? I think so. But can they happen? This is much more doubtful. An appreciation, an in-depth understanding by everyone of the nature of the problems we face, of the consequences of not facing them is a necessary first step. We should be aware of the enormous costs of postponing action. And here, of course, we come to the need for education.

Education is at the bottom of all this. Yet, education systems in most countries are already outdated. Teachers teach what their teachers taught them and often do not keep abreast of change. This was understandable in an era of less rapid change. Today it means being prepared to live in a world in which the quality of life is rapidly deteriorating and the existence of the planet is in jeopardy. The Club of Rome Report entitled, *No Limits To Learning* stressed these problems and particularly the need to make education participative in the sense of dynamics between teachers and pupils. Even more important perhaps, is the need to gear education to anticipate future needs, prospects and limitations for the economy, society and personal life. It is an urgent and enormous task—a task which universities for one, as well as governments, industry and individuals, must undertake. Universities, in particular, are well placed. Multidisciplinary action in the social sciences, natural sciences, agriculture and engineering could come together in relation to the major world problems. The notion of thinking globally and acting locally is becoming more and more important. The task is difficult but also far more challenging than anything that has ever been done. The time to start is now.

Dr. Alexander King is President of the Club of Rome.

William McNeill

Technological Lessons of History Speak to the Future

Dr. Wiseman is absolutely correct. I come before you as an imposter because the task that I accepted when he wrote to me is plainly impossible. He asked me, and I read this literally, "to speak about the impact of technologies," {in the plural}, "throughout history on agriculture, industry, social values and lifestyles, with an emphasis on key transitions," and this, in thirty minutes. Thirty minutes to speak of the impact of technologies throughout history is more than anyone could undertake even with emphasis on key stages of transition. I suppose you were thinking of the rise of agriculture and that of industry when you wrote those vast words. That sort of simple typology seems to me not very satisfying, but of course, the challenge of your invitation is to do something other, and in short enough compass to fit into the time you afford.

It is true that the standard eras, that is hunting and gathering, followed by food production, agriculture and then industrialization, are important landmarks in history. Each of these transitions carried with it an appropriate adjustment of institutions, attitudes and behaviour and the discipline of the farmer saving his seed rather than eating it, because he had to save it to plant next year. This was so utterly alien to the timelessness of hunters and gatherers and the discipline of the factory worker who has a factory whistle to call him to work and an assembly line to keep his fingers busy and so very different from the self-regulation of the craftsman or the farmer of the ex-cultural era.

You can look at this really as a series of progressive enslavements—tighter constraints upon human nature, upon human impulses, on natural and inherited aptitudes. Civilization, in other words, becomes a disease, hunting and gathering was the Eden from which our ancestors were exiled because their numbers became too great to sustain them by that mode of life. All the same, I feel that this is so general and disguises so many local qualitative differences that it is not very helpful. It doesn't carry one very far. The different styles of agriculture, the difference between rice paddy cultivation versus the open fields of medieval Europe for example; the enormous differences between iron and steel, mining or textile industries in the industrial era are vast. Moreover, factories were not statistically the most important locus of human activity even in what we call the industrialized age. Transport and services always outnumbered other industrial activities, even in the cities, and then you have to count the whole rural population, the peasant mass of humankind as persisting into the industrial era. So this assertion of presumed stability and commonality within each stage, a stage that runs across many thousands of years in the case of hunting and gathering, and hundreds of thousands of years in the case of the agricultural era, seems to me not very helpful. So I thought instead it might be worth looking, not at eras and assumed stability or series of benchmarks, but at technological change instead. Here,

I think, you can speak of three eras, and they are, I believe, very important to understanding our current situation.

In the long distant past when human beings lived by hunting and gathering, each man seems to have lived a life very like that of others. The principal evidence is stone tools or the remnants of stone tools. Although they did change across millennia, the change was very slow indeed, and for many thousands of years there was an apparent uniformity across very large distances of the surviving equipment. There was near uniformity of stone equipment among early bands. That does not mean that every man had an exactly identical culture, but it does mean that technological change was very, very slow indeed. By the same token, when technological change occurred, the improvements did spread so rapidly that we have no idea when or where it started or how it spread. The bow, for instance, doesn't exist and then it does. There is no evidence of where it was invented or how it spread.

A new pattern arises with the rise of civilization. We see occupational specialization and significant differences of skills from community to community. Henceforth, this became the main stimulus to technological change. Skills, however, became concentrated in the heartland of a civilization. The surrounding peoples, who lacked some of those skills, were weaker, less wealthy, less capable of transforming material things in the direction that civilized people could. When that happened, quite a new kind of technological change became possible, and it seems to me to have been the motor of historic change.

When a stranger out in the periphery encounters someone who possesses some of these skills, it is at once threatening and entrancing. One then has the choice of trying to catch up, imitate, and adapt to one's own purposes, the skills that this stranger embodies or carries with him, or hold him at a distance by somehow strengthening one's own institutions, practices and skills to be able to hold the other back so he will not threaten your culture, your autonomy or your independence. This ambivalence in encountering strangers with different sets of superior skills seems to have become the motor of most historic changes throughout recorded history. The net effect of this process was the spread of skills, within what I think of as fields of force radiating out of the civilized centres toward other people and lands. The net effect of the spreading of skills within culture "fields" and radiating out from skilled centres towards the peripheries was enormously faster technological change. This induced a persistent instability. Society does change and suffers periodic exposure to disasters. It is coincident that with the rise of civilization we have wars. Now there is something worth plundering and natural disasters become much more threatening when society depends upon rather elaborate extraction and exchange of goods and supplies coming from faraway cities. The great defence against that sense of instability is the rise of organized religion which protects people against disaster through prayer and invocation and reassurance. It controls fears, it gives life meaning, it stabilizes human existence, but in so doing, it creates, it builds into the civilized process a tension because the clerisy—the people representing the organized religion, its spokesmen, its defenders—obviously looked with considerable distance upon anyone trying to upset the apple cart. Any new innovation, any significant innovation, and I would suggest that this conference, now taking place in Guelph, is a modern reaffirmation of that very ancient polarity within civilized society: on the one hand trying to increase your wealth, increase your power, respond to stimulus coming from without by appropriating to yourself that which others have or even surpassing them; on the other, holding fast to those things that make life truly good, safe and moral.

When civilizations arise they arise in multiple places not just in one. There are a multiplicity of civilizations in Eurasia and in the New World as well. Civilization began about 3000 B.C. and for the next 4500 or 5000 years, there has been a rise of ever more intense cross-cultural contact creating an ecumenical system of interaction embracing several different civilizations and peripheral societies in an ambivalent relationship to the civilized centre. Of these, by far the most powerful was that of Eurasia simply because the land mass involved was so much larger than anywhere else. Within the Eurasian ecumenical system, one can detect, as I point out in my book, *The Rise of the West*, migrating metropolitan centres. In the early Middle Ages, it was the world of Islam which was the centre of this ecumenical system with its caravans and ships moving out East and west toward Europe and toward China. Then about 1000 A.D., China took over as the primary centre, and then after 1500, it was western Europe that took over that role. This Western metropolitan centre eventually decapitated other more local systems within the Americas where you had a comparable system around Mexico and another around Peru, not to mention Australia or smaller islands like New Zealand about which I know too little to make dogmatic statements.

As these contacts multiply and as the pace of trade and communication and transport intensifies, the diffusion of technologies also accelerates, and I would suggest to you that as you look at the shift from Islam, to China, to Europe as the dominating centres within the Eurasian ecumenical system, you can determine the migration of key techniques, key technologies. The rise of China depended upon the incorporation of the Chinese practice of, what I call, "bazaar techniques"—the techniques of a trade, a small-scale family trade, the migratory merchant—techniques first perfected by the Moslems. The rise of Europe depended, as we have known ever since Francis Bacon, upon gun powder, printing and the compass, every one of which comes from China into Europe. And now we see Japan's rise rested upon the import of certain techniques from the West. We have here a general pattern at work which is probably still in force.

Moreover, with the increasing technological pace and through intensified contacts, there is more to borrow and more to adapt. Consequently, the very idea of technological change as something that could be deliberately organized emerges, and this represents a third stage throughout the civilized era. Where inventions initially came about more or less at random from encounters with new skills, unintended by-products of war, trade, missions and so forth, we have reached a stage of deliberate invention to keep ahead of the game. The idea that you should sit down and invent something that has never been done before is a very recent idea. The earliest that I am aware is the 1840s with the rise of German industry and research in the marrying of the die industry with academic chemistry. The electrical industry followed in the 1880s, again principally in Germany rather than in the New World. But the idea of maintaining a research staff which is going to simply invalidate perfectly good patterns and destroy the value of existing machinery was not the norm before 1914. In fact, even today, it is an idea which is not universally accepted. The Japanese automobile industry is a case in point. The American automobile industry lay back on its oars after the 1930s and were surpassed by the Japanese. A more conspicuous example still is what happened to the railroad in North America. They just rested on their oars which enabled the trucking industry to take over much of the transport business which had once been theirs.

It can be argued that the notion of deliberate invention became widespread and generally accepted only in the course of the First and Second World Wars. It certainly became systematic as never before, and if it should be maintained in the future, it will mark a new era, one indeed comparable to the civilized era of skill differentiation, in the pace of technological changes, character, range and power. But I also suggest that there are very strong countervailing forces in society. The pressures for conservation are very strong. Therefore, it is not a self-evident proposition that deliberate invention will continue to flourish and accelerate the pace of technological transformations in daily life such as that which has prevailed in the twentieth century. Craftsmen's innovations have always been under a cloud, especially if they tended to call into question the received sacred traditions of the society or the clerisy. Clerisy is a term I used previously. I rather prefer it to clergy as it is broader in meaning. It does not simply imply priests and religious officials but those who specialize in words and deal with values. They are wordsmiths and are more a combination of clergy and intelligencia—the phrase the Russians invented to describe people who were not clergy but had somehow become educated and started to have ideas about social problems. This clerisy has the role of upholding social stability. Their actions help to hold together human beings in the face of sporadic disaster and technological change. However, the intensification of technological change and the resulting insecurities of life means that the clerisy is facing an unprecedented challenge to its role in upholding social stability. In putting ethical considerations into balance, as this conference proposes to do, we are suggesting emphasizing or considering one way of limiting or redirecting, and probably slowing technological change. In other words, this clerisy is proposing to reclaim part of its turf from runaway technologists who, since the First World War, have had remarkably few obstacles to innovation.

In fact, in the First and Second World Wars, we see a turn-around of what in ordinary social circumstances is a conservative force into a revolutionary force, that is government bureaucracy. Bureaucracies, both governmental and private, have veered away from their traditional role of holding things stable to becoming revolutionary forces transforming arms, weaponry, and supporting all kinds of technologies which have had peace-time and war-time applications. Bureaucracy actually forwarded research on the atomic bomb and other such projects, thus transforming international relations and the psychological/social insecurities that we have lived with in the past. This is a most exceptional turning inside out of the normal role of bureaucracy. This inversion of what was once a stabilizing force has let technology loose on a scale, and with a pace that has no analogue in earlier history. The special interests that are threatened by change is not just the labour unions and management, but ordinary human beings outside the industrial process. Those affected and concerned are now beginning to voice more clearly their reservations, their uncertainties, their sense of endangerment by what has been happening around them. Therefore, it seems to me that it is not at all clear that deliberate organized invention—the invention of invention—will mark a lasting departure.

A thousand years from now it may appear as a sort of short-lived explosion, a result of the extraordinary release of the strengths of technological development. I would suggest that we are now living through a rather peculiar transition. The metaphor that comes to mind is—what happens when an airplane passes through the sound barrier? Pressures for change are at a maximum, and resistances to change are rising also; for instance the explosion of religious fundamentalism, not just in the Moslem world, in our own, in Hindu and in other societies, represents an expression of that mounting resistance to change. It means that the future is very much up for grabs and very emphatically undefined. This, I think, is the definition of living in what subsequent ages will call a Golden Age, an age when patterns for the future are laid down whether we want to or not. There are so many things up for grabs, and the decisions, the facts, the practices that will emerge from our insecurity are very likely to become routine patterns of the future for some indefinite time ahead. It also means that living through that Golden Age is a painful and confusing existence because insecurity, uncertainty and anxiety are the costs of innovation. Innovation has been thrust upon us tumultuously, and we are in the midst of it whether we like it or not.

All this does not mean that it is not worth trying to understand what is happening around us. Quite the contrary and it is precisely that which gives reason to a conference like this. I trust that our thoughts will be clear and to the point, and help to define our attitudes and outlook in order to make our future actions more purposive, and ideally, more effective. The result, I suspect, would be to control and contain technological innovation, or at least, give it a more human face than it has had in the past 70 to 100 years. However, I would say in parting, that unless I misunderstand the process—the passage of humankind—process is sovereign over purpose. We project, we have ideas, we have ideals, we set goals, we attempt to attain them, and we change the world by our actions as a result of this pursuit of purposes. But the purposes are never completely, or very seldom, completely realized. All sorts of side effects and unexpected new difficulties arise from the very success we have had in changing ourselves and the world around us. As a result, the ecological process, the overwhelming interaction of everything on the face of this globe, takes over and produces a new situation. This is when our intelligence starts to tinker, tries to set new goals, new ambitions, new directions, and then again, has new problems to solve. That is what human history has been. Purpose has been the greater "disturber." This is the way human social process, human historic experience has in fact progressed. I do not think we will ever escape from that because no matter how smart or advanced we are, no matter how clear in our purposes, no matter how sharp our vision of what we must do, should do and can do, we, or our successors will find that we have created new problems, and worse, the redefinition of goals and purposes of the next generation.

Dr. William McNeill is Professor of History Emeritus at the University of Chicago.

Paul T. Durbin

Ethical Issues in an Age of Pervasive Technology

To commence, I would first like to take apart the title, "Ethics in the Age of Pervasive Technology." I will consider first the latter half of the title and focus attention on a dozen serious problematic areas of modern life in which the problems seem to stem directly or indirectly from technology. The shape of the problems, in fact, is peculiar to countries with a technology-based economy rather than the so-called developing countries—though one part of an ethical response to development theory might be to help developing countries avoid problems of just this sort.[1]

(1) The first and some would say most pressing problems are those associated with the proliferation of nuclear arms. Defenders say that improvements in armaments promote peace. However, the consequences would be so great for planet Earth if something went wrong that the arms race—including such alleged peace-promoting developments as the Strategic Defense Initiative—can be considered a serious threat to human survival. The arms race is also problematic in that it eats up incredible amounts of research funding that might better be spent elsewhere.[2]

(2) In my opinion, the nuclear generation of electricity, as a problem, belongs with nuclear weapons proliferation. However, I will bow to custom and list it among environmental or ecological concerns. High-level wastes from nuclear plants (military or civilian) are simply the longest lasting and most toxic of the substances that have been polluting the earth in ever increasing amounts since World War II. Many people consider this as much of a threat to survival as the arms race.[3]

(3) Some relatively extreme critics of technological development see another threat to human survival in bioengineering. What they seem to have in mind especially is cloning and similar threats to the traditional understanding of what it means to be human.[4]

(4) Closely related to bioengineering, as a threat to what it means to be human, might be certain developments in artificial intelligence. Presumably the threat here is to the ability of humans to control technology rather than the other way around—as suggested in innumerable science fiction scenarios.[5]

(5) As the most serious threat to "the good life," rather than to survival, I would list the rapidly increasing disparities between the rich and the poor in technological societies, and between rich, high-technology countries and poor non-technological countries. Many people also

worry about the destruction of traditional cultures as poor countries attempt to follow the path of Western development. This is a very, very complex issue.[6]

(6) Other issues connected with the world of work in high-technology economies include hazards in the workplace, lack of meaningful jobs, and inequities involving certain classes of workers—such as women or immigrant labourers.[7]

(7) Computerization and automation might seem to belong under the previous heading, but there are numerous other problems that are peculiarly associated with societies that have become massively dependent on computerized and automated equipment. One obvious problem is potential vulnerability to sabotage or terrorist threats of sabotage; another is an increasing potential for electronic snooping that may invade people's privacy, not only on but off the job.[8]

(8) Families seem particularly vulnerable in technological societies—or at least vulnerable in particular ways not found in pre-modern societies. Most obvious are mental health problems, although there are also problems such as increased divorce rates. As a result, children are often left alone to fend for themselves, while women offered new types of employment, find that their ability to raise their children as they would like to, is threatened.[9]

(9) Education at all levels, and especially higher education, has become one of the most problematic areas of contemporary life in high-technology nations. There is widespread alarm over lack of education or miseducation—particularly in terms of the failure of schools to prepare vast numbers of young people for work in the jobs required by a high-technology society. On the other hand, there are equally pressing concerns about the failures of schools, colleges and universities to educate students in ways that will help them become citizens of the future who can effectively control technology in a democratic fashion.[10]

(10) The media represent another part of public education, however much people complain, for instance, about television as depressing public tastes. And certainly the modern media are technological if anything is. What seems problematic to me about the modern high-technology media is precisely the kind of values—mostly of a consumption-oriented sort—that they tend to promote.[11]

(11) Another negative impact of the media is on the fabric of democratic societies. For instance, during election campaigns, not only TV but computerized mass mailings and a host of other technology-related changes have affected the way campaigns are conducted and seem to many to threaten democracy itself. In any case, almost all critics agree that in the U.S. there has been a steady erosion, over a period of decades, of voters' confidence in the major institutions of democracy—including voting itself.[12]

(12) Finally, technology is held by some to have a deleterious effect on traditional cultural institutions. This can include over-commercialization of the arts, bureaucratic constraints on

traditional artistic creativity, even a further diminution in the impact of religion in a technological society.[13]

Are these ethical problems? I will argue at the end that they are. For now, what I can say is that many people in our technological world make impassioned claims about the unethical or immoral behavior of not only individuals but also of institutions in all these twelve areas.

Now to the "Ethics" part of the title. Here I would like to provide a mini-history lesson. Our words "ethics" and "morality" come originally from Aristotle. For Aristotle, ethics meant disciplined discourse about the best means of attaining a set of limited goods. The background was provided by his teacher, Plato, with whom Aristotle agreed that the state of Athenian society was a disgraceful chaos of partisanship and factionalism where justice was most *unlikely* to prevail unless at least the leading citizens were trained in ethics. Where Plato attempted to impose order on chaos by appeal to the ideal of Absolute Goodness, Aristotle's ethics proposed more down-to-earth standards.

Once Aristotle had introduced the name "ethics" for discourse about how to be good in generally bad societies, Plato's dialogues could be reinterpreted as already containing a treatise on ethics. In this case, it would mean a more radical attack on relativism in the name of the highest ideals of human conduct. Furthermore, it then became possible as well to defend the relativism of Greek democracy as a kind of ethics—as I. F. Stone has recently done in his popular book, *The Trial of Socrates* (1988). And Athens' popular teachers—the so-called sophists despised by Socrates and Plato—can be seen as proposing a kind of atomistic/scientific cost-benefit analysis that would pave the way for the later Greek and Roman ethical theories of the Stoics and Epicureans. Once the fashion of attaching the ethics label to theories of the good caught on, it even became possible to speak of "religious ethics" in describing the mythological systematizations of traditional customs or public mores that the Greek philosophers had rebelled against as superstitious or irrational. In short, Greek philosophical ethics was typically critical of public mores, but the term "ethics" came quickly to be applied to any and all theories of the good life. Thus, throughout the Christian Middle Ages, philosophical ethics was scarcely distinguishable from moral theology.

After the Cartesian revolution that launched modern philosophy, ethics took its place beside metaphysics and epistemology as a science that could be elaborated without any help from divine revelation. Benedict Spinoza's ethics, for instance, did not put forward any drastically new ethical principles, but it did derive its principles from the data of human consciousness alone in strict axiomatic fashion. Spinoza thus shared with Descartes the ideal of vanquishing skepticism, in those turbulent post-Reformation times, by appeal to human reason alone (however much both thinkers agreed that the Divine Substance guaranteed the veracity of human thought). In similar fashion, those British enemies of Cartesian rationalism, John Locke and David Hume, defended very traditional norms of religious ethics, now on the grounds of empirical science rather than on either reason or divine revelation. Immanuel Kant, who gave "critical philosophy" its name, also defended ethical principles that are quite traditional and conservative; his aim was to avoid Humean skepticism while supporting not only traditional ethics and religion ("within the bounds of reason") but also modern science. In short, for these leading philosophers of the modern period, ethics was a matter of siding with the scientific "moderns" against the unenlightened "ancients" of the Middle Ages; the grounds were different, but the ethical principles defended were largely the same.

In the nineteenth century, ethics became even more clearly a matter of social reform. G.W.F. Hegel was reactionary in going back to an absolutist (and ultimately religiously oriented) grounding of ethics, but he was motivated at least in part by what he saw as immoral excesses of the new Mechanical Philosophy. John Stuart Mill was clearly a social reformer in the tradition of his father and Jeremy Bentham. And Karl Marx's diatribes against the immoralities of capitalism, as he explicitly said, were meant to change the world, not just understand it.

This reading of the history of ethics is slanted, admittedly, and I have slanted it to support a claim of John Dewey, that *public affairs is the real motivator of philosophy.* Dewey tried to show

> ... that philosophy grows out of, and in intention is connected with, human affairs ... [This] means more than that philosophy ought in the future to be connected with the crises and the tensions in the conduct of human affairs. For it is held [here] that in effect, if not in profession, the great systems of Western philosophy all have been thus motivated and occupied.[14]

There is, however, another interpretation of the meaning of ethics to which I want to allude. For several decades, it has been the approach one is most likely to encounter in a college or university ethics course. There was a time, not too long ago, when the approach was honestly labelled "meta-ethics"—the meta or second-order theory of ethical theories. Nowadays, one is more likely to encounter the somewhat more deceptive term, "theoretical ethics." By whatever the name, the approach is the same: to avoid ethical judgments entirely, and to concentrate instead on the analysis—especially logical or linguistic—of other people's ethical judgments. And the purpose, to state the matter positively, is to be sure that in making ethical claims those who do so are not guilty of contradicting themselves or otherwise saying things they do not mean to say.

Here I have no inclination to give another mini-history lesson. Instead, I want to focus on an odd sort of claim that has been made, increasingly in recent years, that out of this uniquely academic approach to ethics might come some uniquely fruitful applications that would, or at least could help us to make better ethical decisions on concrete cases that come up for public debate. The most interesting claim is that of Thomas Perry, in *Professional Philosophy: What It Is and Why It Matters* (1986).[15]

Perry begins by noting that there is a "rather common but false belief that professional philosophy is now only a collection of technical exercises that could hardly be of interest to anyone but the philosophers themselves." What evidence does Perry offer that this belief is false? He seems to think that one of the most important proofs is to be found in so-called applied ethics, and one of his principal chapters "ends with a discussion of the special qualifications which analytical philosophers can bring to the clarification of public issues." In his conclusion, Perry restates this claim: "Contrary to the common accusation that [analytical philosophy] is a merely technical and conservative game, useless to outsiders, it can and does make valuable contributions to other areas of intellectual and practical life."[16] Once again his most telling example is applied ethics where he includes a great many issues of practical policy on which analytical philosophers have recently contributed to public enlightenment: war crimes, civil disobedience, conscientious objection, freedom of expression, imperialism, racism, school desegregation, sexism and women's liberation, affirmative action, abortion, problems of medical ethics and animal rights—with references given in almost every case to a single journal, *Philosophy and Public Affairs*, and what goes on in those kinds of discussions.

I would like, rather briefly, to follow up on this suggestion of Perry's and see what sort of clarification analytical applied ethics might provide in our dealings with the sorts of technosocial problems I listed at the outset. And more particularly I want to focus on the claim of a small number of ethicists that they can apply standard theories to analyze the *responsibilities* that *technical professionals* have to deal with the concerns of society.

I should note in passing that a great many representatives of technical professional societies today feel that scientists and engineers have special social responsibilities[17]—and that if they meet them we will go a long way toward solving some of the major social problems facing our technological society.

To my mind, the best philosophical treatment concerning the ethical responsibilities of scientists, engineers, and such other professionals as physicians and nurses is to be found in Michael Bayles's *Professional Ethics*.[18] His primary focus is on professional misconduct and how poor a job professional organizations have done in dealing with it (or even understanding its dimensions).

In an interesting conclusion, Bayles talks about alternatives to the ways professional organizations have gone about assuring compliance with ethics codes. He lists several alternatives: involving more laymen on regulatory boards; more effective enforcement (including changing the grounds for disciplinary action, better reporting of violations, better investigational procedures, and due-process approaches where applicable), and preventive measures—including ethics education during professional training, and collegial pressure or an "ethical climate" in organizations. He later adds two more obvious but unspoken alternatives: government regulation and lawsuits.

Another book, an anthology on professional ethics edited by Joan Callahan,[19] provides a handy summary of the ethical-theory presuppositions of this approach. With references to Richard Brandt, Norman Daniels, Ronald Dworkin, Kai Nielsen, John Rawls, and Stephen Stich (among others), Callahan proposes as the basic theoretical approach a method of "reflective equilibrium:" first propose a set of moral principles, then compare them with basic moral intuitions about appropriate behavior in concrete situations. Sometimes our intuitions will have to be brought in line with moral principles, but at other times moral principles will need to be adjusted to accommodate real-life applications of generally accepted moral intuitions. Callahan's ethical-theory sources include a number of "deontologists" (philosophers for whom moral rules always trump consequences) and utilitarians (for whom consequences determine acceptable rules), but she also refers to an older but recently revived tradition, the "virtue ethics" of Alasdair MacIntyre.[20] It is safe though perhaps controversial to summarize this approach—which is the norm in almost all recent applied ethics work—by saying that Callahan believes that moral reasoning is a matter of subsuming particular cases under general moral rules. The "reflective equilibrium" part is brought in to assure the flexibility of the approach, in contrast to older dogmatic or absolutist philosophical approaches to ethics.

In my opinion, these approaches are fine as far as they go. I find the "virtue ethic" approach especially promising.[21] But it seems to me that there is a still better approach that shows even more promise as an effective way of dealing, in an ethical way, with the major technosocial problems I listed at the beginning. This is the approach once made famous by John Dewey and best articulated by George Herbert Mead. It is now largely ignored, even by philosophers such as Richard Rorty who claim to have an affinity with Dewey.[22] This approach would have philosophers get involved, working with others—here, especially activist scientists and engineers, along with other activists concerned about problems associated with science and technology—to solve urgent social problems that impede social progress. What Dewey and his fellow American Pragmatists called this approach is "creative intelligence." Its thrust is not, as with the philosophers mentioned so far, to make moral decisions from the heights of ethical theory—even in an "applied ethics" or "reflective equilibrium" fashion; rather, it attempts to work out or through the problems, collaboratively, in the most intelligent fashion possible at that particular stage in history, given the body of reliable knowledge available at the time.[23]

While activist pragmatism of this sort is rare today among philosophers in academia, and although the political mood in much of the developed world today seems anti-liberal, progressive liberalism of this sort is by no means dead. It is alive especially in public interest activist groups of all sorts who have taken it upon themselves to do something concrete and practical about the nuclear arms race, about environmental degradation, about problems of poverty and hunger and homelessness (often in the midst of technology-driven abundance), about economic injustices and political corruption (often involving high-technology industries providing weapons or materiel for governments), and so on.[24]

Mead has an interesting commentary on this sort of approach. Attacking two of the favourite theories of the theoretical ethicists, he accuses utilitarian ethics of being poorly grounded. Typically, it assumes a selfish individualism that is at odds with the altruism presupposed by progressive social action. He also points his finger at Kantian ethics as providing no guidance. In the end, real guidance for him comes from the democratic process of balancing competing values, not from some set of transcendentally deduced Rational Duties. Mead contends that *real* ethics is to be found in the progressive social problem solving of the community:

> The order of the universe that we live in *is* the moral order. It has become the moral order by becoming the self-conscious method of the members of a human society ... The world that comes to us from the past possesses and controls us. We possess and control the world that we discover and invent.[25]

The highest order of this ethics-as-progressive-community-problem-solving is to be found in the arena of international cooperation.[26] Mead died in 1931 and so could only support international cooperation of the League of Nations sort. Had he lived into another era, however, he would clearly have supported the United Nations—as Dewey did—and would have, even more so, supported still more effective international bodies that might have a real chance of solving such technosocial problems as the nuclear arms race, transnational pollution, or improper technological impositions on Third World countries by multinational corporations.

Conclusion

I need to end with a reference to applied ethics literature. Do such philosophers, such academic philosophers, with all of their narrowness have *nothing* to contribute to the solution of technosocial problems? Though Dewey often attacked academic philosophy, I think he and Mead would agree that even the most ivory-tower philosophers *could* make a contribution. Clear definitions of the sort that analytical philosophers are so good at providing are often important in solving social problems. The same applies to those things philosophers of other schools strive for—empirical justification, comprehensiveness, encyclopedic compendia of existing knowledge, even the "authenticity" prized by Existentialist philosophers. *But*—and this is an all-important proviso—these contributions can only be effective if they are somehow communicated to real-life decision-makers. And the best way to do that would be to join in teamwork with others trying to solve urgent problems.

The ethical issues facing us in our technological world are enormous—and the social problems requiring ethical input for their solutions are even more enormous. A good beginning has been made in recent work in applied ethics, but a great deal more could and should be done.

Dr. Paul Durbin is Professor of Philosophy and Director, Centre for Science and Culture, University of Delaware.

---

[1] I have an article in the pre-print for this conference that suggests some of the bibliographical background for what I want to say here. I will not repeat that material here except to say my message is the same: Ethics is only useful if it means doing something about the social problems that critics lament so loudly today. Paul T. Durbin, "Examining the Record: A Bibliographical Note," in J. Nef, J. Vanderkop, and H. Wiseman, eds., *Ethics and Technology* (Toronto: Thompson Educational Publishing, Inc., 1989).

[2] See Jonathan Schell, *The Fate of the Earth* (New York: Knopf, 1982); and *The Abolition* (New York: Knopf, 1984).

[3] Many people trace environmentalism to Rachel Carson's *Silent Spring* (Boston: Houghton Mifflin, 1962), but since then many scientists, e.g., Barry Commoner, in *The Closing Circle* (New York: Knopf, 1971), and Paul Ehrlich (with others) in *The Cold and the Dark: The World After Nuclear War* (New York: Norton, 1984), have joined the crusade. See also Dorothy Nelkin and Michael Pollak, *The Atom Besieged: Extraparliamentary Dissent in France and Germany* (Cambridge, Mass.: MIT Press, 1981).

[4] The issues are summarized and the alarm sounded by Jose Sanmartin, in "Limits to the Manipulation of the Human Genome," in P. Durbin, ed., *Philosophy of Technology: Broad and Narrow Views* (Philosophy and Technology, volume 7; Dordrecht: Kluwer, forthcoming). Jeremy Rifkin, in *Algeny* (New York: Viking, 1984), is of course the loudest voice on this issue.

[5] Science fiction often hints at warnings as well as predictions. My favourite example is still Arthur C. Clarke's *2001: A Space Odyssey* (New York: New American Library, 1968).

[6] Albert Borgmann, in *Technology and the Character of Contemporary Life* (Chicago: University of Chicago Press, 1984), is one of the few non-Marxist philosophers to make this a crucial issue.

[7] Dorothy Nelkin and Michael E. Brown, *Workers at Risk: Voices from the Work Place* (Chicago: University of Chicago Press, 1984), is a useful source, as is the anthology edited by Gertrude Ezorsky, *Moral Rights in the Workplace* (Albany: State University of New York Press, 1987).

[8] A handy bibliographical summary can be found in Carl Mitcham's "Computer Ethos, Computer Ethics," in P. Durbin, ed., *Research in Philosophy & Technology*, volume 8 (Greenwich, Conn.: JAI Press, 1985), pp. 267–280. Donn B. Parker, in *Fighting Computer Crime* (New York: Scribner's, 1983) and other works, is often taken to be the leading voice on social problems associated with computers and automation—though he is not really very critical.

[9] Vance Packard, in *Our Endangered Children* (Boston: Little, Brown, 1983), summarizes the issues. A stronger advocate is Letty Cottin Pogrebin, in *Family Politics: Love and Power on an Intimate Frontier* (New York: McGraw-Hill, 1983).

[10] Issues of this sort are raised most acutely at the annual technological literacy conferences of the National Association for Science, Technology, and Society—the proceedings of which are

usually published in the *Bulletin of Science, Technology, and Society* (Pennsylvania State University).

[11]David Halberstam's *The Powers That Be* (New York: Knopf, 1979) is an indictment of the corporate character of the mass media.

[12]John W. Gardner, in *Common Cause* (New York: Norton, 1972), long ago set the agenda for this sort of issue, and Common Cause, the citizen group Gardner founded, publishes the hard-hitting *Common Cause Magazine*.

[13]This is a sadly neglected area. Daniel Bell, in *The Cultural Contradictions of Capitalism* (New York: Basic Books, 1978; original, 1976), raises some fundamental issues, but his approach to the solution of the problem seems to me reactionary.

[14]John Dewey, *Reconstruction in Philosophy* (Boston: Beacon, 1948; original, 1920), pp. xi-xii.

[15]Thomas D. Perry, *Professional Philosophy: What It Is and Why It Matters* (Dordrecht: Reidel, 1986).

[16]Perry, *Professional Philosophy*, pp. ix, xiii, and 195 (with reference to p. 176).

[17]See especially Mark S. Frankel, ed., *Science, Engineering and Ethics: State of the Art and Future Directions* (Washington, D.C.: American Association for the Advancement of Science, 1988), and Rosemary Chalk, Marx S. Frankel, and Sallie B. Chafer, *AAAS Professional Ethics Project* (Washington, D.C.: AAAS, 1980).

[18]Michael D. Bayles, *Professional Ethics* (2d ed.; Belmont, Calif.: Wadsworth, 1989; original, 1981).

[19]Joan C. Callahan, ed., *Ethical Issues in Professional Life* (New York: Oxford University Press, 1988).

[20]Alasdair MacIntyre, *After Virtue* (Notre Dame, Ind.: University of Notre Dame Press, 1981); see also Michael Slote, *Goods and Virtues* (New York: Oxford University Press, 1983), and P. French, T. Uehling, and H. Wittstein, eds., *Ethical Theory: Character and Virtue* (Notre Dame, Ind.: University of Notre Dame Press, 1989).

[21]Though he does not refer to MacIntyre, Christopher D. Stone's *Earth and Other Ethics* is a clear appeal for a broader and more diverse ethical approach to the solution of environmental and other social problems.

[22]See Richard Rorty, *Philosophy and the Mirror of Nature* (Princeton, N.J.: Princeton University Press, 1979), and *Consequences of Pragmatism* (Minneapolis: University of Minnesota Press, 1982).

[23]Dewey's best books on the subject are *Reconstruction in Philosophy* (note 14, above) and *Liberalism and Social Action* (New York: Putnam, 1935).

[24]See Michael W. McCann, *Taking Reform Seriously: Perspectives on Public Interest Liberalism* (Ithaca, N.Y.: Cornell University Press, 1986).

[25]George Herbert Mead, "Scientific Method and the Moral Sciences" (1923), reprinted in G. H. Mead, *Selected Writings*, ed. A. Reck (Indianapolis, Ind.: Bobbs-Merrill, 1964), pp. 248–266; passage cited from p. 266.

[26]See Mead's *Mind, Self, and Society* (Chicago: University of Chicago Press, 1934), Part IV.

Geraldine Kenney-Wallace

Scientific Research and Social Values

I am both challenged and honoured by being on this platform today to talk about ethics and technology, and to try and share with you a direction in which I believe we must go—with science, with technology, and unquestionably with wise ethical choices. I am going to elaborate these arguments in some detail, but first, let me deliver a prologue on the conference.

When Henry Wiseman came to see me this time two years ago, I had been Chair of the Science Council for barely two months. A mutual colleague had put us in touch, and a few phone calls later, we sat in Ottawa and had an animated discussion on ethics and on the possibilities of this as yet unshaped conference. The Science Council of Canada became a co-sponsor in an act of faith as much as an intellectual and business decision because we believed in the general thesis of the argument. Ethics *is* everybody's business, and yet too little attention is given to this theme.

That is in a sense what this conference is about: making value judgements in a highly complex and rapidly changing technological society. Sometimes not all the facts are in, not all the plans are in shape. But you must move ahead, make decisions and get on with life. How to do that wisely is intimately tied up with choices, with technology, and in particular, with cooperation and collaboration among traditionally different groups of academe, business, labour and government.

Thus, I want to congratulate the organizers of this conference, all the other sponsors and the delegates. All of you have had the insight to participate in what promises to be a stimulating few days, whose impact on you, as individuals or institutions, may very well shape the way you personally enter the twenty-first century.

I am neither professional philosopher nor professional historian, but I am fascinated by one reoccurring theme which reflects on our disciplinary culture. We will probably all agree that "it is self-evident," and "history has shown" are loose statements just as dangerous as "science has proven!" We all work on what we believe is the nature of evidence, but the way we assemble our evidence varies between philosophy, history, and the physical or life sciences. We translate our ideas beyond the facts and data and in doing so enfold beliefs and values. As a physical scientist, I am constrained in my interpretations by the (so-far) constraints of the universe or the laws of physics. There is no ideology attached to the speed of light. There are, however, values in interpreting history. We must share an understanding of our disciplinary cultures in order to move ahead in the wider debates on ethical choices.

My theme today is very simple: *"The Global Village is Restless."* We are electronically tuned to each other like a giant nervous control system. But the reasons for the restlessness are a little confused. Thus I would like to present my remarks today in the context of these global events and from the *perspective of discovery*.

As a scientist, I am intrigued by the act of discovery. The essence of being alive scientifically is to ask questions and shape solutions. This process is a voyage of intellectual discovery in which uncertainties and judgement play a major role. Discovery is intrinsically a human activity of choice and one in which we revel. We rejoice, in an often surprisingly generous way, the first time we discover a range of events that have a fresh personal meaning. Let me give you some examples:

- Discovery that a child can link words haltingly into a full sentence;
- Discovery that a disease may have hope for a cure or be eradicated, such as the case for polio in the 1950s and 1960s.
- Discovery that against all competitive odds, the race was run and won;
- Discovery that a new author can transport the imagination and light up our minds;
- Discovery that a space probe can transport us to images of another universe, at least electronically;
- Discovery that the tax bills are less than projected;
- Discovery of personal tranquillity;
- Discovery that human warmth can eventually heal the pain;

From such a perspective of discovery, let me state the three central points I wish to make and elaborate in the context of ethics and technology.

(1) Discovery through Nature: The science and technologies of tomorrow to which we must respond, positively and wisely, are here because the scientific principles are already well established. What neither I nor you know is the breakthroughs that may occur, indeed, will occur, over the next decade or two. Science and Technology must progress wisely in order to maintain harmony in times of almost bewildering change. In biotechnology, for example, every breakthrough will cause further restlessness unless ethical consideration keeps pace.

(2) Discovery through Human Society: both individually and collectively. The issues of ethics can be grouped into a set of four umbrella issues which refer to the needs of society. These are material needs, social needs, the needs of the interface of human and machine, and finally, the needs inside of each one of us. The latter need is to express and to fulfil our human potential which is the single and possibly loneliest voyage of discovery each one of us takes. It is critically important we do not confuse one need for another. Nor must we let the failure of society to grapple with one need delay the progress on others by default.

(3) Discovery for the Future: Can we identify the grand questions that have achieved marked prominence today as a consequence of globalization of news, markets, medicine, ideas translated into dozens of languages, books, trade and technology, scientific research and educational goals, and environmental challenges? Our restlessness is heightened because of the decentralization of decision-making in all sectors and because of knowledge-driven economics that open markets in the face of crumbling ideologies. It is indeed a time demanding courage, conscience and confidence. We must identify and understand the questions of the future. Perhaps the most important question is about ourselves. Is our human software up to this? Yes, I believe it is, but as humans we have also shown remarkable resistance to change. Complacency is not an option—that is a point on which we might all agree. Evolution or revolution? That is always the question, and the point upon which there will be debate.

I believe the answer is that we need a blend of both evolution and revolution. In those issues where an evolutionary or environmental change is appropriate to move individuals or society ahead, a radical change will have disastrous consequences; and in those issues where "more the same" is a pathway to obsolescence, intellectually or economically, then clearly revolutionary concepts are needed to shift the paradigm. Revolution can be peaceful, as the extraordinary events unfolding in October 1989 in Hungary showed us, in contrast to the tragic events of 1956. It is political and public will that determine the difference.

In other words, change must be accompanied with a clearly articulated set of clauses which I will call sunrise and sunset. These must be discussed when considering our voyages of discovery whether they be in research terms, societal terms or in individual terms. To give a concrete example: keeping an older technology facility fully operational in a hospital, although it has been overtaken by far newer techniques capable of similar or better results for the patients and doctors, seems to be a waste of hard-earned tax-payers' money. The important skilled human resources could be applied elsewhere. When the newer technology is less invasive and more effective in diagnostic terms, surely the decision in "cost-benefit" terms should be clear? But if maintaining the older technology means limiting patient access to the newer facility because constrained hospital operating budgets result in cutting down the hours of access, then this becomes an ethical issue as well. Do not blame the technology. Ask who is accountable in setting hospital priorities. Where are the barriers to common sense decisions? Unfortunately, this is too common a problem in the health care sector.

Evolution or revolution? Sunset or sunrise? Keep these in mind when, in the conference workshops, you look carefully at the ethical choices and the wise actions that you would recommend in the context of rapidly changing and pervasive technologies. To be wise you need to be informed before choices are made. Therefore, let me now move back into my modes of discovery.

(1) Discovery through the Natural Sciences

First of all I would like to analyze the title of the Conference, "Ethical Choices in an Age of Pervasive Technology." As a scientist, I thought: every age is an age of pervasive science and technology, every age is an information age. It is what you *perceive* as science and technology that changes.

Consider a rather different timescale than that of rotation of the earth and sun. Consider a timescale from a state of magic to a state of art, from a state of science, a state of technology, a state of convenience, a state of antique, a state of *objet d'art*. Let me illustrate this timescale and show how perceptions of technology change.

In 3000 B.C., Babylonians had a superb sense of mathematical symmetry and pattern recognition that is the envy of modern robots. Look at the jewellery, the copper and bronze tools and armlets, or at the trumpets they blew. We do not call this advanced materials, metallurgy, acoustics, differential equations and symmetry theory. We call this archaeology now, and exhibit just such artifacts in museums as art, and as beautiful, eloquent expressions of the age.

In Renaissance times, Michelangelo painted the Sistine Chapel magnificently. He must have worked in an empirical way. He and the members of his atelier were smart and experimented extensively. It was natural for them to discover. Michelangelo knew, as an artisan, that what we now call inorganic transition metal pigments lasted longer and could withstand the bleaching of the sun. He used them literally to brilliant effect on the ceiling in contrast to many other painters of the time, and since, who used organic pigments which indeed bleach and fade rapidly. Secondly, he also knew as an artist much about the science of optics, perspective and illusion. Close to the ceiling, the larger than life figures are immensely distorted, but on the chapel floor, looking up, the three-dimensional images stand out clearly and naturally.

We see here a brilliant blend of art and science at a time when creativity flourished and the arts and sciences were sponsored by major institutions such as the Church, the State, the Court, the Medicis, and a range of other private sponsors or patrons. Some citizens were prepared to pay or could afford to pay; many more over the centuries have enjoyed the results.

They are now restoring the ceilings covered with 500 years of smoke from flickering candles and bustling human activity that brought the dust and grime of daily life into the Chapel and eventually on the surfaces of the walls. The ceiling restoration is astonishingly beautiful, bold in colour and alive with imagery. The chapel is closed to the public now and will be for some years. A Japanese company has the rights on the filming and release of pictures of the new cleaned ceiling, to be revealed in a few years time. It has invested in the rediscovery of this art. While some may grumble about access during the 1980s and 1990s, no one else was prepared to foot a bill of such magnitude. There is a moral here, analogous to the familiar free lunch story, in both the hospital and chapel anecdotes. There is no access without cost and that can be an ethical issue, if access *is* the goal. But then, citizens must be prepared to pay the cost, financial or otherwise, if it is unethical to impede access to the science and its technological applications which are of a public good nature.

You might be surprised to realize that it is only over the past two decades we have learned why inorganic transition metal compounds are so colourful and stable. The answers lie in quantum mechanics, spectroscopy, and the excitation of electrons. Indeed, some of these pigments are doped into crystal lattices and polished to make rods for lasers. This rather unexpected blend of science and art today underlies a 10 billion dollar global industry built upon lasers and optoelectronics. In many areas, lasers have become commonplace. Medical applications abound, from ophthalmology or treatments of eyes in outpatient clinics to laser photoradiation therapy treatment of skin cancer. Lasers, communications, satellites and fibre-optic networks: these are the components of the global communications network through which we live, do business, receive information and are challenged today. These dramatic changes are all sources of our restlessness as well as our wonder.

In a society based upon socialized medicine, there are few access problems in principle. In practice, we have to have policies that answer the question wisely, "access to what?" The ethical issues arise from privacy and access to information. Who has access to medical information as a consequence of the diagnosis and treatment? There are ethical issues arising from invasive surgery, when the choice is, perhaps, no surgery at all. There are issues on priorities of funding, on fiscal allocation and on human resource allocation, in days of competing technologies in hospitals and clinics. These all happen after the discovery-through-nature phase and should be discussed and widely debated. These issues should not be used as a vehicle to prevent science and discovery from moving on. Today, without a car, or public transportation, you would be surprisingly inconvenienced. This may change in the future. The rapid diffusion of information technologies may soon see us back in the equivalent of electronic cottage industries as work, decisions, manufacturing and services become increasingly decentralized and globalized. You may not identify with radar, which emerged from World War II, but you would not like to give up a microwave oven. It is now a matter of convenience.

Do our perceptions of risk change along this state of magic to a state of modern convenience time-scale? Undoubtedly yes! But science is and always has been part of our culture. Technology is, and always has been pervasive. It is our perspective of what Science and Technology are, how pervasive technology is, and our personal knowledge base that are changing all the time. More and more people are exposed to a greater store of knowledge over which they are not necessarily in control, or empowered to control. Thus our notions of risk change and evolve in this context of discovery and uncertainty. Today, the global village is electronically wired and pervasiveness is constantly impressed upon us. Sharing other peoples' risk by proxy, through remote control of television drama or environmental devastation around the world, is in itself a source of restlessness to many in the global village.

(2) Discovery through Society: Issues of Needs

Let me now move to some modern examples of the science and technology affecting our lives but which have come about through our societal needs. First, let us look at material needs, and through a few specific examples to identify the demands on technology and science-based innovation.

Canada is a country which historically has relied on trading its natural comparative advantage in raw materials and wealth of natural resources. In days of intense global trade challenges, the market issues of competitiveness focus on the need to put value-added into that resource base. The resource sector is in a period of trade deficits, and there are plentiful alternative suppliers to the world markets. The nation's economy is at stake.

Through biotechnology, in particular through advances in genetics over the past two decades, transgenetic experiments are now taking place which have an impact on fish, trees, plants, insects. There is, furthermore, a new movement towards sustainable agriculture in Canada. The degree of transgenetic research and its implications are not fully known. This is a modern cellular version of grafting orchard trees to produce fruit through hybrids. But in watching the most fundamental research move ahead, and in acknowledging the needs of society for a stronger resource base, there are still voices of disquiet. Now scientists are working at the DNA, RNA, and cellular level, across previously distinct species. They are beginning to touch matters very close to the human being, to life in all forms. The ethical choices will lie in how we apply the results. The closer the results come to us, the more complex those ethical choices seem to be ... or are they? Let me give you an example of what I mean by "close to us." Consider the already proven and partially available genetic screening. A person's disposition to genetic-based disease can be mapped out, a little like finger printing. This is a wonderful breakthrough towards early diagnosis and the prevention of certain genetic-based diseases, if treatments are known.

However, a few moments reflection raises very important questions. Who does the screening, and who pays? Who gets the information, and who acts? Who is liable if refusing to act? These are profound issues of privacy, control, and health care economics which could lead to the setting of targets and priorities in a health care system. Should we prevent genetic research for screening? No. In any event, it is too late. Articles on genetics appear in business journals and fashion magazines. But we must debate the ethical issues clearly, and soon, before we get too emotionally involved because it is "close to us."

Thus a marvellous leap forward in genetic medicine, giving hope for some individual lives, must be thought out carefully from a perspective of individual rights, freedoms and responsibilities. Society, too, has a collective responsibility to build on our knowledge, to utilize science and technology for the greater public good. Health is a key public good responsibility in modern industrialized societies. In the developing world, health is an economic factor which encompasses a broad range of issues from food security to disease prevention. From agriculture, to vaccines, to safe water supplies, biotechnology, biosciences and genetic research have revolutionized the way we can meet the legitimate demands and needs of society. The ethics of meeting those needs still requires debate and thoughtful action on the standards, regulatory practices, codes of behaviour, and priorities in research to allay fears that a Brave New World is too "close to us."

I believe we, in 1989, are really dealing with the most revolutionary and evolutionary of human activities: the management of transition and change in real-time in our global village. Information technologies sharpen the focus on the decentralization of decision-making, on the dramatic geo-political shifts in our village, on the swell of democracy, and on the fluidity and rapidity of response in fiscal markets.

To accomplish this, we are realizing that we must go beyond the village borders, beyond the bounds of conventional wisdom, beyond the bounds of isolated academic disciplines, or yesterday's science and older technology, beyond the long established divisions of private and public sectors. We are compelled to acknowledge that the pervasive nature of technology has challenged us, and our village peace is disturbed because our values and ethics need to be assessed or reaffirmed. And the greatest unease can often be found at the human-machine interface because it is there that our personal sense of control, of being empowered to freely make decisions, is most often questioned or vulnerable to challenge.

Finally, let me say a few words about our inner individual needs. What do you personally want to do or to be or to give to society? What are the personal ethics that drive your human engine? Science and technology have opened up incredible vistas for each one of us and forced us to deal with a remarkably wide set of choices for personal action. Knowing and not knowing is a debate that carries on in our conscious and subconscious mind, leading us along a personal voyage of discovery from uncertainty to confidence and back again. Developing our human potential is the loneliest, and yet the most extraordinary experience each one of us survives. We make choices all the time, sometimes by default.

(3) Discovery for the Future

Little free time is spent on things that are free today, and little free time is spent freely. Life seems rushed. I have tried to imagine the future world and pose questions that undoubtedly will absorb whatever free time we may choose to spend in trying to answer them. In the new realm of work, the conventional old lines of demarcation and responsibility will at first sight seem blurred. The old rules and old management styles do not always work. I hope we are clear in our goals, in what evidence we see, because if we are, we will ask the right questions. Ethics are not an add-on to this future. Ethical issues are central to decision-making and codes of behaviour which are set by, and also govern the norms of society. From the electronic board room to the computerized factory floor, ethical behaviour is everyone's business.

In the future, we will still sense that the bounds of time and space are collapsing. Stock markets now communicate around the globe in nanoseconds (10^{-9}s) and the space probe Voyager II launched a dozen years ago, has left our universe as this remarkably robotic vehicle travelled 4.6 billion miles, passed Neptune on its way, and now continues to another universe. Ice sheets, 500 km in length and 50 km wide are found in space and the frontiers of our galaxy continue to tantalize our minds.

The new work realm is digital but culturally we seem analogue in response. In the research world, whether in space or on earth, we are trying to understand what happens to the materials at the atomic level. The atoms and molecules can influence or scramble the encoding and decoding of information from electronic or optical sources. Versatility is the hallmark of our future capability. We must be both digital and analogue, both precise and uncertain, but always know our direction.

Whether deforestation, excessive grazing, or depletion of resources as demand escalates beyond delivery, both industrialized and developing countries share the global commons and the mutual responsibility for environmental integrity. What is ownership? Ownership of the broadcasting frequency spectrum, of space, of deep ocean floors, of the environment, must all be considered as much as ownership of firms or intellectual property. These are very interesting and important questions which have ethical dimensions in an age of pervasive technology. Once again, courage and conscience must meet imaginatively in our decision-making on ownership, public and private good issues.

Finally, imagine in our future world, the very real scenario that the store of human knowledge (such as the U.S. Library of Congress, the Canadian National Archives, the Bodleian, the great yet still hidden libraries of other cultures) comprising facts and interpretations, history and future trends are all stored holographically in a device the size of a sugar cube. Who has access to the sugar cube? How do you as individuals have access to the sugar cube? What do we do with the overwhelming volume of knowledge? Technology may be pervasive, but how pervasive is our understanding of all the facts, of the management of human change and our own personal voyages of discovery?

Science and technology are agents of change. Like love and betrayal, whether of ideas, or a country, a person or a personal future, science and technology carry a duality. They have already made us reflect upon, and be motivated by rapid changes in our village which have propelled us into a global realm of unprecedented opportunity. As developed and developing countries come to grips with opposite sides of a complex and environmentally common global coin, let us all commit to individual and societal leadership in placing ethical issues as high on our new agenda as education and the global environment. Science is a pervasive way of thinking about our culture, and so is ethics. Tension can be creative, not destructive. Atoms and molecules, at the microscopic level, move with uncertainty according to the laws of physics manifested in quantum mechanics. Learning to live wisely with change and uncertainty and to embrace the sense of discovery in nature and science is perhaps after all part of our natural order in this universe. We are part of this symbiotic sugar cube in the galaxy. The future challenges are ours to accept, and ours to decide.

Dr. Geraldine Kenney-Wallace is President of McMaster University, Hamilton and formerly Chairman of the Science Council of Canada, Ottawa.

John Kenneth Galbraith

Ethical Concerns in the Relationship Between the State and Technology

My concern today is with the relation of the state, of government to technology, not excluding the ethical concerns that there arise. It is a subject marked by perhaps the greatest inconsistencies, even absurdities, of our day. Very possibly one is more successful in identifying these inconsistencies than in persuading one as to their correction.

The relation of the state to technological innovation, in the common definition, the application of science to practical objectives, defies any broad generalization. It is, in general, wide-ranging and politically much celebrated in its role. But in large and important areas of economic life, it is limited, even rebuked, as an unnecessary extension of government activity into what is properly the domain, or is held properly to be the domain, of the free enterprise system. While some publicly sponsored and supported innovation is effectively exempt from calculation as to eventual return, some is subject to rather severe cost-benefit analysis. And while some publicly supported technology is held to be wholly above attack on ethical grounds, some is subject to severe criticism. Let me seek to be more specific.

In Canada and the United States, to take a locally relevant case, there has been for more than a century now strong public support for technological innovation in agriculture. There has also been strong support for carrying this into active, practical use through the extension services. Nor is the result in doubt. Productivity gains in farming have far outstripped those in industry. Some, perhaps much of this, is to be credited to the development and use of mechanical equipment, of crop hybrids, gene engineering, and to, as some have called it, the nitrogen revolution. The latter has contributed to reducing the number of farmers from a large to a relatively small part of the employed population. Moreover, if less significantly, a smaller role in national policy is to be attributed to the work of the colleges of agriculture and, as anciently designated, the agricultural experiment stations.

There is a similar acceptance of state support in other fields, notably in that of health. It is taken for granted that the response to any major threat to national health will be a public responsibility. This has been the case with cancer and AIDS, as it once was with malaria, yellow fever, infantile paralysis, as it was then called, extending down even to the common cold. This intervention no one condemns. Were anyone to do so, his voice would not be heard amid the cries for more extensive, more effective and, inevitably, more costly investment.

The yet stronger, and in fact strongest public support for technological innovation is on behalf, needless to say, of military development and application. It is here by far that the largest sums are appropriated. In the United States, it is this that has the most powerful economic and political constituency. We accept that it is politically dangerous to be "soft on defence," a peril that extends to any serious question of presumptively innovative expenditure. The research and development budget of the Department of Defence in the United States is now in the range of forty billion dollars a year. This compares with around twenty billion for all other R & D expenditures of the Department of Energy and National Aeronautics and Space Administration or NASA. Expenditure for purely peacetime purposes, including that for cancer, AIDS, the environment, agriculture, and all the rest, such as expenditure for the study and control of acid rain, totals about fifteen billion, or but a third of the military outlay. Nor is it essential that the particular military expenditure have any clear relation to either need, or possible success. The B–2 or Stealth bomber has its justification only in that it is invisible to Soviet radar, although not apparently to effective satellite surveillance. The Strategic Defence Initiative, more commonly known as Star Wars, is believed by virtually all detached and competent scientists, physicists and other observers to be without serious prospect of success. There has not been, however, a decisive objection to its development. Expenditure on military technology, to repeat, has a rationale unrelated either to need or to result.

Another, perhaps obvious point must be emphasized. Public support for innovation in health protection has a strong humanitarian, which is to say, ethical appeal. This looms large in its justification. Innovation in weapons development, on the other hand, has as its primary purpose, the more efficient euthanasia of people and, indeed, of the population of the planet. This, however, produces no *decisive* ethical objection. Those who object, though both articulate and fairly numerous, are thought to be out of touch with modern political and military reality. Occasionally, as in the long span of memory from Ypres and the vast and terrible killing fields of the First World War, there remains a special concern, a special residual concern over innovation effort. This has long applied to poison gas and its manufacture, and likewise to the residual and uncollected wastes from the development and production of nuclear weapons. Even these concerns, however, although well publicized and a deeply felt part of the culture, are still not decisive.

Such is the powerful and effective case for state support to technological innovation. I come now to the large area of modern economic and social life where such support is either episodic or even suspect. And where this is so, at no slight economic and political cost, it is part of the case for technological innovation in military matters that reaps a civilian spin-off. Aircraft development, that of the commercial passenger jet, is specifically and repetitively cited in this regard. Likewise, if less confidently, is the civilian use of atomic energy, and the approximately thirty million dollars of military R & D expenditure that is presently being devoted to high-definition television in the United States. It is my impression that these cases of a civilian application of military technology are cited as much for their rarity as for their importance, but I pass over that point. The more important matter is that while regularly citing these rewards, we do not allow them to justify any organized public support for improved industrial technology in general.

Some more than incidental public support has, of course, long been accepted. In the United States, the legislation that brought into being the agricultural colleges also provided support for the general development and application of the mechanical arts, thus the A & M colleges or universities, as indeed some are still designated. But increasingly with the passage of time, it has come to be assumed that in contrast with agriculture, or in contrast with health, the industrial firms themselves will carry on much of their own research and development and much that is needed by society. Anything involving automobiles is for General Motors; anything concerning chemicals or synthetics is for Du Pont; anything involving environmental matters is, of course, for Exxon!

There is little doubt in the public mind that this has been beneficial for technical change and for progress as customarily defined. It has also established a close nexus between development and use, for it was the need for the latter that normally inspired the technology. Parenthetically, looking at these matters in the Soviet Union some years ago, I noticed that technological development went ahead without use. I was impressed by the seeming gap between publicly sponsored technical development and its practical employment. The flaws in this design are, however, not specific to the Soviet Union. The fact that they can lead to industrial "hit or misuse" is increasingly evident in our time.

There is, first of all, the accidental character of technical development when thus entrusted to private enterprise. In the classically competitive market of small firms, development—as in the case of agriculture—is usually beyond the resources of the individual firm in cost and, since quickly copied, also quite possibly of fleeting advantage. In the large corporation to which, in the distant company of Joseph Schumpeter, I have attributed the resources and market power necessary for, or conducive to research and development, there is also, we now know, a serious uncertainty as to whether effective investment in technology will, in fact, be made. As in the case of the American steel industry, there can be acute bureaucratic sclerosis which effectively excludes innovation. For long periods, managerial complacency can rest contentedly with things as they are. Development investment can also have a low priority because it is not directly reflected in early earnings or immediate solvency. The current acquisitions and leveraged "buyout insanity" has created debt structures in many corporations that will effectively command revenues which would otherwise be available for technological development. All this is shielded from the public and official concern by the ancient ideological commitment to *laissez-faire, laissez-passer* and the equally old and established belief that somehow there is an association between such large-scale financial transactions as leveraged buy-outs, mergers and acquisitions, and higher human intelligence.

In leaving technological concerns to the industrial world and to the broad encouragement of the market, we also ensure that socially urgent, as distinct from privately advantageous, lines of development will be systemically, even systematically excluded. Such socially urgent expenditure will not usually be of advantage to the individual firm. There was no market inducement to the automobile companies in past times to design and develop a vehicle that minimized pollution. There was no market advantage in the safe disposal of industrial wastes. A midwestern utility has no market incentive to develop measures for the retention of the components of acid rain. Technical development comes only under social pressure and eventually at the behest of the state. In the case of acid rain, one notes the high substitutability of extended study of the subject over effective action as an excuse for inaction. A quick remarkable manifestation of research is used in direct conflict with the action that would reflect strong ethical concerns.

I come now to what should be done. It is clear that the relationship between the state and technological development is complex, in marked degree chaotic, and in the distribution of technical resources absurd. In the case of weapons development, it can be not only ethically questionable, but socially disastrous. In civilian economic activity, it can be systematic and comprehensive, as in the case of civilian industry, while socially damaging in its absence, as in the case of environmental or other social effects.

I do not turn optimistically to government action, especially considering that government in the United States and Britain, and perhaps in some measure in Canada, is now in the hands of those who dislike and even seek to discredit public action. But reality must be faced; there is no other course. I would urge, needless to say, a greatly reduced technological commitment as regards weaponry and defence. In the American case, such a commitment draws technical and capital resources from urgent civilian and other public purpose. The Pentagon, it has been estimated recently, now pays the salaries of around one-third of all American engineers and scientists. Conversely, the availability for civilian use of these resources and associated capital has played a large role in the economic success of Japan and the German Federal Republic since World War II. Their economic success can be traced, in no small part, to the military constraints that were the result of losing a war. Military defeat was the prelude to economic victory.

I would urge further that all modern governments have an organization that maintains an eclectic and systematic surveillance of the industrial economy. It should be in constant search for unexploited technological opportunity and should command the financial resources that, directly or indirectly, be committed to that end. This should not be a purely scholarly exercise in surveillance, as to some extent is now the case with the National Science Foundation in the United States. Rather, it should be a major department of government disposing serious revenues in areas of possible, useful and competitive technological development, or in defence, against socially damaging development. It should have a long view of the future and thus serve as a countervailing force to the most damaging of recent public and private tendencies, which are to sacrifice future problems and prospects to short-run comfort and convenience.

What I here suggest is not an especially radical step. It is the course of action we now follow when there appears to be military opportunity, even of the most exiguous sort. As I have noted previously, we celebrate this for its civilian byproduct.

The high level of cooperation in Japan between state and industry in the last forty years represents the least celebrated and one of the most important advantages that country has over the English speaking countries. We, here, are in the tradition of conflict between state and enterprise that goes back to Adam Smith and is still reflected in the works of any considerable number of unduly vulnerable minds in our own time. In contrast, the young Japanese read Marx and accept therefrom that the state is the executive committee of the capitalist class. Although this is not a point I strongly applaud, one result is nevertheless the close technological collaboration in Japan between state and industry.

Immediately urgent also, is the need for the state to devise ways and means for dealing with the social consequences of economic development. This, more than incidentally, is a task that cannot be accomplished without effective cooperation between the affected lands. Since we share the same planet, there must be shared responsibility and action for its preservation.

We are just beginning to recognize this need for public action as we seek technological and regulatory means for remedying past default. That is good, but it hardly speaks well of our earlier perception of these problems. We have the scientific and technical competence to foresee, as one example, the problems of urban atmospheric pollution that we now face. We should have had the public foresight and will to have acted before, rather than after the fact. The suffocation of Los Angeles, the second, maybe third largest metropolis on this continent, did not come without warning. It was something that was fully anticipated. Only the resulting action was lacking. The final technological and public imperative is to foresee, and then act, on our foresight.

Let me end, however, on a more hopeful note. I have stressed especially, the diversion of technical resources and competence to destructive and sterile military use and purpose in these last decades. The essential and indomitable Ruth Leger Sivard has just estimated that world military expenditure for 1988 reached a new high of just under $1000 billion. But now, for the first time in forty years, there are winds of change. To the considerable discontent of many entrenched interests, the cold war and the associated support for military technology is easing. There is here, to use a much used phrase, a window of opportunity, and even a small opening is large in such circumstances. A five per cent reduction in military spending by the superpowers (as they are still denoted), and elsewhere around the world, would allow a doubling of health expenditures for four billion people in the Third World. This is the miracle of leverage. But this, or any redistribution of resources will not come easily. Military spending, as I have noted, has now a vested life of its own, more or less unrelated to the reality or threat of danger. Nonetheless, the opportunity exists. We must see that it is relentlessly pursued. The clear opportunity and need is for a large reduction in the technical and other resources devoted to weaponry and warlike purposes, and their equally large reallocation to urgent civilian and peacetime need. Part of the reallocation I would urgently wish for, would be that the Eastern European countries include the Soviet Union as they seek to make this very perilous transition from a static bureaucratic economic society back to a more flexible structure. It would be a sad thing if liberalization in that part of the world were identified with, and seen as causing economic hardships. Having just returned from East Germany, there is a sense of urgency that requires the bringing together of all Western resources so that this transition to a more liberal society is not identified with increased hardship.

Dr. John Kenneth Galbraith is a Paul M. Warburg Professor of Economics, Emeritus, Harvard University.

Richard Falk

Technologically Driven Defence Policies

I feel both honoured and intimidated by the conference theme and the challenge in trying to say some general things about how to best approach it. I am also struck by the frequency with which things now are viewed in a terminal mood. Part of the explanation could be that we think things are coming to an end because of the approach of a new millennium. In one way, this is encouraging in the sense that there is a receptivity to more drastic ways of conceiving what is desirable and necessary and possible for the future. If we accept that the severity of the problems posed by the relationship of human activity to the well-being and sustainability of life on the planet is increasing, then we need to be as open as possible to drastic thinking and analysis. Without the latter, we will not make the changes in behaviour and institutions that are required. It does no good to exhort, one needs a politics that is transformative, that flows from the analysis, but the analysis must also be there. Therefore, part of the role of a conference like this is to help fashion the kind of consciousness that can produce that sort of transformative politics.

Two of these discussions to this end are quite fascinating from a cultural perspective, and have caused an enormous recent stir in the United States. One is an essay by Francis Fukuyama called "The End of History." What is meant by this title is not the end of the world, but rather, it is a celebration of the end of the Cold War on terms favourable to the West. What that really implies is that the end of history equals the death of socialism and the removal of any serious competition to the ideological orientation of the West which is a combination of a commitment, constitutional democracy and market oriented capitalism. It is not accidental, I suppose, that the author of the above-mentioned essay, which has received such celebrity, is Deputy Director of the Policy Planning staff of the U.S. State Department. One can read this essay as a mixture of celebration of economic liberalism and a kind of Thatcherism and Reaganism mix. It is nice to please your employer by giving it such a philosophical sound as if the whole force of history is behind this development. But I think it does represent a very widely shared view that we are at the end of the post-war world—that kind of world that emerged after 1945 and was dominated by the sorts of ideological rivalry that the East/West struggle embodied.

The question posed then, becomes "Where does one go from here—what does that tell us about what comes next?" As for Fukuyama and much of the thinking on the part of Western governments, it is time to "mop up," to continue to do the work of spreading successfully the ideology of the West. That, however, has its good points but also includes some disastrous things. The good things are the emphasis on human rights and political democracy. The bad things are the uncritical materialism and the presuppositions that the main driving force of history is going to make economic practices more efficient and more in control of the planet as an integrated market place. The kind of capitalist utopia where the whole world becomes one unit, is in a certain sense, the shadow side of the dream of human unity under a progressive political perspective. This view sees the future evolving in the direction of what is sometimes called the "common marketization of the world." In other words, the driving towards increasing concentrations of capital organized around basic market principles. It is expected that this would lead to a mixture of safe and societal forms of cooperation to manage some of the global problems, including those of the environment.

This is essentially a top down view of the future in which technology is the driving force. To the extent that there are ethical consequences of a positive sort, they basically flow from the continued productivity of a technologically driven civilization and the spread of that civilization to the globe. What is also intriguing about the Fukuyama vision of the end of history is that it has no place for the poor. They have no relevancy nor are they given choices except to either politely die and disappear or to engage in parasitism. Those are the options that this vision implies for those who are not part of the common marketization of the world. What this produces is not the remedy that this vision supposes will result, but rather something that is more closely approximated by the phrase, "The Lebanonization of the Third World." Lebanon is not just a tragic circumstance of political, economic and social disintegration. It is a warning about some very fundamental tendencies that are occurring throughout the non-Western world. India or Pakistan could easily become the Lebanon of the early twenty-first century and Sri Lanka has already anticipated that kind of evolution to a significant degree. So that is one dark side of that view of the future. The other is that it is pre-ecological, if that can be imagined. This conception of common marketization implies only the most modest adjustments in economic and governmental practices. It essentially sees the future in terms of this unfolding of productivity and simply finding new technological fixes for the problems that are generated by technology even looking to genetic engineering as one of the positive prospects in coping with whatever difficulties arise in the areas of energy or food scarcity. In other words, the vision rests on technological determinism as the basis for conceiving what is possible in the future.

The second vision, as outlined in Bill McGibbon's book, *The End of Nature*, is very dissimilar. There is no dialogue between these two presentations of the future. What McGibbon sees is a path of plunder—planetary plunder—that cannot be sustained given the carrying capacity of the planet. He regards the planet as becoming uninhabitable long before it runs out of resources even if there are no problems generated with respect to something like nuclear war or some other form of wider catastrophe. In other words, the McGibbon view is one in which fundamental shifts have to occur in our personal outlook if we are to have any prospect of coming to terms with global problems. The most basic shift is one from what I would call a fear/greed axis that rests on the fundamental idea that human experience is about conflict and that we must protect ourselves with means to inflict pain and violence in order to deal with or to achieve security. The fear/greed axis is what is embodied in our institutions and therefore, we cannot hope those institutions will change without changing the political climate within which they operate. What we seek, I think at this stage of history, is what I would call a hope/needs axis. That is a view in which the prospects for human cooperation, both between societies and between different parts of the world, enters into the centre or core of our consciousness and influences the way we shape organizations and institutions in the search for some form of viable global government. What this entails, this end of nature, if it is to be the beginning of hope rather than the culmination of fear, is, indeed, some movement of a deliberated sort toward a structure of global government that is supported at the state and grassroots levels.

Let me in closing, make some suggestions about why there is a basis for hope. We are at a point in time now that we have not had for a very long time, and may not have again. This creates an urgency of challenge that I think is represented by the very fact that a conference of this sort is occurring. I would mention at the very outset, the emergence of a leadership in the Soviet Union that accepts the McGibbon understanding of the priorities in the world. It is almost a miracle of bureaucratic evolution that a system as dead as the Soviet system could turn out a leader as in tune with the needs of the future as Gorbachev seems to be. It is not an argument for authoritarianism but when one looks at the leaders that we have had in the United States, emerging out of a free society, one begins to wonder what has become of the connection between democracy and leadership.

The second factor is that the ending of the Cold War and the spread of human rights and democracy, as is taking place in Eastern Europe, does create a capacity to focus now on the real challenges confronting the planet. We have been diverted by the luxury of this geo-political conflict over the last several decades. Now we are given an opportunity to really address the challenge of poverty, the challenge of sustainability, the challenge of an obsolescent organization of political life on the planet.

Thirdly, there is emerging, as evidenced by such things as the Brundtland Commission report, and the almost surrealistic note in the unexpected "greening" of Mrs. Thatcher—a real consensus about the seriousness of the environmental challenge and the importance of addressing it at this stage.

Fourthly, there is a widespread appreciation of the failure of war as an instrument of social policy: the Soviet Union in Afghanistan, the United States in Vietnam and now Central America. It is true you can invade a little island and declare it a victory but that almost proves the point that superior military power cannot be translated effectively into political results. To continue to devote the resources we do to this obsolete and scandalous human institution of war is a sign of moral decadence at the very core of civilization at a time when we face the sort of challenges we do. War has become as scandalous for the late twentieth century as slavery was in the last century. Until we wake up to that politically, we are not going to be able to address, for resource and attitudinal reasons, the problems.

Fifth, there is a renewed confidence in the United Nations as a peace-making organism and as a global framework which can grow to respond to the greater needs of a complex interdependent world and provide a much stronger institutional presence at the centre.

Sixth and finally, there is this extraordinary revival of relevant action within civil society throughout the world. It is not only the human rights and environment groups in the West, like Amnesty International and Greenpeace, that have done more than governments have done to create the kind of consciousness that is necessary to address the future, but it is also the developments of these great movements in Eastern Europe, the Philippines and elsewhere that have re-established the power and potency of popular democracy and popular sovereignty. It is also the awakening, I think, of a new religious consciousness such as liberation theology in many forms in the Third World leading to base communities and new forms of social organization. But it is also the increasing feeling that unless religions share their focus on the sacredness of creation, the future of any kind of spiritual life on this planet is destined to be doomed and degraded. So I think one does approach the ethical choices with a very positive set of forces and the most important element, I would stress in closing, is that we take these favourable developments in order to create the kind of societal consciousness that will build the sort of "ego-oriented greenish" politics that can overcome the gridlock that continues to operate at the level of most political institutions of the world.

Dr. Richard Falk is the Albert G. Milbank Professor of International Law and Practice at Princeton University.

Jim MacNeill

Sustainable Development and "Ethics-as-Usual"

It is just recently that I spent four years directing a global enquiry into the state of the world, a sort of international *royal* commission which has become known as the Brundtland Commission, after our Chairperson.

The nine hundred days of our enquiry were spent in wrestling with a series of "ethical choices" stemming from this "age of pervasive technology"—to borrow the theme of this conference. The choices confronted us in every issue we considered: energy, agriculture, industry, international economic relations, environmental threats to peace and security, the global commons, international relations.

These choices have become very difficult. The power of human numbers and human technology have combined very quickly to alter radically the conditions for life on Earth. We have experienced a sudden acceleration of interrelated events on several fronts simultaneously—the economic, the ecological, and now, considering *glasnost* and the tidal shift in East-West relations, the political.

This set of circumstances is forcing profound changes in the relationships between peoples, nations and governments, as well as in the way we view and think about the management of the planet as a whole. It is also forcing ethical questions on professions, industries and governments; questions which until recently were considered at best, irrelevant, and at worst, subversive.

The need for more sustainable forms of development have become an imperative. This imperative stems from the fact that we are on history's most rapid growth track. The key figures are familiar. Since 1900, the world's population has multiplied more than three times. Its economy has expanded twenty times. The consumption of fossil fuels has grown by a factor of fifty. And most of that growth, about four-fifths of it, has occurred in just the last four decades.

The pace of future growth could be even more stunning, driven in part by a further doubling of world population within the lifetime of today's 20 year olds. We could act to stabilize population at a lower level, but our efforts to date as a world community clearly do not measure up to the challenge. If human numbers do double again within the next fifty years, we can estimate that a further five to ten fold increase in economic activity would be required to enable humanity to meet its basic needs and minimal aspirations; aspirations, as we all know, are as important as needs.

The gains in human welfare during this century have been breathtaking. If we continue to avoid world-scale conflict, then the potential for future gains is even more awesome. Biotechnology, just one new branch of engineering, could itself change the world as we know it. Information technology already has. We now have potentially unlimited access to information and the advent of global communications makes it possible for people to begin to exercise responsibility for every part of the planet.

The processes of development that produced these gains are also provoking major unintended changes in Earth's atmosphere, biosphere and hydrosphere. Millions of people in dozens of countries have suddenly become aware that much of what God created, man is now destroying. Most of us are familiar with the dismal trends. But they will raise a horde of ethical dilemmas.

Take world poverty and the growing imbalance between the North and South to start. The growth of the last forty years has been concentrated in the North. With twenty-five, soon twenty per cent of the world's population, industrialized nations consume about eighty per cent of the world's goods, and generate about the same proportion of its environmental destruction. That leaves more than three-quarters of the world's population with less than one quarter of its wealth, thus increasing tensions with the South, and leaving ever larger numbers of people poor and vulnerable. Pervasive poverty at a time when the means and experience to eradicate it clearly exist is the greatest single failure of any civilized society. It is also both a major cause and major effect of environmental degradation and economic decline.

These bleak trends have shattered the simple faith of our fathers in the permanent order of nature. If we glance at some of the recent titles on the best seller lists and op-ed pages of the western press, their titles abound with terminal metaphors; metaphors like "the end of nature," "the end of forever." We all sense that there is a very high probability that most of the world's children will not know the richness and variety of Earth that poets have celebrated down through the centuries. The world's economic and political institutions are seriously out of step with the workings of nature.

If Earth is already crossing certain critical thresholds—and I believe it is—how is it going to accommodate a further five to ten fold increase in economic activity over the next fifty years?

A five to ten fold increase over fifty years sounds enormous. Given the magic of compound interest, it actually reflects annual rates of growth of only 3.2 and 4.7 per cent. No government, developed or developing, aspires to less than that and, in fact, in many developing countries, it is hardly enough to keep up with projected rates of population growth, let alone reduce levels of poverty.

But all this translates into a colossal new burden on the ecosphere. Take energy, for example. If nations were to employ current forms of energy development—if it is "business-as-usual" in the energy field—energy supply would have to increase by a factor of five just to bring developing countries, *with their present populations*, up to the level of consumption now prevailing in the industrialized world. Critical systems would collapse long before reaching those levels.

A transition to sustainable development will not be possible if we continue with "business-as-usual." A transition to sustainable forms of development will require a fundamental reorientation of dominant modes of decision-making, in government and industry, and on the part of individuals who buy, consume and dispose of the world's goods. It will also involve significant changes—many of them politically very difficult—in economic, fiscal, energy, agricultural, trade, security, and foreign policies which guide national, corporate and private behaviour. Of course, it will also entail fundamental changes in the ethics underlying these modes of decision-making and policies.

Can these changes be made—and in time? The answers to that question are by no means evident.

No one can predict the future. I learned long ago in OECD that "he who lives by the crystal ball must learn to eat ground glass." So no one can rule out a future of progressive ecological collapse. This is something that we in the Brundtland Commission did not do. After all, the Four Horsemen are at work in parts of Africa, Asia and Latin America, fed in part by growing population/environment pressures. Threats to the peace and security of nations from environmental breakdown are today greater than any foreseeable military threat from conventional arms. They are increasing at a frightening pace. Local, even regional conflicts based on environmental disruption, water and other resource scarcities could well become endemic in the world of the future.

It is easy to get bogged down in prophecies of doom, and it is sometimes tempting—some Canadian experts are making a profession of it—but it really does not accomplish anything. We preferred instead to explore the possibility, as we saw it, of a "new era of development"—not the type of development that dominates today, but sustainable development, based on forms and processes that do not undermine the integrity of the environment on which they depend.

The maxim for sustainable development is not "limits to growth;" it is the "growth of limits." Some limits are imposed by the impact of present technologies and social organization. But many present limits can be expanded through changes in modes of decision-making, changes in some domestic and international policies, and through massive investments in human and resource capital.

In relation to the theme of this conference, I would like to cite four examples of areas, where, in my view, rapid change is needed for a sustainable future.

First, there are the values and attitudes underlying human behaviour. These are shaped by many things—family, school, religion, events, media and so forth. Let us take religion as an example.

Many of the world's religions have taught and continue to teach us to believe that humans are lords over the planet and all other species, and they urge us to "take dominion" over the earth and to "subdue it." We have done so. We are now literally skinning the planet alive and, in the process, we are eliminating species at a rate of 50 a day and climbing. If the world's religions wish to play a more positive role in securing a sustainable future, they should rethink many of the doctrines that unconsciously shape human attitudes to nature, and going one step further, that shape attitudes toward the role of women in society.

Second, we have to take another look at the market. Human behaviour is strongly conditioned, often decisively conditioned by the market. The leaders of Eastern Europe, China and some other countries are doing political handstands today to open their economies to market forces. They have finally discovered that the market is a most powerful instrument for driving development. What they have not yet discovered, however, is that it can drive development in two ways: sustainable or unsustainable. Whether it does one or the other is not a function of an "invisible hand," but of man-made policy.

Energy is a good example. If future energy needs are to be met without adding further intolerable pressures on the world's climate, nations will have to make efficiency the cutting edge of their energy policies. Productivity gains of one to two per cent a year are quite realizable and would buy the time needed to increase the use of renewable forms of energy and to develop some new and more benign forms of power.

The major obstacle to this is the existing framework of market incentives—subsidies, taxes, and other policy instruments. We have found that they are all pervasive; backed by enormous budgets; and they usually promote the very opposite of what is needed for a sustainable energy future. They underwrite coal, tar sands, oil and gas; they increase acid rain and global warming and ignore the costs of pollution; they favour inefficiency and waste; and they impose enormous burdens on already tight public budgets. We have got to turn them around—but can we?

That, I think, depends on whether we can change the way in which we have traditionally organized our institutions. Our economic and ecological systems are totally interlocked in the real world, but they remain almost totally divorced in our institutions. That is the greatest single barrier to sustainable development. Environment must be brought into the centre of economic decision-making in government, industry, and in the home where individuals choose consumer products.

But that alone will not necessarily change anything. There are strong, value-laden forces within society that compel our political institutions to capture the benefits of an economic activity—jobs, income, profits, tax revenues—for today's electors, and then to transfer the costs of managing the wastes from that activity to somebody else.

The *Not In My Backyard* syndrome is one expression of this. When an entire nation catches NIMBY, the aggregate result is what I call NIMNY, the *Not In My Nation's Yard* syndrome.

Having captured the economic benefits, what do we try to do with our PCBs? We try to send them to Wales, and in mid-October, we did in fact send a cargo to France. The Italians try to hide their toxic wastes in Nigeria, the Singaporeans in Thailand. Nations try to transfer costs to a neighbouring country or to the global commons. Strong countries transfer the costs to weak ones. And every day, politicians face the irresistible temptation to transfer these costs to the weakest group of all—future generations.

This is what I call "planetary-management-on-the-pay-later-plan." As William McNeill said at this conference, bureaucracies are notorious for finding ways to sidetrack, stonewall, and postpone awkward decisions. The problem with this now is that the future generation in the calculus is already with us. On a global plane, 50 per cent of the population, more than 2.5 billion people, are under the age of 25. They do not have the option to pass on these costs to later generations. And politicians are beginning to discover that they vote.

Finally, there is an urgent need for new and stronger forms of international cooperation. The massive changes occurring in the relationships between the world of nation states, the Earth and its biosphere have not been accompanied by corresponding changes in our international institutions.

Legal regimes have been rapidly outdistanced by the accelerating pace and scale of change. New norms for state and interstate behaviour are desperately needed. At a minimum, the world community requires some basic norms for prior notification and consultation with neighbouring states on activities likely to have an impact on them. States must accept an obligation to alert and inform their neighbours in the event of an accident which could be harmful to them. Basel, Chernobyl, Exxon Valdez are cases in point. States should also be under the obligation to compensate those affected for any damage done. Similar norms and obligations are needed for the global commons.

Governments and the United Nations require some kind of office, perhaps an external office supported by non-governmental bodies, with a mandate to act on behalf of the commons and future generations. This could be a sort of environmental ombudsman. We have just received the annual report of Canada's Auditor General. With an independent capacity for assessment and reporting, I suggest that the annual report of a Canadian Environmental Watchdog would be at least as interesting as that of the Auditor General.

A rich menu of options for new forms of international cooperation are under consideration. Some of the ideas floating around build on existing institutions; others propose more fundamental changes involving some expansion or pooling of national sovereignty. This is essential. If we are going to address climate change, for example, we will have to be prepared to accept an international regime that would lead in time to a more equitable sharing of the Earth's limited capacity to handle greenhouse gases. This regime will have to recognize the growth imperative of developing nations. It would have to monitor and report upon the performance of nations, providing incentives for good performers and penalties for bad ones.

This could only be done within a framework that expands and pools national sovereignty. The weakest link in the chain of obligations imposed by any international agreement is enforcement. Invariably, enforcement is left up to individual nations. If nations insist on their historic sovereign rights to sign conventions and then ignore them, the climate change scenarios will unfold inexorably.

William McNeill mentioned earlier that "process is sovereign over purpose." I agree with that. But we know that decision processes can be changed, even harnessed to purpose. If we change the way we make decisions, we could change the decisions we make. And conversely, if we don't, we won't. The optimism underlying *Our Common Future* is based on the assumption that we can change the way we make most of our decisions. If that assumption is wrong, and it may well be, then the Earth, the World's economy and we, ourselves, are all in a heap of trouble.

Some recent signs suggest that this assumption may not be entirely wrong. We have witnessed a sea-change in public opinion on these issues. It has forced them to the top of political agendas in the United Nations, in Washington, London and other capitals around the globe, not to mention in some multilateral banks, and in many of the board rooms of the Fortune 500. During the first full year after our report was presented to the General Assembly, more heads of state converted to environmentalism within the new context of sustainable development than converted to Christianity or Islam in any single century when conversion was assisted by the point of a sword.

Public opinion, I believe, will remain ahead of government on these issues. Global warming alone will ensure it. The politics of greening will continue to drive the greening of politics—and ethics—well into the 21st century.

Dr. Jim MacNeill is Director, Program on Environment and Sustainable Development, Institute for Research on Public Policy, Ottawa.

Digby J. McLaren

Science and Culture for the 21st Century: An Agenda for Survival

In this presentation which I had occasion to present at the UNESCO Symposium of the same title in September 1989, I would like to consider five themes, and to generalize from them in the context of ethics and technologies. They include: (1) Science and the New World View; (2) Predicting the Elements, the Evolution and the Cultural Dimensions of Change; (3) Reconciling the Diversity of Interests with Social Freedoms, Human Rights and Human Values; (4) Determining Remedial Activities; and finally, Ethics and the Responsibilities of Scientists.

Science and the New World View

I choose to take the term "new world view" literally and look at this planet as we perceive it today and as it has developed through time.

Our ideas about the Earth have changed since James Hutton first gave us a model two hundred years ago. He recognized the existence of an earth system and correctly outlined a pattern of on-going change through small increments over an enormous time period. He thus paved the way for Darwin's still broader biological conceptions on the same basis. Hutton's model, however, was not evolutionary, and he really did make the oft-quoted remark, "We find no vestige of a beginning—no prospect of an end." It is ironical, today, when we are at last approaching an approximation to a new model of the Earth that we are faced with the very real prospect of an end to the current era of human dominance. We now see the Earth as a small planet in space that is inherently changeable. Its liquid core and mantle are heated by radioactive elements that still remain from its origins some four and a half billion years ago. This heat induced on-going crustal and mantle movement is described under the term of plate tectonics. Within this system there are many sub-systems of change acting at different rates, some rhythmic others episodic. As a consequence, it is beyond our capacity to predict future changes accurately. Some are manifest in earthquake and volcanic activity on land and at the ocean ridges. They are linked to change in the relative position of the plates leading, in turn, to changes in climate and ocean circulation, and in the ambient life forms at or near the surface of the planet. All are on-going and currently unpredictable.

The planet, with its life forms, is part of the solar system and is thus influenced by the sun, and by variations in earth tilt and orbit round the sun. These induce further changes in atmospheric and ocean circulation, and therefore climate. Finally, the planet has been constantly bombarded by material in the form of meteorites and comets; some large enough to cause further massive changes in the Earth system and its biomass. We are far from being able to tie all these variables together into a coherent model.

Life has played an important role in shaping the physical and chemical nature of the planetary surface and atmosphere. Life developed in balance with the changing environment as a result of an evolutionary process driven by those changes. In the very recent past, the emergence of the human race has begun to cause change in the environmental flux more rapidly than, and in a different manner from, the established system. With essentially free energy supplied by fossil fuels, our race has become, during the last two centuries, a dominant force for change on Earth by any measure we may apply.

We are now able to chart past and current environmental changes, and techniques recently developed enable us to view the land, oceans and atmosphere from space, and measure secular changes in climate, cloud and ice cover, soil moisture, and marine and land bio-productivity. Ice cores have furnished an accurate record as far back as one hundred and sixty thousand years of global temperature, levels of atmospheric carbon dioxide and variations year by year in wind-borne sediments, including volcanic events. Other techniques allow us to penetrate more deeply into the past.

Direct measurement may now be made of the accelerating effects of quarrying by humans of soils, forests and ground water, encouraged by an economic system not yet adjusted to evaluating the sustainability of a resource, commonly assumed to be renewable, by overuse to such a degree that recovery will not occur on a human time-scale, if at all.

The scientist may point out and measure many of the changes that are taking place in our immediate environment and in a time scale of our own lives. But it will take very much more than science to change our current system, and persuade us to learn to live in balance with earth's ecosystem.

Predicting the Elements, the Evolution and the Cultural Dimensions of Change

In the present world, we must take certain facts into account that are not open to dispute in assessing the cultural dimension. The physical reality is that the ecology of the planet is out of equilibrium and change is out of control. This must surely be dictated by human behaviour. The facts are:

Population Growth. The world reached its first billion in population about the middle of the last century. In this century, it has increased to 5 billion, and, barring catastrophe, will double within the next thirty-five to forty years.

Energy Use. The use of fossil fuels in this century has increased twelve-fold, and the rate of increase is accelerating. This accounts for about seventy-nine per cent of the world's total energy usage, but more than three-quarters of these fuels are used by less than a quarter of the world's population. The increase of carbon dioxide in the atmosphere, generated largely by fossil fuel use, has reached danger levels and cannot continue for very much longer. This also is largely the waste from the minority—the so-called developed world.

Biodiversity Reduction. We are in the midst of a major extinction event comparable to some of the largest in the geological past. By eliminating wildlife habitat we condemn animals and plants to individual extinction. We now use and therefore interfere with forty per cent of all the net primary productivity of the Earth. It is this activity above all others that is inevitably changing the ecological balance of the total biosphere—an activity largely unplanned and without regard for the consequences.

Global Military Expenditures. These now total about one trillion dollars a year. In the light of problems facing the world today, these figures represent an enormous, almost unimaginable, waste of resources and human ingenuity.

Contemplating these facts, we observe that the global economy, this century, has grown twenty-nine fold, and is expected to grow another five times during the next doubling of the population. The largest growth in human population takes place in the tropics, but North Americans, for example, use two hundred times as much energy per capita as a citizen of Bangladesh or Bolivia, and produce the equivalent amount of pollution and CO_2.

There is one major observation that may be made concerning the changes we are inducing on Earth: almost all the disrupting phenomena, from CFCs in the stratosphere, acid rain, greenhouse gases in the atmosphere, quarrying of soils and soil erosion, quarrying of ground water, overconsumption of energy and resultant further damage to the atmosphere, are reversible. We may not choose to do so, but they could be stopped, repaired and/or recovered if we took measures today. We are technically fully capable to undertake this task. It is simply a question of political and economic will, of rethinking our cultural values and taking the ecological warning signals seriously. The destruction of the forests and other wildlife habitats, however, is irreversible. The current accelerating extinction rate, if it continues for a hundred years more, will equal the massive extinction of seventy to eighty per cent of all species on Earth that took place sixty-five millions years ago at the end of the Cretaceous—the well-known end of the dinosaurs. It takes millions of years to recover from such extinction events and the ecology is never the same. This is perhaps the greatest single danger facing this planet, and humankind.

Reconciling the Diversity of Interests with Social Freedoms, Human Rights and Human Values

Certain things are very difficult for us to grasp today, and are becoming more difficult:

(a) The worth of a human being is inevitably associated with things that we value most ourselves and that we recognize in others. We send food to the starving, but if we truly valued those who receive our help, then we would try to prevent the situation that they are faced with from happening. In fact, by our current actions we are contributing to the onset of much greater starvation than the world has ever known.

(b) It is necessary to understand what is meant when we use the word "we." In all discussions on the future, "we" is always present, even though it may be unvoiced. When we claim that humankind is emerging or advancing or mastering their environment, does this mean all humankind? In fact, proportionally, most of our claims for the "we," as it is tacitly assumed, are false. Those living in the privileged corner of the world cannot encompass the fact of five billion people on Earth and the fact of ninety million babies born each year and all that this demands of us. How may "they" become "we?"

(c) Our system of thought has grown out of our background, our history. But we have nothing to learn from history today. Indeed, we must forget it if we are to come to terms with the exponential growth currently, but temporarily, dominating humankind in resource use, waste production, soil erosion, water depletion, and so on.

Some of us alive today will live to see the end of growth. How will this come about? By planning, education and control, by famine and disaster, or by war on an unimaginable scale? Growth, surely, cannot continue, so that culturally we must come to terms with the idea that we live on a finite planet, and that most of us (the "we") are living lives of ultimate degradation, and that it appears very likely that this will get worse while growth continues. We (local) must recognize our legitimate diversity of interests and reconcile them with ideas of social freedoms, human rights, or human values. In each case, we must ask for whom?

Determining Remedial Activities

Science may be entering, or is already in a period of history for which we have been preparing since the Greeks who suggested about 2600 years ago that perhaps nature is intelligible. We find we are now faced with a task which is more difficult than anything we have ever contemplated: to decide how we may continue to live on this small planet. The human being is an animal that has moved out of ecological balance with its environment. Man is a wasteful killer and a despoiler of other life on the planet. This normal and apparently acceptable behaviour is licensed by a belief in God-given resources and encouraged by an economic system that emphasizes short-term profit as a benefit, and has not learned to put a real cost on the resources we consume. If we depart from an ecological balance to the extent that we destroy most of the remaining life on Earth, then, surely, we are dooming ourselves to a similar fate. In other words, we must live in balance with the world in which we find ourselves.

There must be a price put on such commodities as soils, as well as groundwater, surface waters, atmosphere and biosphere—or the sum total of all kinds of life on Earth. Such a price must include the cost of protection, replacement and substitution. Current economic thinking appears to be caught in a system which assumes limitless resources and ignores the production of waste products. This system worked when resources did appear to be limitless and when waste was easily disposed of and self-cleansing. Neither of these variables exist any longer.

The economic subsystem takes in resources and excretes wastes, and is thus irrevocably and closely linked to the ecosystem. Both input and output are finite and the main variable is the one-way flow of matter-energy. Such a way of looking at things raises the question of how big the economic system should be in relation to the physical dimensions of the global system. This also necessarily questions the concept of growth economics and the impossibility of generalizing current Western standards of living to the world as a whole. An important factor must be included: human welfare and equity.

If we begin to think this way, we shall be confronted by some extremely hard decisions, which may not be taken. But we shall also be confronted by a massive questioning of the current beliefs, axioms and myths, which lie behind much of today's economic and social thought, and we may look to the emergence of new understandings of what constitutes our enlightened self-interest.

Ethics and the Responsibilities of Scientists

These remarks may be considered presumptuous on the part of a scientist, but we are all in this together. I believe, therefore, that it is perfectly proper to appeal for an inductive approach in looking at our present condition on Earth, to draw empirical conclusions, including constructing some worst-case scenarios, and to attempt to put probabilities on them. I began these remarks with the Earth System, and I find that the human species has taken over. I suggest that we do not know enough to decide how to run this planet. We are forcing our will upon it, using the depleting resources and increasing waste discharge, while at the same time claiming that we must aim for sustainability. May we attain this globally, or have we passed the limits within which it may be achieved?

Perhaps a way might be found to judge our actions by a new principle: the health of the planet. Perhaps the economy could be seen as being within the environment, and not the environment within the economy. Perhaps we should ask the question of any action that we take: "Does it increase or decrease survivability?" The problems in relation to this way of looking at things would be scientific and social, and in their solution, we would strive to discover reality.

The term "quality of life" might take on a new meaning. We could try to limit our own needs in keeping with a consciousness of global resources and needs in the broadest terms. We could live in balance with all life, and crop and harvest according to preference and needs, provided that this does not reduce the capacity of future generations to also do so. In agriculture, food could be produced through appropriate land use in balance with the capacity of the environment to supply, rather than imposing our will on it by force for short-term benefit. Such an approach does not require a high degree of altruism, although it does require some degree of sacrifice. It is inevitable that what we now consider justifiable freedoms may be seriously constrained.

In a similar way, we may look on sovereignty in a different light. We may assume common cause with all people on Earth against a common enemy—action that threatens balance within our environment, or reduces our legacy to future generations. Somehow, a way must be found to permit us to look, for one brief moment, at the world without the filters of belief, axiom, model or political theory. During this moment, we could observe the planet and draw conclusions from our observation as to the health of our planet and the probability that life may be self-sustaining indefinitely into the future in terms of human lifetimes. We must examine the presuppositions that lie behind all our beliefs, and realize that sustainability is the ultimate criterion by which we judge our actions in our use of Earth resources and our discharge of wastes within the confines of our planet.

Dr. Digby J. McLaren is past President of the Royal Society of Canada, Ottawa.

Shimwaayi Muntemba

The Social Impact of Technological Advances in the Third World

Mr. Chairman, I bring the University of Guelph greetings from the Environment Liaison Centre International which is a global coalition of non-governmental organizations and voluntary organizations working on environment and development. Currently, its membership is drawn from 70 countries, north, south, east, west, ranging from on-the-ground actors, i.e. community operational organizations to research institutions, lobbyists and advocators. While less than 500 pay dues, and therefore have a greater role in directing the policies of the organization, the ELCI has a constituency of about 9,000 local organizations, all concerned with sustainable development, a development, we believe, in which economy meets ecology and environment, and where people mutually relate to nature.

I was asked at this presentation to focus on the ethical foundations of technology in International Development. For our organization, the World Commission on Environment and Development which Jim MacNeill referred to, strengthened our efforts by putting on the global political agenda our understanding of sustainable development as, and I quote here from the Commission's Report:

> Development that meets the needs of the present without compromising the ability of future generations to meet their own needs.

This definition of sustainable development raises fundamental and, if you like, ethical questions of how to attain that development, and another question of, to what end? ELCI's current strategy for sustainable development states, among other things, again I quote:

> The ELCI believes that lasting solutions for sustainable development will probably come out of a genuine interaction between modern technology and emerging grassroots, societal forces that are trying to reclaim control over their own destiny.

In my view, underlying both these quotes are the notions of equity and needs, that is equitable access to resources which will lead to global acceptable standards of living for the global family. I wish here to underline the fact that the former speaker, Richard Falk had emphasized poverty.

The Commission's definition, in my view, also challenges us to pause, to take stock of how we manage and modify the life-support systems of land, fauna, flora and air. Modification of the life-support systems implies technology and the relationships between the various actors in the process of development. Never once should we forget that for the majority of people in the economic South, sustainable development really means having secure livelihoods. Of course, the ultimate goal is this as well as sustainable development as defined by the Commission. The question of livelihood security is one component and is as important for people in the economic South as is global sustainable development.

I want us also to take stock of the concept of "relations" when we speak about sustainable or international development, and the mechanisms of attaining this development. We have social actors. Herein lies the notion of ethical foundations. How do technologists and those who transfer technology relate to the intended end-users of that technology? What processes should be put in place to ensure participation? I believe that participation is very central to the ethical foundation of development and technical motivations. What should be borne in mind is how to ensure that technology does not ultimately destroy the very foundations of development i.e., the environment and the natural resource base.

First, let's talk about the social basis of technology. Until very recently in this century we have been pre-occupied with the notions of the objectivity of science, objectivity of technology, of research, and of information. This objectivity is now under question. I know that in my earlier teaching days, my post-graduate students challenged, and today some of our Southern members are challenging, the objectivity of research and the objectivity of technology. In particular, technology is now seen as a carrier of cultural domination, thus a powerful weapon which destroys the social and cultural basis of sustainable development. Most of our members believe that there has to be social and cultural diversity just as there is, and should be, biological diversity. If this be the case, and I share the view that it is the case, the challenge to technologists as we enter the twentieth century is to determine what pathways must be followed for a technological development that will be a genuine tool for accomplishing global sustainable development? That is a challenge that we should address at this conference.

It is in the context of such concerns that the ELCI sees as necessary, the interaction between new modern technologies and emerging people's forces as a viable combination for modifying the basis of development.

But we may ask, how can this be accomplished in the real world? It is maybe a dream but it is herein that we are faced with the challenge of how to transfer technology or, if indeed, we should transfer technology. What are the ethical reasons for transferring that technology? Should the basis for international cooperation not be a shift towards placing greater focus on institution-building and human resources development in specific countries or sub-regions and, where possible, in eco-climatic zones? I think this deserves a little more reflection than is possible in plenary sessions and may be picked up in one of the workshops. Suffice it here to emphasize that technology for sustainable development must be built on firm ethical foundations of respect and dignity for the value systems of the end-users. To ensure that this is the case, international development agencies will have to work with technologists.

In the last two years, in particular, we have been tutored in the linkage between ecology and the environment. Hopefully, some of us have become converts. We also have come to realize and accept the interdependent nature of environmental and development concerns. Until recently, we thought that the issue of the environmental basis of development only concerned rural communities, mainly in countries of the economic South where livelihood security and development remain directly linked to viable natural resource bases such as land, water and forests. Now we know that the global family is sitting on dynamite greater than the nuclear threat—dynamite which is largely of our own making: depleted and contaminated soils and water, poisoned air, depleting the ozone layer, global warming leading to sea-level rises and so forth. We all know them. Most of these ills have resulted from the spread of careless technologies. The panel that I managed on the World Commission came to the conclusion that the spread of careless technologies has rendered greater threat to the natural resource base than we have been made to believe. I want to emphasize that the spread of this careless technology, while increasing the standard of living of the middle and upper class people, particularly in the North, has created a garbage culture—a culture of waste which, through technological and cultural export, is being transferred to other countries and societies.

There are, in my view, two sets of ethical questions in this regard: (1) Is it ethical for the perpetrators of this garbage culture to persist in so doing, knowing full well that this culture is undermining the foundations of sustainable development globally? What would it cost us to review and change our lifestyles as a personal contribution to global sustainable development? and, (2) What technologies need to be put in place that will not undermine the very basis of development and human survival, and how can this be done?

These are ethical questions which interest groups within nations and nations themselves must address and answer now. What is heartening to me is to see the awareness of these issues over the last two or three years and the concern expressed by many groups from scientists, technologists, academics, young people, industrialists to policy-makers and, of course, by the NGOs and the media. The latter two especially have been at the forefront in spreading these messages to the world. What is also heartening, although it is just beginning, is to see that at such conferences, we all come together to discuss, think through and learn from each other in order to realize our dreams of sustainable development in scientific and technologically accepted ways. The message underlying this is twofold. One is the essence of participation. Whatever technological pathways we choose, there has to be an element of participation in the decision-making process. How to do that is a question which we will pose to our industrialist friends. The other question is one of integration. How do we make sure that input by the end-users of that technology, particularly the poor in countries of the economic South, is incorporated in the decision-making process?

I believe that the greatest challenge here is first to acknowledge that the poor are not ignorant. For instance, our organization is coming up with information that shows that women in most African, Latin American and Asian societies know how to select seed and conserve soil and water. They are the seed banks. What we need to do is to develop technologies which will build on the technologies that peasants have already developed. The challenge of sustainable development is for those who own and control modern technology to build and work together with the peasants and women of Africa, Latin America and Asia and with the non-governmental and voluntary organizations who now serve as the vanguard of the relationship between economy and ecology for sustainable development.

Dr. Shimwaayi Muntemba is Executive Director of the Environment Liaison Centre International, a global coalition of non-governmental organizations. She is also the host of Peoples Voluntary Organizations, programme coordinator of a Global Programme of the World Commission on Environment and Development, project manager of the International Labour Office.

James M. Stewart

Ethics in the Use of Technology: An Industrialist's View

I certainly feel like Daniel in the lion's den at this conference—one of the very few industrialists in a sea of distinguished thinkers from academia and the public sector! Yet, industry is one of the main vehicles through which society derives the benefits and sustains the costs and penalties of technology. So industry must play a vital role in ethical decisions on technology. It is also necessary to reflect on the way we, as a society, go about making technological choices and why this process must be improved. Some practical examples from our experience at Du Pont might be useful in helping others comprehend the kind of approach we think should be taken in weighing the advantages and disadvantages of new technologies. Finally, I will offer a few specific suggestions about how industry can make a more meaningful contribution to technological decisions.

I will start with a few of my beliefs:

(1) Technology is neither ethical nor unethical. The ethical dimension comes in the decision-making process on how technology will be used. An ethical decision-making process is one which is fair and open, and gives all those with a stake in the outcome a chance to be heard. Decisions will be ethical only if they are made after balanced and thoughtful consideration of all the implications, by and for all constituencies, and within a short and long-term global context.

(2) By and large, the use of technology by industry has been ethical: a higher standard of living, longer life spans, dramatic reduction in disease, better and more plentiful food, more universal education. These are the important benefits that society wants, and in helping to develop them, industry has acted in an ethical manner.

(3) As a last premise, the survival of industry depends on meeting public expectations. As Peter Drucker has pointed out, "The [business] enterprise exists on sufferance and exists only as long as society and the economy believes it does a job—a necessary, useful and productive one."

Technology can continue to be a positive force for good. Yet today, we face enormous and critical decisions on its use. We are just beginning to understand that in an interdependent world, technological decisions can have far-reaching, sometimes global implications. In this respect, we must ask ourselves whether these decisions will be made in a balanced, thoughtful and ethical way? Will all important constituencies be heard from and their points of view considered? To attain this balance, we are going to have to radically change our decision-making processes.

Although I will be using some environmental examples to outline the decision-making process that takes place at Du Pont, we face similar ethical issues in technology in many other areas. My company, and for that matter myself, are involved not only in technological decisions relating to the environment, but also to the use of energy, worker and community safety and occupational health, employment and job creation, urban development, health care, and Third World development. In few of these areas do we see a really balanced and thoughtful decision-making process. Instead, we can observe a decision-making process characterized by the following traits:

(1) Single issue lobbyists with strong, partisan, emotional biases tend to get the most media coverage. They have a legitimate role to play but they tell only one side of the story.

(2) The public is woefully unprepared and largely uneducated regarding technology. Yet technology is the dominant force affecting our lives. Naturally, fear, often unreasoning fear, dominates the thinking.

(3) Industry, suspect because of its vested interest, and in some cases because of its record, is reluctant to get openly involved. Its essential input is often disregarded.

(4) Most of our politicians do not have the background or knowledge to understand fully the complexities of modern technology or the implications of its use.

In this context, it is no wonder that we stumble ahead uncertainly, unable to really come to grips with major technological decisions.

Industry Responsibility

What can industry do to improve this situation? First of all, we must recognize our responsibility to speak up publicly. It is industry that in many ways has the best information, knowhow, and resources to contribute to decisions involving technology. But we have been too reticent, too secretive, not willing enough to take the public into our confidence, reluctant to share the information needed for balanced decision-making. May be that is because it has seemed easier to try to reach decision-makers through quiet lobbying behind closed doors.

The low-key approach is not working. Politicians are more sensitive than ever to the media and the polls. To make an impact, industry will have to inform and win over public opinion. We will have to speak in terms to which the public can relate—about the concrete benefits and hazards to them in what we do. We must also be prepared for emotional and unreasoned attack, as well as valid and reasoned criticism.

Industry must inform the public that there are important but controversial issues that need to be considered not to mention some difficult balancing of interests. For example, we may all endorse the call of the Brundtland Commission for sustainable development, but translating that principle into decisions and actions is a very challenging task. In the developing world, the balance will be even harder to find since technology is crucial to improving living standards, health and nutrition.

Canadian industry is operating in a fiercely competitive world—an increasingly interdependent world. The health, even the survival, of Canadian industry depends on the aggressive development and application of technology. In many areas, we are already behind competitor nations. If we do not introduce new processes and new products, for sure others will, and Canadians would then solely import the results of successful application of technology elsewhere. All Canadians would be the worse for that through unemployment, lower standards of living, lessened ability to make public investments whether it be as assistance for the disadvantaged in our society or support for the arts. In the developing world, the balance will be even harder to find since technology is crucial to improving living standards, health and nutrition. If groundless fears and ill-conceived arguments deprive Canadian industry of the tools it needs to compete, the price will be high, and ultimately, it will be paid by all of us. Industry must bring forward these considerations so that the tradeoffs can be made in an ethical decision-making process.

At this point, I would like to highlight some specific cases that illustrate ethical decisions on the use of technology at a practical level. At Du Pont, we are producers of plastic packaging materials, so I will address the issue of plastics in food packaging and garbage disposal. Both are, needless to say, controversial subjects. My purpose is to highlight the kinds of questions that we in this company believe must be asked and answered as part of an ethical decision-making process.

(1) The Solid Waste Crisis: Some Practical Examples

Our biggest enemy is the tendency to reach for simple, popular solutions based on superficial analysis. Unfortunately, these issues are anything but simple. It takes rigorous thinking to arrive at an ethical decision that truly considers all implications—long and short-term—by and for all constituencies.

The municipal garbage issue is a case in point. Public opinion has somehow become convinced that plastics are the problem. If only they could be eliminated, recycled or made degradable, the problem would be solved. In the United States and elsewhere, plastics are being singled out for restrictive legislation. But this snap judgement overlooks a whole range of relevant factors. A key point is that plastics make up only about 7 per cent by weight of municipal garbage, although, true enough, more than that on a volume basis.

Advances in plastic packaging, from bread bags to microwave dishes, have not only reduced the costs of distribution and greatly increased consumer convenience. They have also played a major role in the dramatic reductions in food spoilage and disease transmission. It cannot be denied that there have been some frivolous uses of plastics in packaging. These, however, will not survive. On the other hand, the movement to restrict plastic packaging threatens to deprive the public of useful, and in some cases, essential products. It will not help the environment much either, given the relatively moderate contribution of plastics to the solid waste stream. On the contrary, it could be counterproductive if plastics are replaced by containers that are less environmentally compatible.

We need to put the role of plastics in municipal waste disposal into context. The major components of municipal garbage are one-third compost waste (leaves, lawn and kitchen waste, etc.), and one-third paper products. Why are our politicians not working more strongly on recycling the large compost portion? Is it ethical to concentrate on the visible and emotionally charged plastics issue?

Maybe we could learn something from European countries that seem to be handling the solid waste problem more effectively. In the most progressive jurisdictions, cardboard and paper, glass and metal, and some plastics, are separated and recycled; and compost materials are removed for separate recycling. What remains is burned in high-tech incinerators. Even Sweden, which once banned incineration because of environmental concerns, has now found waste incineration environmentally safe and uses energy-from-waste incinerators to dispose of a large part of unrecycled waste. After all, most plastics are made from oil and their reuse for energy saves oil and coal.

Few people seem to realize that every kilogram of polyethylene used to recover energy avoids the use of two kilograms of coal.

What about recycling? All thermoplastics, and they are the ones in everyday use, can be recycled. It is just a question of cost. But that is a big question. An infrastructure is needed to collect plastics in sufficient quantity to warrant building a reprocessing plant. Different plastics have different properties so sorting is a big and costly problem. The net result is that the cost of recycled plastic can be much more than virgin plastic. Du Pont strongly supports recycling where it makes sense. But in some cases, we have to ask if it is the best way to spend our waste management dollars, particularly if the energy value of plastics can be recovered in efficient incinerators.

While the environment is not the only criterion for deciding which packaging to use, it is obviously very important. But assessing the environmental impact of a packaging system is a more complicated task than many people realize.

I believe we must compare plastics with other forms of packaging in terms of the total environmental impact *over the entire life cycle* of the technology. That means considering the effects of raw material production, transportation, use, disposal—in other words—the full span from cradle to grave. Only if we do this objectively and thoroughly can ethical decisions be made. In this assessment plastic packages should survive only if it is the best packaging system, on an ethical decision-making basis.

(2) Plastic Packaging

Milk pouch packaging is a more specific example of an environmental impact assessment in food packaging. Half of Canadian milk is sold in plastic pouches. This system was developed and commercialized in North America by Du Pont and we lead the world in this technology. The main alternatives are the paper carton or the plastic jug. Many consumers, and some consumer groups, favour the use of paper products because they are based on a resource that is at least potentially renewable. Some people propose a return to the glass bottle, believing it to be a more natural, usable container. Which is friendlier to the environment?

The plastic pouch generates less than one quarter of the packaging waste by weight than does the carton. Also, the process of manufacturing the pouch generates 60 per cent less air pollution than does the production of paper packaging for the same quantity of milk. In a landfill site, the pouch takes up less than 10 per cent of the space of the milk carton because it is completely compressed. Furthermore, it can be recycled while the carton cannot. Whether recycling makes economic sense is a debatable point but Du Pont is working on an experiment to find this out.

What about the returnable glass bottle? It appears that a British Colombia dairy is promoting glass as the environmentally friendly solution. But once the total system is examined, glass is quickly rejected. Why? The high energy in its manufacture; the transportation cost for a heavy container; the chemicals, energy and water required for cleaning; the spoilage and health risks. A study done by the University of Minnesota a decade ago compared the environmental impact of glass bottles, paper cartons, returnable polyethylene bottles and polyethylene pouches. Some of this data is shown in the table (on the next page) on an index basis. The study assumed that the glass and returnable polyethylene bottles would last for 25 trips.

It is not difficult to see that the pouch won hands down in all categories. An environmentally friendly winner? An ethical decision?

It should be mentioned that pouch packaging of food products is in use today largely in the rich countries. Should we be promoting it for use in the developing world? Is that not just another example of exporting our wasteful and environmentally damaging

Environmental Comparisons
Various Milk Packages

	Paper Carton	Glass Bottle	Poly Bottle	Poly Pouch
Energy Comparisons	100	36	31	26
Volume of Wastewater	100	24	29	7
Atmospheric Emissions	100	67	50	40
Volume of Solid Wasste	100	27	6	3

technology? Again, a total impact assessment should help us to make an ethical decision.

In Puerto Rico, school milk is rapidly being switched from paper cartons to individual "mini-sip" polyethylene pouches. Why? Cafeteria garbage is reduced 40 per cent and schools pay for garbage disposal on the amount generated. There is a major saving in the refrigerator volume required, thus also, less energy. Kids like it and it costs less. To us it seems an ethical decision.

In India we are working on pouch packaging of edible oil. Edible oil is a huge volume commodity there. It is handled in bulk—in tanks and drums, and consumers take their individual needs home in their own containers. Seems like a perfect environmental packaging system—everything reusable, perhaps indefinitely. But is it? Are we ethical in promoting a switch to polyethylene pouch packaging? The immediate reaction of the environmental critic is predictable. But consider this. In the present system, leakage and spoilage are high—conservatively estimated to be at least 10 per cent or even double that amount.

Consumers face serious hazards through spoilage and contamination. The mass sickness and paralysis from the adulteration of cooking oil by industrial lubricating oil in Calcutta in 1988 was widely reported. But this was just one of a long list of such incidents. There is also the serious problem of consumers receiving both poor quality and suspect quantity.

The plastic pouch is less than half the cost of competing rigid plastic or paper-based containers. Considering all aspects of the present system, the advantages of the plastic pouch system in cost, safety and health and environment, are apparent. It is no wonder the Indian government is enthusiastic about the potential of plastic pouch packaging.

Such mundane examples may seem out of place with more elevated, philosophical concepts on ethics. The examples themselves may even sound self-serving. This was not the purpose. As mentioned beforehand, plastic packaging will survive or fail on its merits. It is just an example with which I am familiar. It is also one where things are not necessarily what they might seem to be on the surface; where total environment impact assessments are necessary so that the right answer—the ethical decision ensues. Without airing the total picture, public pressure might push the decision in the wrong direction.

What Industry Should Do

What can industry do to contribute more to ethical decision-making on the use of technology? There are a number of aspects to be considered in building a set of ethical guidelines:

(1) It goes without saying that industry should view technological decisions holistically, and strive to see that they are ethical.

(2) Business has an obligation to share its knowledge and expertise to increase understanding of the issues and the advantages and disadvantages of proposed solutions.

(3) Corporations should work harder and more openly to break down the barriers of fear and mistrust between themselves and the community at large—including, of course, environmental groups.

(4) Business should participate more fully in open public debates on technology. Our only plea is that we be treated as responsible citizens with honest and valid points of view.

(5) Industry should work harder to promote improved education on the benefits and perils of science and technology. It should provide tomorrow's leaders and voters with enough technological awareness that they can make balanced decisions. Du Pont is assisting in several projects in this area.

Industry has stewardship of capital and human resources as well as environmental resources. It is our responsibility to see that, in the process of making decisions, society considers the full dimensions of the issues at stake and the valid perspectives of industry on these issues.

As I have tried to show with the plastic packaging examples, ethical decisions on technology are often more complex than meets the eye. To make informed, sustainable choices, we need thorough research, rigorous thinking, and an understanding of the total life cycle of the product or technology under assessment. Industry has the analytical tools and the technical knowledge to make a vital contribution to the debate. Ethical decision-making is very much about weighing and balancing. It is the obligation of industry, as far as possible, to see that all relevant factors are placed on the scale.

James M. Stewart is Senior Vice-President of Du Pont Canada Ltd.

Shirley G.E. Carr

Technology: A Labour Perspective

The labour movement believes that advances in the development of capital and technology could be used to greatly enhance the development of people here in Canada and throughout the world. The critical question, however, is who controls these instruments and how will they be used. As the Canadian Conference of Catholic Bishops put it:

> Unless communities and working people have effective control over both capital and technology, the tendency is for them to become destructive forces rather than constructive instruments in economic development. Under these conditions, the worker becomes more and more redundant and a victim of impersonal economic forces. This is the central problem of our times. It is first, and foremost, a moral or ethical problem in the structural order of our economy and society.

A 1987 study by the Canadian Auto Workers on "Technological change in the Auto Industry" sums up the issue very well.

> Corporate enthusiasm for a particular type of technology or a particular constellation of technologies might wane, but the underlying motivation does not. Corporations will continue to reduce costs, improve efficiency and increase productivity by introducing technology; they will continue to use it as an opportunity to restructure the workplace; they will continue to look for labour relation innovations in quarters that do not have strong union traditions; and they will increasingly whipsaw workers while encouraging their individual support and involvement.

There is no doubt that management is currently the dominant actor in labour relations, and technology can be played as a trump card in both economic and ideological terms. The driving force behind technological change is corporate, the cost-benefit analysis narrowly economic. If the goal of technological change is short-term profit and a single-minded reduction of labour costs, the outcome will surely be a deterioration in the conditions of working life; and this against a backdrop of shrinking employment opportunities.

As is so often the case, labour shoulders a weighty responsibility, first in challenging narrow economic interests, and secondly in promoting a broad social agenda. Technological change is a workplace issue, but it is also one of the most powerful social and economic changes of this decade. As such, labour's response to technological change must influence more than the outcomes in a particular plant, company or even industry.

In Canadian industrial culture, one of the most clearly discernible trends is the drive for increased managerial control. New technology is designed to increase management's command over production and managerial authority over producers. The market-oriented policies of government and technological change have in effect created conditions that will not make our task easy. Under these conditions, working people are compelled to develop a new lifestyle for the emerging high-tech market society. With the Mulroney government's emphasis on the private sector as the engine of economic growth, on federal deficit reduction, lower taxes for the rich, cutbacks in social programs, deregulation, privatization, and now, free trade with the U.S., the government's ability to manage our economy and maintain social standards has been weakened. At the heart of this political agenda is a renewed vision of "market society" for a high-tech industrial age. Human relations and people are being redefined in terms of the market place. Certain values and principles—profitability, productivity, efficiency and competitiveness—are the laws by which social relations are governed in a market-oriented society. Under such market criteria, labour, human needs and human services are generally treated as commodities to be bought, sold or exchanged in the market place.

As new technologies are introduced into the workplace, workers are called upon to adapt, adjust, retrain and relocate. As competition for world markets increases, workers in Canada are urged to be "more competitive" by lowering wages and reducing demands on social services. At the same time, the working people are expected to respond to the fantasy world promoted in advertising messages by consuming, spending and accumulating. These are the features of market society and market values today. In effect, the survival of capital takes priority over labour, over people and over communities. Measures to bring down real wages are proposed. These are described as flexible new forms of employment such as job sharing, working at home, and expanded part-time employment.

As we enter the 1990s, we have a system increasingly characterized by production based on advanced technology, unskilled labour and mass consumption. The rapid introduction of labour saving technologies has only intensified the crisis. There is a growing cynical resignation to high unemployment in our society. Under these conditions, capital and technology are being reasserted as the dominant organizing principles in this market-oriented society.

Computerization and robotics have begun to create what may become a new class of people. These are the men and women who are being shut out or marginalized by their functional illiteracy in the new technologies. The most affected are expected to be workers in manufacturing and resource industries. In addition to this new class of people, we have had a dramatic increase in part-time employment as well as an increasing number of permanent plant closures and mass layoffs. The permanent manufacturing jobs that are lost tend to be replaced by part-time service sector jobs, and most of these are in the personal services and unskilled low-wage sector.

One of the most significant features of the labour market in Canada during the 1980s has been the proliferation of low-wage, part-time, insecure jobs. Data from Statistics Canada Survey of Employment Earnings and Hours show that about 37 per cent of the jobs created since 1983 pay less than $10,000 annually—roughly the poverty line for unattached individuals, while 77 per cent pay less than $20,000 annually—the poverty line for a family of three. Only one job in five pays more than $20,000 annually.

It is the middle class which are the most vulnerable to increasing marginalization due to the new technologies. The upward social mobility of the post-wars is rapidly giving way to the new trend of downward social mobility for many people. As a direct consequence, this is likely to contribute to an enlargement of the sectors of poverty and powerlessness in our society.

Coupled with the introduction of technologies that replace people are the vast changes in the global economy. These include the decline in our manufacturing industries, increased corporate concentration, and rapid expansion of multinational corporations.

The last three decades have seen the collapse of the family wage system. Is this yet another signal of the arrival of the two-tiered society? By this we mean essentially, a society with no middle class, one with a large number of poor and a small number of rich people. The bottom fifth of Canada's population now earns a mere 3.6 per cent of all income while the top fifth takes 43.3 per cent. The time has long passed when a single wage could support a family. This trend reflects, among other things, a radical de-skilling of the workforce, the substitution of machines for skilled labour, and a vast increase in the number of low paying, unskilled jobs, many of which are filled by women.

According to a German trade union study, a privileged stratum of elite workers may eventually comprise one quarter of the working population. Another quarter of the working population will be made up of unskilled or semi-skilled industrial and clerical workers holding stable jobs, while half the working population will be on and off the job continually. This "floating population" will be employed mainly in subcontracting and service industries, either part or full-time. In other words, half the population won't have a regular job any longer.

In this changing economic climate, some social historians feel that our society could become torn between the affluent minority and a horde of desperately poor people by the end of this century. Instead of the Third World joining the industrialized world, this new market-oriented society would reshape our society to that of the Third World.

It is often argued that job growth in the service sector can offset the losses in manufacturing employment. Some analysts of the post-industrial era regard this growth as a sign of decadence. Economists who try to prove that job losses due to computerization can be offset by enlarging the service sector in fact advocate a kind of society which many of us would find repugnant. As one influential theorist of the post-industrial society explains: "It is a society based on extreme inequality where the people for whom the social process of production has no use are to sell their personal services to those who have a comfortable income." According to André Gorz, this would take us back to the second half of the nineteenth century when one sixth of the labour force worked as servants and domestic employment. It would create pre-democratic conditions, a kind of South Africanization of society.

Another frequently heard argument from conservative economists is that economic growth will solve the evils of unemployment and the maldistribution of wealth and income. But as one of Canada's well-known critics of public policy, Eric Kierans explains, "More economic growth does not solve the evils of unemployment and maldistribution of wealth and income." He points out that the MacDonald Commission's emphasis on economic growth as the solution to Canadian ills has ignored the history and experience of the last four decades. He points out that over that period, we enjoyed phenomenal economic growth but unemployment increased and the distribution of income and wealth worsened. Kierans reminds us that, "The heart and purpose of an economic system is its principle of distribution. Otherwise our economic policy makes production an end in itself, the pursuit of wealth and power for its own sake and not as a means of serving the needs of the people." He therefore raises an important question when he asks, "Is Canada splitting in two, one part protected under the corporate umbrella and the rest vulnerable, weak, employed and unemployed who struggle for survival? Is corporate power beyond political control?"

The economic disparities between classes and regions are growing. Our future will be shaped less by the nature of technology than it will be by the current political philosophy which favours increasing corporate concentration mergers, take-overs and multinational corporate power with global interests.

Mass unemployment, the declining family wage, and the alarming increase in poverty are fundamentally moral and ethical issues. The official unemployment statistics combined with the number of discouraged workers (those who have given up looking for work), and the number of underemployed workers (part-time workers seeking full-time employment), mean millions of people are being deprived of an adequate income.

Underneath the continuing employment crisis lies a deepening human and social tragedy. The experience of unemployment generates a sense of alienation and power-lessness that comes from a loss of personal identity and self-worth. These personal traumas tend to translate into social crises such as increasing alcoholism, suicides, family breakdown, vandalism, crime, racism and street violence. Personal insecurity associated with unemployment creates a climate of social fear and passive acceptance. There are some disturbing signs of the times emerging in this post-industrial era. The magnitude of the problem is staggering. What we are undergoing in terms of social change is equal to and as dramatic as the industrial revolution. Yet the programs that would help Canadians to adjust are under attack or non existent.

The domination of our industrial system by multinational corporations has meant that whole operations have been moved out of Canada since the free trade deal has been put in place. Moreover, cutbacks in government social programs, such as the massive cuts in unemployment insurance, are indicative of a possible return to a system of privatized social services in a market society. The alarming increase in food banks across the country, from zero just a few years ago to over a hundred, as well as the thousands of homeless, is just one indication of the breakdown of our social support system. The voluntary sector is asked to carry what is properly a government responsibility.

Most of the laid-off in industry are in their forties. They have worked all their lives, they are skilled, live middle-class lives in terms of expectations and combined family incomes. Many who do not find jobs may never work again. Those who do find jobs will be subject to de-skilling, and end up doing something less demanding for less money.

In a recent study, the Science Council of Canada found massive de-skilling as laid-off workers in manufacturing move into the low-skill, low-wage personal services sector. For people who move into poverty in their forties, the social problems are horrendous. It is not only the percentages employed that will decline but the quality and meaning of their work as more and more workers are engaged in mindless, meaningless, and monotonous efforts. Technology itself is a problem, but in a society where the market (or that small number of powerful economic interests) makes the final determination, the social consequences are far-reaching. It is this market orien-tation about which we must be most worried.

In the mid-fifties, the Canadian Labour Congress asked, "If traditional mechani-zation has produced this effect, what will automation do, piled on top of traditional mechanization?" Today, the question is more complex. What will technological change do piled on top of outscouring, overcapacity, rationalization, greenfield production, and threatening developments in trade? In the fifties, the question was at least partially answered by the sixties and a period of economic expansion. But in the eighties and nineties, with increasing joblessness and declining employment, there are few developments on the wider horizon that encourage optimism.

The introduction of new technologies provides a focus for labour's efforts to improve the quality of "work" life. But the conflicting trends and conflicting effects of new technologies make the task more difficult to accomplish. They also make the need to do so more imperative. If the impact of new technologies was solely detrimental, labour could respond with strategies to resist technological change or at least offset its negative impacts. If the consequences were always positive, labour could embrace technology while working to resolve the inevitable frictions involved with its implementation. Neither of these options are practical. Instead, we must recognize technology's conflicting potential. We must be equipped to separate technology design issues from those of implementation, and must influence both. Moreover, we must differentiate technological determinism from corporate authority and challenge both.

As the Canadian Auto Workers' study reminds us, in the fifties, the labour movement in Canada and the U.S. articulated a set of policies which remain appropriate in current discussions. The issue was "Automation" and the threat of unemployment. At the time, most trade unionists accepted automation, and even supported it, as not only necessary, but desirable. Labour argued that its impact made it necessary to develop appropriate public policy responses and safeguards.

In the U.S., the trade union position was expressed by labour leaders such as the late Walter Reuther to the Congressional Hearings that were held on *Automation and Technological Change*. In Canada, the Canadian Labour Congress presented the views of labour to the Royal Commission on Canada's Economic Future in 1956. In a report entitled, *Probable Effects of Increasing Mechanization in Industry*, the CLC argued for a number of seemingly attainable objectives:

- **Shorter Work Time**. We can reduce hours of work. We can increase the number of statutory holidays, and lengthen vacations. We can keep youngsters longer in school and college, and we can retire oldsters earlier.
- **Training and Retraining**. We will require training and retraining … Government or government and management will have to take the responsibility for retraining displaced workers.
- **Income Support and Protection**. Unions can press for the guaranteed annual wage … for higher unemployment insurance benefits, and old age security and family allowance payments.
- **Higher Wages**. Press for higher wages in general … or management will get more than its share of the fruits of technological progress, and the mass purchasing power on which the whole industrial system depends will suffer.
- **Government Policy**. Unions must press for the right government monetary, tax, tariff and investment policies.
- **Full Employment**. We must establish and maintain full employment … That is by no means all that government has to do, but unless it does this, nothing else it can do will be effective.

While there may be some debate on the particulars of any one of these policy proposals, the general thrust remains as relevant a starting point today in responding to technological change as it did in the fifties when labour first confronted automation. But today, debate isn't enough.

Some steps toward union input into technology have been made, but they remain limited. Some corporations have talked about greater worker input, but this still needs to be tested and is simply not good enough. We can no longer accept the process of introducing new technologies as a "management right." We must place the principle of negotiating technological change on the agenda. This means that if corporations can plan the introduction of technological change so methodically and so far in advance, they can also give us the contractual right to advance notice. It means collective agreements that recognize that since technological change is now so integrally related to all working conditions, its implementation must be jointly administered. Above all, it means that we recognize that technology is not simply a "thing," mysteriously coming from the outside, but a product of human activity that is currently shaped by management priorities, but can also be shaped to address workers' needs.

Some will accuse us of overstepping our role as "workers." But just as paying workers for not working (paid vacations) was once thought of as an absurd proposition, just as paying workers who were no longer employees was once considered outlandish (pensions), just as health and safety issues were, not too long ago, thought of as an inherent cost of having a job, technology can no longer be left for unilateral management decisions, nor loosely reserved for management-dependent "consultations."

The issue for labour, therefore, is not whether technology is good or bad, nor whether we are for or against it. The issue is whether we will share in the wealth it creates, the leisure it makes possible, and can we wrest some control from a management determined to subordinate the new organization of work to the goal of competing for profit.

As I said at the beginning of this presentation, the labour movement believes that advances in the development of capital and technology could be used to greatly enhance the development of people here in Canada and throughout the world.

From labour's perspective, our social goals must reflect a renewed national commitment to full employment with an emphasis on permanent and meaningful jobs, new patterns of work with adequate personal or family income. It also entails a commitment to providing social services—education, health care, social security, unemployment insurance and child care. These social objectives, in turn, require a commitment to finding new and more effective ways of redistributing wealth and power among both people and regions in this country.

The fight against unemployment must, in our system of values, remain the primary goal of economic policy. It is the pivot by which social policy and programs result.

Shirley G.E. Carr is President of the Canadian Labour Congress.

Archie Graham

The Technological Either/Or: Technological Optimism Or Technological Realism?

During the last plenary session of the 1989 conference on ethics and technology at the University of Guelph, Eugene Critoph of Atomic Energy of Canada argued that the most significant shortcoming of an otherwise successful debate on the impact and role of technology in society was the separation of conference participants into two isolated and adversarial camps, that of the "technologist" and the "non technologist." While he did not clarify exactly what he meant by this terminology, Critoph made it patently clear that he thought these two groups were mutually exclusive in regard to how they respond to technology, progress and each other. This line of thinking is reminiscent of the "two cultures" argument, that at the heart of the technological problem is a clash between those who view technology as an "unalloyed blessing" and those who think it an "unmitigated curse," those simply "for" technology and those unconditionally "against."

Stated in this way however, the problem is oversimplified and misconstrued. It is not just a question of technology alone, and while the polarity suggested above does in fact exist, it is not based on unqualified acceptance or rejection of the technological system. The problem is more complex and lies much deeper. It is a matter of opposing world views. The proponents of one are unstintingly committed to the ideology of progress and pin their hopes for a better world on developing future technological possibilities. The advocates of the other are suspicious of this ideology and are engaged in an attempt to address more immediate and comprehensive human problems. In both cases, however, technology plays an important part: The former taking an optimistic view based on an enthusiastic confidence in the power of technology to improve and even transform society, the latter remaining unconvinced of the success of the technological system in this regard, and seeking technological reform as part of a larger endeavour to resolve pressing social and environmental difficulties. It is a contest between *technological optimism* and what I will identify here as *techno-eco-logical realism*. These points of view are grounded in opposing ethical principles. The technological either/or comes down to a hard ethical choice between two incompatible ways of life.

Technological Optimism

Technological optimism is not just a hopeful attitude about technology and the technological future, one shared by this group or that—in other words, by the few. It is a value system most of us in the Western world have paid allegiance to, in one degree or another, as a result of history, education, and the collective habits and patterns of the technological society in which we currently live. This value system is shared not only by individuals but by whole nations and even cuts across ideological barriers.

It is characterized, to begin with, by the love of change for its own sake, by the desire for unchecked innovation, particularly in material possessions and in technology itself. The technological optimist is like the undisciplined child who is hooked on novelty and constantly demands new toys to satisfy his unceasing yearning. There is always a new way of doing things, a better way, and where there is a way, there is a tool or a technique that can do the job.

If practical or social problems are so insistent as to command exclusive attention, the technological optimist is convinced they can be resolved by the strategy of the "gadgeteer." Faith in the power of technology is so strong that there is a natural readiness to apply it automatically in response to such cases. Where there is a question of deforestation, for example, forest management techniques are applied to ensure preservation of resources for continued development. In the case of the medical problem of increasing rates of heart disease, to take another instance, the prevailing tendency is to resort to manufactured drugs and where necessary open heart surgery. In respect to such important environmental and medical issues, in other words, the technological optimist looks to the immediate or impending technical fix, while carrying on business as usual in other areas of life.

Perhaps this is why technological optimism is always oriented towards the future rather than the past, though mainly in the sense that it involves commitment to the priority of technological possibilities over practical and social problems. It is inordinately focused on technological exploration rather than on the profound difficulties that technology generates. For the technological optimist, life is most interesting when some anticipated technical innovation is about to happen. He is so eager to exploit such prospects that he fails to take seriously enough the consequences of their actualization. This is partly a function of the fierce competition that lies at the heart of our industrial system. Canadians try to keep up with Americans trying to out-manoeuvre the Soviets, trying to beat the British, trying to edge the West Germans, etc., while everyone is trying to oust the Japanese from first place in the technological race.

The attitude of technological optimism is clearly premised on an often inarticulated proclivity to rate mechanical functions above purely human values. The trend of the modern world towards automation undermines confidence in the skill and power of human beings, especially in respect to the production of necessary goods. It invites us to exalt the technical expertise of collective man as it is embodied in the industrial technological system. As individual human beings we are intimidated by our relative weaknesses in this context, and by the perceived frailty of the human condition. Commitment to the technological system is so reinforced that we frequently act as if it were infallible, and where it is not so, seek with a vengeance to identify the "human error." Consider, for example, the focus of so much of not only media and political but professional attention concerning what were thought to be the root causes of the 1986 explosion of NASA's Challenger Spacecraft: the engineering and managerial mistakes. I am not suggesting that the latter were insignificant, but simply that as technological optimists we have come to believe so much in the strengths of the machine, that our natural limitations are viewed as operative liabilities which the technological system, as such, does not share. This overlooks the ironical fact that it is precisely these so-called liabilities which drive human beings to evolve technical instruments in the first place as a means to overcoming them, and that such liabilities are always present in the process of designing and using such instruments.

All of the chief characteristics of technological optimism can be explained, I believe, by reference to the unstinting faith in progress. I am referring to the kind of progress which derived from, and has prevailed since the Industrial Revolution:

unlimited advance in the material conditions of human life made possible by the continuing innovation in techniques. Closely associated with this notion is an unspoken sense that we are evolving towards perfection. There are some researchers now engaged in the study and development of artificially intelligent systems, for example, who give voice to this utopian sentiment in the most startling ways, prophesying a future populated by robotic slaves which (or perhaps I should say who) will release us from ordinary and menial labour to engage in a life of unadulterated and unparalleled leisure. Whether such a scenario is ever likely to prevail is a moot question, in this context, because the progressive tendency carries on unabated by our uncertainties in this regard: It continues *as if* utopia were to be the end result.

Progress And Technology

We are so used to thinking in terms of this technologically oriented progress that it is difficult for us to imagine life without it. Automation is often viewed not just as one way, but the only way forward. Indeed, progress so understood is sometimes identified with human destiny. Statements like the following are commonplace: "The world is moving inexorably into the third technological revolution, based on computers, telecommunications and the information economy ... Technology is revolutionizing Canada's manufacturing and is introducing a new world of unique mass produced products and Japanese inspired management and organizational methods." If we are to take such statements at face value, we have no choice: human fate is sealed, the automated utopia a forgone conclusion.

We are deeply influenced by progress because it is part of a prevailing, historically entrenched, and largely unquestioned system of ideas successfully transformed into a programme for social action. It is in this sense that we may speak of an *ideology* of progress. This epithet is useful because it suggests the rather rigid and monolithic character of a philosophy which significantly influences the personal and collective life of humanity.

The idea of progress has multiple roots, many of which I cannot trace here. But the peculiar modern sense of the word emerged from philosophical, literary, and scientific sources in the seventeenth century. Francis Bacon in particular lamented the fact that human knowledge had not advanced, in his estimation, since the ancient Greeks. He declared the need for a new, more practically oriented approach to seeking truth. Bacon identified the task involved as one of conquering nature, which for him, had a very specific meaning: To understand the laws of nature, and from such understanding to evolve a means for harnessing nature's powers. Following Biblical prophecy, he spoke of man's need for restoration after the Fall, that is, of the need to recover his rightful place in God's scheme of things, as subduer of the earth. It seems that in Bacon's reading of Genesis, knowledge was not the problem but the answer, a new practical knowledge, in a word, science.

Here is a philosophy which clearly suggests that human beings in some important sense lie *outside* nature, or, at the very least, if they are to become what God has given them the potential to be, they must engage in a struggle to rise above nature and establish control over this wayward mass of creation. We are encouraged thus to view ourselves as creatures quite independent of our natural surroundings, indeed, to accept the role of competitors in a contest with a rather inhospitable agency, and to exercise authority where none could have been expected before. As Bacon tells us in the *New Organon*, knowledge equals power. And power is exercised by the application of techniques which imply a radical separation between the user and the used. It is a question of mastery of, or by nature, which by implication is something less than human spirit—mere matter, to be precise, or mindless energy.

While the concrete development of the new knowledge was left to the "practical philosophers," most notable among whom was Isaac Newton, Bacon himself, along with Valentin Andreae and Thomas Companella, they revived a traditional mode of thinking first systematically explored by Plato, the envisagement of the ideal society. In *New Atlantis*, *Christianopolis* and *City of the Sun*, we see scientific knowledge applied to the renewal of society. It is pictured as the foundation of a heavenly inspired transformation of collective human fortunes. Science was thus established as the vehicle not only of human advance but of a kind of heaven-on-earth, a veritable utopia. The new optimistic faith in scientifically propelled progress was given a firm voice which was to resonate throughout the subsequent centuries.

It was the practical men of the eighteenth century who put this philosophy into action. Scientists came together with manufacturers, businessmen, and inventors in a variety of new societies committed to the application of science to industry. These organizations were instrumental not only in adapting the new knowledge, however, but in developing the meaning of progress by stressing the importance of improvement in material conditions as the means to the betterment of society.

An unremitting faith in such progress fuelled enthusiasm for the development of industry during the Industrial Revolution, industry that was made possible by what Toynbee calls "the substitution of scientific for unscientific culture in the agricultural sector." The organization of farming improved the mechanical efficiency and scale of agricultural output while at the same time serving as a vehicle for transformation of the domestic system into the factory system. The same kind of organizational principle was applied to manufacturing, the earliest factory being essentially an organized collection of steam-powered machines run by human operators and centralized under one or a small group of owners. The factory was so designed to permit more effective control over industrial production, to reduce costs, and above all, to increase efficiency and output for a mass-market. It became the motor of all progress, and progress was now intimately associated with the development of industrialization.

When we speak of technology in the modern world we think of it in the context of this tradition which we have inherited, a tradition focused on the industrial production of goods, implemented in two distinct but interrelated systems of operation, mechanization and automation. The principal effects of the mechanical mode of production are the contraction of human input and the specialization of labour: human beings are required to perform tasks which are strictly limited by extensive powers of the machine, and made uniform by its repetitive operations. This involves standardization in both the process of production and the product. The end result towards which mechanization has tended ever since the Industrial Revolution began is clearly implied in this description of its mode of operation. It involves two interconnected factors: the minimization of human labour and the maximization of production, the one understood as the means to achieving the other.

Automation has not altered the direction of this general tendency, in spite of prophecies to the contrary by Marshall McLuhan. In fact, the most noticeable change brought about by the automated phase of industrialization has been the augmentation of the mechanical mode in a critical respect. Whereas the latter minimizes human labour, the former minimizes human *control*. The combined effect on the process of production is the virtual elimination of the human factor. All of this is undertaken for the same largely unexamined end, maximized output.

Man, Environment and the Ethic of Domination

Clearly, progress in its fullest sense is premised on the ascension of homo-sapiens from the "jungle" of nature. The term ascension is appropriate here because of its theological connotation. The early proponents of the idea of progress perceived science and industry as the emblems of God's glory, and vehicles of the quest for heaven-on-earth. While the divine incentive may have vanished from the contemporary scene, the sanction has not been repealed: We no longer see ourselves heading towards heaven, but soaring, nevertheless, through outer space. Whatever the goal, the process is the same: a grand triumphant, upward spiral separating us from the earth.

Man has not been restored, however, as some of the originators of progress predicted, to a grander paradise, but is perched precariously on the edge of the abyss of his own ignorance, secular lord of a questionable creation. Nature has been transformed in our minds and in fact current terminology reveals how it figures in the hierarchy of human values. Even the relatively benign word "environment" suggests something peripheral to the purely human, a context apart from what we ourselves are. Thus it is easy for us to think of it as a "commodity" to be "consumed" or "raw material" to be "purified" and "refined" for human use. In general, we speak of a "natural resource" as something to be "exploited" in order to satisfy not simply necessary needs but manufactured wants.

It is this relationship of "exploiter" to "exploited" which reveals the ethic underlying the ideology of progress, the ethic of domination. Even if we do not think consciously about it, this ethic is entrenched in our mental habits and patterns of action. We design technology to master and manipulate. Tools are used to exercise power over nature and harness it to our own use. This ethical bias is illustrated with a vengeance in the thermonuclear weapon, which is clearly designed for indiscriminate destruction of vast tracts of nature. So designed, in fact, that it cannot be used in any other way. Such an instrument discloses a deep-seated contempt for nature—including human nature—embodied in the ethic of domination.

This is the ethic of the controller who imagines himself in absolute control, an ethic which sanctifies the conquest of nature as a means to what is perceived to be the common good. The irony is, that the controller himself is in fact out of control, and ends up in a position where his abuses are generating a reaction from the abused: nature refuses to be governed by man's ethics and subjugated entirely to his will.

Techno-ecological Realism

Technological optimism and the ideology of progress have been outlined in such a way as to point up its shortcomings, not only for the sake of demonstrating the bankruptcy of this point of view, but also with a view to defining what may be called techno-ecological realism. It is precisely because of the difficulties inherent in technological optimism that a new approach to technology is required, one based on a new realism which may be more clearly formulated in contrast with the insolvent optimism. What I will present below is an attempt to articulate some of the primary philosophical underpinnings of this alternative outlook.

The new realism does not amount to a rejection of technique or technical innovation as necessary and important factors in human life. But it does challenge the point of view which takes these as leading priorities of social development. I refer here, in particular, to the overriding concern with technological possibilities—prospective technical innovations or impending technical developments—which so often involves the neglect or deliberate dismissal of ensuing practical and social difficulties. The new realism insists on giving precedence to the consideration of such difficulties, not simply on an *ad hoc* basis, addressing this or that specific problem, but as a matter of practice. It is an approach which is premised on the notion that only by so doing can we expect to sustain the quality of human life or the integrity of nature on a lasting basis, simply because it takes account of these factors first and foremost, prior to whatever technology is projected for development.

This, of course, entails rejection of the strategy of the gadgeteer, whose solution to problems, whether technological or not, is automatically to invent a gadget to do a job. The attention of the new realism is not primarily focused on the tool, as such, or even the mechanical technique, which presumes a radical separation, as we saw, between the user and the used. It is concentrated, rather, on the prevention of such dilemmas in the first place. Not all human problems can be solved before they begin, of course, and immediate difficulties often necessitate immediate technological responses which, under present circumstances, is often all we have at our disposal. But techno-ecological realism holds out the promise of a radical alteration in the long-term relationship between humans and the world we live in, by establishing as critical standard the principle that the key to survival and ultimately to enriching human existence is not to change our surroundings so dramatically, but to change human character and lifestyle instead.

An essential factor in such change is the recognition of ultimate limits. I speak here not simply of the limitations of the individual, which the technological optimist is so quick to acknowledge and disparage, but the limitations of the collective human enterprise (which involves the whole industrial technological system) operating under conditions imposed by the ecosystem which is nature itself. I am speaking here of ultimate ecological limits, natural necessity, that beyond which no advance can be made. Becoming conscious that there are in fact such limits does not at all imply the devaluation of the human being relative to the mechanical device that is characteristic of technological optimism, and the consequent damning of the "merely" human as "weak" and "erratic." On the contrary, it involves more confidence in our humanity *per se*, and can lead to a greater enrichment of the human condition. On the one hand, it requires us to tap our extensive powers of cooperative creativity to find more comprehensive solutions to common problems. On the other, it enjoins us to a more intense and appreciative enjoyment, even celebration of what we have, because this is all there is. Techno-ecological realism encourages restraint not merely for the time being to deal with an immediate crisis but as a way of life because, over the long term, it promises to improve the quality of human existence.

This realistic attitude does not compromise the future for the sake of the present. Living fully includes acknowledgement that the immediate circumstances are inextricably linked with both the past and the future. What techno-ecological realism does take issue with in this connection, however, is a certain lack of awareness of this very fact. I refer here to an ignorance which is often accepted as part of the emotional if not conceptual framework of technological optimism. It takes the form of a reckless disregard for the past, or an overwhelming confidence in the future, or both. Such responses are not solutions, but part of the problem.

The latter is not principally a problem of techniques. It is not even a question simply of how we use technology or how, as McLuhan would have it, it uses us. Either way, it comes down to a matter of design: we abuse much of our technical expertise, and the resulting technology, in turn, abuses us, but only because we have designed it in such a way as to make this scenario inevitable. According to the new realism, the problem of technology is primarily one of knowledge and a sense of values. It has evolved from an impoverished outlook on who we are as humans and the ethical capitulation of means to ends: we have failed to recognize that we are part of nature and in setting out to conquer it, we have lost control of ourselves, having all too willingly relinquished responsibility for our own destiny to the technological system devised for the conquest.

Conservation and Technology

The kind of realism that is described here is founded on a rival concept to what is customarily called "progress," with its emphasis on the inevitable march of technique to ever greater heights of refinement, and the unlimited advance towards a material cornucopia. Progressive change, as it is understood in the contemporary industrial world, is a function of the automatic expansion of the technological system and the endless consumption of goods, which fails to allay—indeed, only serves to perpetuate our collective anxieties. It is merciless change, uncontrolled change, change without meaning or purpose beyond what it is, change which has value in and of itself. Progress, as it is understood here, is the sort of change that dissipates rather than sustains, and is in this respect, the opposite of the kind of growth that is referred to below.

The latter may be defined in terms of conservation, which can be clarified, in part, by distinguishing it from preservation. The term preservation suggests that something already dead is being kept from decomposing. Conservation, however, implies the perpetuation of life, and the deterrence of death. It does not preclude change and should not be confused with stasis. In fact, it involves change in the form of qualitative improvement, or enrichment. The prefix "con" meaning "with" or "together" contributes to the suggestion that this is a cooperative affair, characteristically organic.

The new realism involves the establishment of a different set of social priorities, in particular, the promotion of conservation over progress. This does not mean that all forms of change must come to an end, but that these evolve from a different kind of relationship between man and environment, the former coordinating with, rather than acting against the latter, as if he were its conqueror. This would have to include not only a redefinition of environment, but of man, redefinitions which are consistent in this regard: that they incorporate the notion of the latter's inclusion in the former.

We cannot adequately understand the environment until we begin to see it as nature, the class of all species which includes ourselves. And we cannot understand ourselves until we recognise that humanity is only part of the whole complex of the natural world.

A realism based on the priority of conservation is inherently ecological, and as such, entails a technology which evolves from different principles of design than its industrial precursor, *techno-ecology* as opposed to technology. Techno-ecology should be conjunctive rather than disjunctive, joining us to, rather than separating us from the earth. It ought to do so by nurturing the interrelationship of the parts to the whole, of each species of animate and inanimate life to every other. Techno-ecology would be designed with this emphatically in mind, considering the "raw material," mode of operation, and product of the system of production in relation to the whole ecosystem in order to foster rather than deplete or destroy the ecological complex. It would not be consistent with the objectives of mechanization and automation which are intended to usurp the functions human beings can and want to perform in fulfilling their needs. In fact, it could re-humanize work by linking us to nature in a way which not only generates, on a lasting basis, the products we require, but which enriches our experience by contributing to a greater understanding of its diverse and unequalled powers. In the best of circumstances, the techno-ecological implement should meet human needs pragmatically as they arise, and lead to the reduction, not expansion of industry and waste. Designed to avoid the production of surplus, a techno-ecological system would meet the ultimate objective of conservation, the minimization of the exploitation of nature.

Nature, Humanity, and the Ethic of Collaboration

There is a need for a redefinition of the terms "environment" and "man." I suggested earlier the usefulness of recalling "nature" and "humanity." The task is to understand, without romantic sentimentality or appeal to divine magic, how we are part of nature and how nature is an extension of ourselves. Much of the groundwork for the completion of this task has been laid already by many thinkers in the past. So when I speak of an organic or ecological concept of the natural world I am conscious of a history of thinking about nature, not as a kind of enemy to be conquered, but as a consort to be esteemed. In this context, it may be characterized as a loosely defined agglomeration of interconnected processes, one which is inclusive of human beings.

Understood in this sense, nature is not an eternal agency which lies behind temporal phenomena consigning these to a single, predetermined fate, but a concrete organism, each species of which (including each member of each species) is a process that emerges to its own individual fruition, dissolves, and ceases, in tandem with every other. These processes are all interdependent, each one feeding from and into every other, forming a union to be sure, but not a totality, because the whole is never fixed or predictable. The ceaseless confluence of such processes as each individual one strives towards its own completion entails constant evolution of the conditions which make consistent lines of development of species possible. Each process weaves together, from its relations with other processes in its vicinity, a sum greater than its parts, a new synthesis which is added to the many already coursing towards their respective conclusions. Nature, in other words, is a dynamic and creative ecosystem, its emerging forms of life involving a limitless capacity for novelty and diversity.

The species of human beings is one particular form of such organic life. With the ability to choose and to reason, humans exemplify and enjoy nature's creativity to the full, because they are not merely subject to the conditions under which they emerge in the ecosystem, but can affect these in process. We make a mistake, however, when we believe that we are somehow the independent sources of this creativity, are able to manipulate these conditions without cost, and are thereby capable of conquering nature. Humans are one interactive cell in a larger organism, and our creativity is a function of the interdependence of species. The more we study nature without the filter of the ideology of progress, the more we may discover, perhaps, that no species dominates, precisely because each one is dependent on, and significant to the emergence of the others.

Perhaps the ethic which is most consistent with the principles expressed here is an ecological one in which creative elaboration is the critical standard. "Collaboration" here refers to the conscious act of humanity to "co-labour," so to speak, with nature, as opposed to competing. The adjective "creative" in the same phrase refers to the capacity for nurturing compatible realization of independent purposes. Human beings who lived by such an ethic would meet their own needs in a way which was consciously modified to be consistent with the continuing health of the ecosystem as a whole. This involves acknowledgement of ecological limits, ultimate limits, limits which impinge on human progress in such a way that we must stop trying to do what cannot be done without dire cost to the whole of nature, including ourselves. But it does not necessarily mean a life of diminished enrichment. If freedom refers to the application of reason to the realization of potential established under the evolving conditions within the ecosystem, clearly it implies a sense of responsibility as well, an awareness of the effect of individual actions upon the world. Thus, when the freedom of the part is matched by a sense of responsibility for the whole, the result is a quality of life at once enriched in two principal ways: by the expansion of human potential through a more intimate understanding of nature, and by the establishment of a life-promoting equilibrium among the diverse forces of nature, including those peculiar to the human race. The ecological ethic involving the creative collaboration of humanity with nature is life-enhancing in a comprehensive sense.

Dr. Archie Graham is an instructor in Philosophy at the Ontario College of Art and President of the Faculty Association.

REFERENCES

1. *Ethical Choices in the Age of Pervasive Technology*, University of Guelph, October 25–29, 1989.

2. Emmanuel Mesthene, "The Role of Technology in Society" A.H. Teich (Ed.) *Technology and Man's Future*. (New York: St. Martin's Press, 1981) pp. 99–100.

3. Charles J. McMillan, "Technology: A Canadian Strategy" in *Inside Guide*. (Toronto: Winter 1988) p. 65.

4. See J.C. Davis, *Utopia and the Ideal Society*. (Cambridge: Cambridge University Press, 1981) pp. 124–125.

5. See J. Bronowski, *The Western Intellectual Tradition*, ch. 18. (U.S.A.: Dorset Press, 1986) pp. 323–335.

6. See Max Weber, *The Protestant Ethic and the Spirit of Capitalism*, ch. IV. (New York: Charles Scribner, 1958) pp. 155–183.

Carol Anne Letheren

Technological Pursuit in Sports

Growing up in sport, one of society's institutions, is like growing up in many other fields of endeavour—religion, the arts, the business and financial communities: we become part of an in-group, an inner world that, by its very nature and needs, sets itself apart, has its own language, ethics and values.

While sport is practised by many, it continues to be difficult to define. Slusher once suggested:

> ... play is the raw material for sport but sport is more than play. It includes devotion, care, respect, concern and responsiveness to the desired outcomes. It is serious. Sport is woven into man's existence, and like most phases of life, it has evolved into a task of the living. Sport provides the challenge of existence, the situation for attainment of high level being. It lets you know how good you really are.

Olympic sport has a stated philosophical base and is guided by the identified olympic ideals or the aims of the olympic movement. These include:

- international peace and brotherhood
- the development of physical and moral qualities such as fair play
- a concern for others

Sport at the top level is this and more. At these levels, it is truly a business.

The individual who pursues sport at the highest levels is pushing his/her physical capabilities to their limits. They are concentrating, focusing all of their "being" (physical, mental, spiritual and emotional) on one outcome. They invest a lot of time (often 7 days a week, 5–6 hours a day, for 10–15 years), sacrificing some of the day-to-day pleasures of adolescence and growing up. They are looking for the *edge*—the way to be the best they can be, to establish themselves as the best. There is little margin for error or slippage. There will only be *one* gold medal. The giving, the sacrifice is often difficult to comprehend, and it starts at a very young age and impressionable age. There are few life experiences like it.

As the athlete grows and develops, the pressures and demands change. Top competitors are constantly surrounded by a support team of coaches, managers, medical personnel and so forth. They move from pressures of a more personal nature, often family directed and close to the athlete, to more distant pressures coming from mega-institutions and organizations such as the media, the political and corporate worlds. By living *through* the athlete, they all stand to gain money, votes or an acclaimed reputation.

Each athlete's story is different and each one is effected differently by their development. Ben Johnson's story is a case in point. There are many young people, who like Ben, started their involvement in sport at a very young age and often because of an older, role model. In Ben's case, it was his brother who is also a renowned Jamaican sprinter.

Ben's Story by Ben Johnson

In my early years as a boy in Jamaica, play and sports were always a part of my life. I played a lot of soccer and to get enough money to go to the movies, my friends and I would race each other around the block betting 10 cents for first place. I suppose you could say that was my start in track.

But a constant in my life, my source of confidence and love was then, and is now, my Mum. We are a close family always helping each other out.

Although I took part in school sports, including track and field, running 100 m in 11.3 second and 200 m. in 23 seconds at age 14, it was my older brother who first suggested I come to his club and train properly. He was a track and field athlete who trained with Charlie Francis.

I started competing in world wide competitions in 1978 and placed fifth in the semi-finals. In 1979, I was the top junior in the world and won the 100 m in 10.60 at the national championships in Vancouver. Despite some upsetting losses in between, by 1984, I won the Bronze medal. This was a turning point in my life. I wanted to do better and better. I was one of the first runners in Canada to lift weights and use strength as a major factor in my training as a sprinter. The Gold medal in Seoul was what I wanted badly and it was within my reach. It became an increasingly important goal for me. With my Father in Jamaica, my oldest brother in Texas, I was the man in my family and I saw an opportunity to provide for my family.

However, I got swept up in a tidal wave—a lot of success—swept up with what it seemed everyone was doing. I trusted and followed and I am responsible. I took steroids to help me achieve my goal. I knew many others were and I thought I had to do the same in order to win.

I want so much to be able to compete again—to show I can do it in a fair and honest way using the natural talents I still have. I let down a lot of kids who had become an important support group for me and I want to show these kids I can do it and do it clean. I want to tell them and show them that drugs are not necessary and cheating is wrong. I was lucky to get caught and put an end to that era.

I have learned much through what has been a tough experience. I have disappointed many people including myself. I really knew better. But whatever, the choice was mine then and the choice is mine today.

High pressure situations such as these stretch the limits and push us to make choices in very critical areas. Sport is not alone in this situation. Competition, a part of all aspects of ours lives forces us to consider the cost of coveting the gold medal, of making a million dollars. We have a need to gain the *edge* in whatever we do. It is at that point, however, that all of our foundations are challenged. Certainly, our sense of fair play is challenged, and we make choices—choices that will impact on our own value system. We have witnessed the results in Seoul. As Canadians, we have felt it.

International competition exposes cultural differences—differences in values, ethics and approaches to the same subject. We have to recognize in the world of sport that the ethics and values of many countries are subservient to their political goals and goals of conquest at any price. The stakes can be very high—lifetime pay-offs. Athletes who win medals from such countries as the GDR, Soviet Union, China, even to a degree South Korea, are provided with cars, apartments, monthly stipends for life. Only a very few of our Canadian amateur athletes experience such extrinsic rewards, and when they do, they are often accompanied by corporate demands or government pressure to continue performing at the top.

Progress and advancement in our society have made it possible for us to seek greater heights. Technology and the communications industry have pushed us, stretching the boundaries into global boundaries.

Technology in sport, in equipment, training methods, sports medicine, clothing, and drugs have all contributed to the knowledge that with these tools, these innovations, the hitherto perceived levels of achievement can be transcended. The four minute mile can be broken, the triple twist in gymnastics on the exercise floor is now commonplace, quadruple jumps on the ice are possible, man's mystery of his body appears to know no limits. We want to see and experience the impossible in our lifetime.

But we must ask—do ethics and morality determine the nature of our technological advances, or is the process such that our technology in actuality shapes our ethical and moral behaviour?

The need to control some of our most serious mental disorders resulted in much research on psychotropic drugs which have unlocked the doors of our mental institutions and allowed many patients to live normal lives. This technology, which was meant to do and did so much good, is now responsible for epidemic overdrugging. Many who are anxious, opt for a quick fix rather than undertaking the longer term search for the root cause and its solution.

The events during and after Seoul have made us realize the extent to which we in sport had compromised our ethics to stay in the race. We did what we perceived everyone else to be doing; what an emotional jolt to our national psyche.

But from the ashes of defeat and despair, we have looked in the mirror. We have exposed ourselves and out of all this will come recommendations; some will be for censure and punishment. But if the history of censure and punishment to reform can provide any example, we must do more than that. We must develop another technology—a spiritual and psychological technology that helps us to actualize our potential in an acceptable, legitimate and fair way. Increasing the number of anti-doping tests and the timing of these tests is not the only answer. It will only make the laboratories happy. But surely, what we are striving for is a generation of athletes, of young people who, when faced with a choice say, "No thank you, I can do it my way which is a clean way. I am not interested in breaking the rules." Or are we faced with a generation of athletes who either go further underground and use yet a newer technology to mask a substance, simply find another substance not yet on the banned list, or refrain from using drugs *only* out of fear of being caught? What we need is a reaffirmation and adherence to a value system and a set of principles that will help us make wise choices no matter what technology provides.

The mind has unlimited potential. We have not yet harnessed the power of the intellect and the emotions to break the barriers of performance. Skill training and psychological preparation are both part of the equation for success. The potential is great.

A little over a year ago, we in Canada, indeed people world wide experienced one of our lifetime highs and lows. The substantive issue was ethics and technology. Ben and I were two of the participants. Ben's story has been told. He has lived many hells, albeit self-imposed, and not condoned by any of us. But a spirit still burns and is trying to rekindle itself. Ben is aware of how many people he has let down. He wants to make it up playing within the rules and using his god given talent. The message is powerful—the cost of choosing to cheat! The potential in the message is tough to beat.What is happening, however, is not the story of one man only but of hundreds of thousands of starry-eyed young athletes.

There are many agendas in sport and government that have to be cleaned up. We as adults, leaders in sport, must reaffirm our ethics. The sport system is somewhat out of control. We must bring it back. Our beliefs and standards must focus on legitimate technologies—those that are fair, constructive, and will help us unlock all of our human and natural potentials. This must be our legacy.

The fabric of the olympic ideals has been challenged, yet the spirit of the olympic games lives on. It remains a good training ground for young people. It remains an excellent preparation for life. The games are expensive and other than preparing for them, they consume energy and time. The pay-off derived from being involved in them should be cherished and nurtured. They inspire and fuel many youngsters all around the world to stretch their physical and mental limits through sport. They provide living legacies for those who participate that transcend medals, victory ceremonies, and the national medal count. Lifelong friendships are made. One hundred and sixty countries shared the same cafeteria, the same laundry facilities, the same playgrounds, buses and so on for four weeks in Seoul.

How do we protect such a prize? How do we develop an air-tight value system that cannot be violated, cannot be unlocked by the newest technology?

At what time do we also recognize that sport cannot do it alone? Yes, we have a captive audience in sport—many of the youth of the world. Yes, we have a responsibility. But we are *part* of a whole, part of a total society—a society that needs to review its own values and ethics—a society in which there are perhaps too many mixed messages.

Is there a single and consistent guiding light—from the banks and the major financial institutions to industry and its leaders, to governments and to religion itself—where is the role model? What is the message? How can we in sport expect young people to make the desired fair choices if the signals in life around them are confusing and even contradictory. If sport is perceived to be, and many of us believe it to be, one of the best schools in which to promote and teach the values of fair play to youngsters from all around the world, then it must have support. It cannot do it alone.

For me, witnessing the intellectual strength and desire of the people at this conference to grapple with the issues involving ethics and technology, I suggest that some of the potential for encouraging change rests in your hands. You have so much experience and knowledge in your ranks that the capacity to produce an action platform that by its very content and backing must be heard and considered is here.

Ben and I are honoured to have been considered for this event—honoured to share our message and our hope for the future. An opportunity lies ahead of us. It would be tremendous if this conference produced a solid, consistent, and powerful direction and approach to ethics in the age of pervasive technology. It is needed, the conference is timely, the results of it even more timely. The challenge is truly yours.

Carol Anne Letheren of Mathieu, Letheren Associates, Toronto, was Chef de Mission of the Canadian Olympic Team, Seoul, Korea and is a member of the International Olympic Committee.

Right: **J.M. Stewart**, Senior Vice-President, DuPont Canada.

Below: **Eugene Critoph**, Vice-President, Strategic Technology Management, Atomic Energy of Canada Ltd.; **Reverend Roland de Corneille**, Priest in Charge, St. Pauls Runnymede Anglican Church; **Henry Wiseman**, Conference Chair; **Ben Johnson**, Canadian Olympic Sprinter; **Jack MacDonald**, Vice-President Academic, University of Guelph.

Below left: **Paul Durbin**, Professor of Philosophy and Director, Centre for Science and Culture, University of Delaware. *Below right*: **Jim MacNeill**, Director, Program on Environment and Sustainable Development, Institute for Research on Public Policy, Ottawa.

WORKSHOP REPORTS

WORKSHOP 1: Technology and Ethical Choice in the Food Systems: Agriculture

Coordinators: Dr. Frank Hurnik, Animal and Poultry Science, University of Guelph; Dr. Hugh Lehman, Department of Philosophy, University of Guelph.

Chairs: Dr. Freeman McEwen, Dean, Ontario Agricultural College, University of Guelph; Dr. Hugh Lehman; Dr. William Hughes, Department of Philosophy, University of Guelph

Rapporteur: Dr. Evelyn Pluhar, Department of Philosophy, Pennsylvania State University

Session #1: *Overviews of Concerns about Food Systems*

Major Points Raised by the Speakers

(1) The public is increasingly concerned about the safety of its food and the impact of agricultural technology upon the environment. Who should bear the costs of decisions made in view of that concern? Is it ethical and consistent for the public to make these demands while continuing to expect cheap food and ever higher standards of living? The Canadian government has the responsibility to ensure the preservation of our agricultural resources and the safety of our food. It should do so by consulting all stakeholders, then making decisions which are factually rather than emotionally based. Public emotionality is hard to counter. The recent controversy over the use of alar on apples is an example of too much emotionalism and too little rationality. The apple farmers have had to bear the brunt of the resulting costs. Government should take it upon itself to inform a frequently misinformed, panic-stricken public.

(2) Agriculture is a technology, and as such it is a dimension of culture. In making our ethical decisions, should we take a *rights* approach, a *utilitarian* approach, or a *deep ecology* approach? Who has the ultimate moral responsibility? Should the farm operator be the owner? Is the production of cheap food our goal? Can we feed the world's people? Yes, but this is the wrong question. The real issue is balance in the human control of nature and of humans.

Discussion

While there was general agreement that taxpayers rather than the farmers alone should pay for land preservation and changes in methods demanded by the public, some in the audience thought that agricultural technologists and government bureaucrats have rightfully lost public credibility in some cases. Some objected that the problem is not a misinformed, overly emotional public. People may have different views on risks and how risks should be analyzed (e.g., voluntary vs. imposed risks). A member of the audience charged that government regulators are very paternalistic in their views of the public. There are other approaches to agriculture besides the standard benefit/risk analysis approach. It was agreed that far better communication was needed between government officials and "stakeholders."

Session #2: *Problems with Modern Technology*

Major Points Made by the Speakers

(1) Modern agriculture is pervaded by presuppositions borrowed from the outdated model of classical Newtonian mechanics. The atomistic, mechanistic, assembly-line approach in agricultural technology has led to the degradation of the environment, enormous animal suffering, loss of jobs, and the disintegration of some indigenous cultures. The *holistic* approach, which is reflective of good science, should be adopted instead. We should move to "agroecosystems" for the production of our food. This paradigm change would be ecologically and ethically preferable to the agricultural *status quo*.

(2) The assurance of an adequate, nutritious, safe food supply is a basic function of any organized society. The public desperately needs to be well-informed about the facts, but such information is extremely hard to come by. Advertising hype and media irresponsibility have led to massive public misinformation. Public fears and anxiety have led to unprecedented public concern about food safety (e.g., pesticides and other food additives, cholesterol).

(3) Pesticides are a tool which have been and can continue to be extremely beneficial when *properly used*. Public fears about pesticide use should be put in context: death and poisoning rates related to pesticides pale beside those due to car accidents, for example. However, we should work toward reduction in the use of pesticides (e.g., by adopting the policy of "Integrated Pest Management").

(4) Those involved in the teaching and practice of agriculture have been for the most part ethically responsible. The problem is that public demands are changing. Biotechnology offers tremendous opportunities in animal agriculture. If we do not pursue it, other countries will. A "black market" would likely result. Biotechnology, responsibly pursued, will help to "tailor the product." It was said that agricultural animals are "food production units," and we should use whatever means are available (robotics, computer science, cloning, genetic engineering) to maximize yield and quality. We must face ethical choices about animal welfare, the legitimate concerns of farmers, and the demands of consumers.

(5) Consumers demand excellence and wholesomeness from their food. However, consumers are very uninformed about pesticides, other residues (e.g., hormones, antibiotics), and proper diet. All food consists of chemicals, after all. Prices would be unacceptably high if we rejected standard techniques. Ethics is an individual responsibility. Consumers should become better informed about the issues and the consequences of their demands, for they are powerful.

Discussion

Several objected that the analogies drawn between risks from use of pesticides and risks from other sources were faulty. We must disentangle different concepts of "risk." The "bottom line" conclusions about the need to use pesticides and certain food additives *may be* correct, but the analysis needs work. A more fundamental objection was that bad management strategies have been pursued in our insistence on greater yield per acre/hectare, cow, or chicken. For example, insecticide use has gone up, but loss to pests has increased. We lose four times more corn than before to pests, although we have increased our use of pesticides by a factor of 1000. Farmers have been the scapegoats for bad decisions by food technologists (e.g., the abandonment of crop rotation). Farmers should receive public assistance to change to sounder methods.

Several in the audience spoke in favour of a "holistic" approach to agriculture, and indeed to much more than that. It was agreed that much better information is needed. Quick media fixes which raise ratings and sell papers, as well as deceptive advertising, have taken their toll. We would all be better educated if we could only speak to each other more. The separate workshop structure of this very conference was criticized by some for fostering an atomized approach. The one conclusion to which everyone agreed was that a "black market" in biotechnology is a horrifying notion.

Session #3: *Impact of Agricultural Technology on Third World*
Food Systems

Major Points Made by the Speakers

(1) When there is scientific uncertainty about the consequences of applying a particular technology (e.g., the use of pesticides to kill African desert locusts), the values of those involved become the decisive factor. Values actually influence one's perception of the facts, and determine one's view about where the burden of proof should lie. Development policies must give great emphasis to the issue of *consent*. The affected parties in developing countries have virtually no say at present about the use of potentially hazardous technologies.

(2) Political barriers trap persons in environments which become deficient. Developing countries which try to make more of their land production are often guilty of creating the opposite effect. Populations shift to urban areas and formerly agricultural land is used for other purposes (e.g., as a summer resort for rich people from the cities). Indigenous peoples are often displaced rather than helped: this has been the case in the North African desert countries. Non-renewable resources such as fossil ground water deposits are being exploited. For whom is development?

(3) Those who approach developing countries in order to offer them "appropriate technologies" often have a blind, uninformed, condescending attitude. Instead, those offering assistance should adopt the Gandhian "swadeshi" approach: understand the people, their language, and their culture. "Appropriate technology" is often defined in too narrow a way: it should be more than gadgets. Any changes should be tailored carefully to systems and cultures already in place. Natives should be consulted: they know far more than the typical "experts" who come from developed countries.

(4) Developing countries want biotechnological advances, and developed countries have the responsibility to help them achieve them. Regulators should proceed with great caution: safety cannot be guaranteed but should be maximized. We should take a risk/benefit approach and abide by informed consent. A consistent international approach to the offering of biotechnology to developing countries is desirable.

Discussion

Some suggested that it was unethical for agricultural technologists to impose certain technologies on reluctant developing countries (e.g., the export of modern poultry breeding and management techniques to Indonesia). It was replied that agricultural experts sincerely want to help disadvantaged people and are doing so in a responsible way. Some (themselves from developing countries) pointed out that persons in the *governments* of developing countries might be requesting biotechnologies, but that this does not imply that the people in those countries want it. What is "appropriate technology?" Who decides what is "appropriate?" Several concluded that the people in the countries themselves should make the decision about what is desired.

Control and *empowerment* underlie these ethical choices. Consent is indeed critical and frequently lacking. However, this can be *implied* consent rather than consent based on direct information on the part of every individual.

Desires and perceptions of what is needed are powerfully affected by *marketing,* in both developing and developed nations. Biotechnology, e.g., is being aggressively marketed at present. Unfortunately, there is much misinformation, and media irresponsibility promotes it. Another member of the audience retorted that we have only ourselves to blame for this: we should stop blaming the media, and complain if we spot distortions. Concerning the demand for better consumer information about marketed products, she added that she, for one, would prefer *not* to know all the ingredients in her beer.

Concerning the well-intentioned efforts by developed countries to send food aid to famine-stricken countries, it was observed that these efforts often do much long term harm by killing initiative. Aid which stresses agricultural *development* would be far more beneficial. This would be appropriate technology.

FINAL WORKSHOP REPORT

Three Concluding Recommendations

(1) The organization of agriculture should be such that resources are widely held while decision-making is widely dispersed.

(2) Evaluation of a new technology must centrally include a consideration of indigenous technologies, as well as socio-cultural and ecological contexts.

(3) The creators of agricultural technology have a moral obligation to engage in dialogue with the community in order to establish their needs and concerns. Channels to facilitate this must be created.

Three Concluding Questions

(1) Should agriculture be considered a social service rather than an industry?

(2) How can the decision processes regarding the use and transfer of agricultural technology best reflect participation of small scale stakeholders?

(3) How can we ensure that all stakeholders affected by agricultural policies are sufficiently informed?

WORKSHOP 2: Ethical Choices and Technology in Animal Husbandry

Coordinators: Dr. Frank Hurnik, Animal and Poultry Science, University of Guelph; Dr. Hugh Lehman, Department of Philosophy, University of Guelph

Chairs: Dr. Franklin Loew, Dean, School of Veterinary Medicine, Tufts University; Dr. Ole Nielson, Dean of Ontario Veterinary College, University of Guelph; Dr. Don Grieve, Department of Animal and Poultry Science, University of Guelph; Dr. Lawrence Milligan, Dean of Research, University of Guelph

Rapporteur: Dr. Jeffrey Mitscherling, Department of Philosophy, University of Guelph

Themes and Issues

In the brief description of this workshop distributed in advance to all participants, it was stated that "The discussions will include an in-depth examination of issues ranging from animal and human welfare to the environment. Discussions will consider how problems perceived in contemporary uses of technology can be solved." While the promise of an in-depth examination was certainly fulfilled, consideration of solutions to current problems was quite limited. In retrospect, this is not surprising, for a good deal of our time had to be devoted precisely to the *perception* of the problems. In our fourth and final session we attempted to bring those problems into clear focus by identifying the central concerns underlying all of the various issues that had been examined in our previous three sessions.

In preparation for that task, the following list of twenty-eight issues was prepared under five headings (which may be regarded as "Themes"):

- **A.** Nature, Goals and Moral Obligations of Research, Technology and Food Production;
- **B.** Welfare of Animals;
- **C.** Welfare of the Environment;
- **D.** Welfare of People;
- **E.** Welfare of the Economy.

The decision to include an issue under one heading and not another is, in each case, based largely an the context of the discussion in which the issue was raised. The list not only conveys the broad scope of the interests of the participants but also points to the relative importance accorded by the participants to matters that have clearly to do with animal welfare as opposed to those having to do primarily with technology and food production. The overriding concerns of the participants will become more evident below, in the survey of "The Essence of the Debate."

A. Nature, Goals and Moral Obligations of Research, Technology and Food Production

(1) The impact of technological progress on social progress

(2) Technological development and "productivity" (maximum as opposed to optimal)

(3) Development, testing, and distribution of biotechnological products

(4) The non-neutrality of technology

(5) The goals of agricultural research: increased productivity and efficiency of production

(6) Embryo handling and gene transfer

(7) The irreversible reduction of genes

(8) "Husbandry" as opposed to "Production Technology"

(9) Ethical obligations of Agricultural Research, given its commonly recognized goals of increased productivity and increased efficiency of production

(10) The irreversible reduction of genes

(11) The family farm

(12) Stewardship/Husbandry

(13) The role of management

B. Welfare of Animals

(14) Welfare of animals

(15) Companion animals

(16) Animals & crops

(17) Animal/human nutrient competition

(18) The moral status of animals

C. Welfare of the Environment

(19) Ethical obligation towards the environment

(20) Sustainability of soil and of agro-ecological systems

(21) The ethics of consumption

D. Welfare of People

(22) Population control

(23) World hunger

(24) The testing of biotechnological products in the Third World

(25) The Third World and the exportation/importation of technology

E. Welfare of the Economy

(26) Full costs of food

(27) Short- and long-term economy

(28) Tax tools

The Essence of the Debate

As suggested by the number of entries under each of the above headings, we do indeed live in an age of "pervasive technology." Issues having to do with primarily technological concerns outnumbered those dealing explicitly with animal welfare by more than two to one. A few of the participants noted in our final session that our workshop, which had ostensibly to do with the topic of animal husbandry, had actually dealt with that topic only peripherally. While this assessment was not in fact true of our first session—where the discussion following the papers was devoted largely to concerns of animal welfare with regard both to livestock farming and to animal science—it did hold true for our second and third sessions.

A brief summary of the debate carried on through all of the first three sessions will indicate the general direction which the discussion followed. (The intention here is not to summarize the contents of the papers themselves, but rather to give some sense of the discussion to which the papers gave rise.)

The general topic of the first session was "Overviews of Issues Confronting Animal Agriculture," and the three papers presented by Donald Shaver (CM, Honourary Colonel, National Defence, Ottawa), Victor Wageman (Mutual Products, Morrisburg), and Bernard Rollin (Professor of Philosophy, Physiology and Biophysics, Colorado State University) initiated a lively discussion that focused on ethical obligations toward the environment, the failure of current food production practices to translate technological progress into social progress, and the welfare of animals. Most of the discussion concentrated on issues having to do with animal welfare, with specific attention paid to livestock farming and animal science. With regard to the former, it was noted that the effects on animal welfare of technological development in livestock farming have been at least to some extent negative, doubtless as a result of the fact that moral value judgments regarding animal welfare continue to be secondary to concerns having to do with the economic welfare of the farmer. It was also pointed out that, given the understandable concern of the farmer with efficiency and productivity, animal science itself will find it difficult to adopt a greater interest in animal welfare.

With specific regard to animal science, discussion turned to its moral basis. After acknowledging the difficulty involved in identifying what constitutes cruelty to and suffering of animals, it was suggested that we consider veterinary medicine, which enjoys a natural regard for the moral status of animals. Underlying this regard is a newly developing ethic which, it was suggested, extends also to animal science. This ethic demands the radical restructuring of animal science and livestock farming, a restructuring that will incur considerable expense. While no general consensus was reached on the topic of the session as a whole, five "conclusions" were tentatively agreed upon during the course of the discussion:

(1) Major companies should appoint an Environmental President reporting directly to the CEO;

(2) The Ministry of the Environment must enjoy a senior portfolio in every government;

(3) Farmers are concerned with animal welfare and are willing to work towards improvement;

(4) Criticism of current farming practices and proposed solutions must be based on scientific and economic proof that balances human and animal welfare; and

(5) Costs incurred in the restructuring of livestock farming must be borne not by the farmer but by the consumer.

Underlying the last three of these conclusions was a concern with animal welfare that was not clearly to emerge again until our final session. The second and third sessions focused increasingly on matters having to do with technology, the environment, and economic factors involved in food production.

Discussion of the general topic of our second session, "Problems Concerning Modern Animal Technology"—introduced by papers presented by Brian McBride (Department of Animal and Poultry Science, University of Guelph, Ontario), Eric Beauchamp (Department of Land Resource Science, University of Guelph, Ontario), Daniel Goldstein (Professor, Biological Sciences at the University of Buenos Aires Argentina), and E.E. Lister (Director, Animal Research Centre, Agriculture Canada) focused on the implications of new technologies and on problems concerning the environment and soil sustainability. It was stressed that we must control the development, application and employment of new technologies; that we must, for example, ensure product safety and take into account social considerations. Attention was also directed toward the Third World. It was agreed that the ethical issues involved in the development of new biotechnologies concern not only animals, farmers, consumers and the environment in the West, but also in the Third World, a fact which raises urgent ethical issues that must be addressed immediately. A number of such issues revolve around current practices in the testing, development and distribution of new biotechnological products in the Third World, which not only has little money for investment in new foreign technologies, but also has no pressing need for importing these technologies.

Environmental concerns were raised in the context of soil sustainability where the central and most provocative question had to do with the role played by animals in an agro-ecosystem. It was suggested that, when investigating the effect animals exercise on soil sustainability, we not lose sight of the fact that animals, soil and crop plants are all interactive parts of the general agro-ecosystem. Following this line of investigation, we find that there exist reasons both for and against regarding animals as a necessary component of an agro-ecosystem—in other words, it is not clear that animals are needed in order to sustain soil productivity. With this in mind, the session concluded with the observation that the interaction between animals and crops, as well as their relative importance in considerations of food production, is a topic that should be recognized as central to this workshop.

In response to papers presented by Kenneth Dahlberg (Professor, Department of Political Science, Western Michigan University, USA), Ann Clarke (Professor, Crop Science, University of Guelph, Ontario), Paul Siegel (Department of Poultry Science, Virginia Polytechnic Institute and State University, USA), and Morris Freeman (General Manager of Semex Canada, Guelph, Ontario), the discussion of our third session raised questions that ranged far beyond its stated topic of "Future Developments in Animal Technology." Acknowledging the impact of agricultural technologies on rural regions and farmers—with special regard, again, to the Third World—it was agreed that the ethical implications of the non-neutrality of technology demand our immediate attention, and that we must concentrate on determining precisely what constitutes morally proper behaviour in the development of new technology. The urgency of these demands is reflected in the dramatic increase in the world's human population, which is giving rise to an increasingly brutal competition for basic resources. This competition for resources, in conjunction with the recognized imperative to meet the needs of farmers, producers and consumers alike, confers urgent significance on the notion of "sustainability." Sustainability, while playing a central role in the current debate, is itself in desperate need of elucidation.

"Sustainable agriculture" is synonymous neither with "soil sustainability" nor with "sustainable agro-ecosystem," and the notion of sustainability in each case seems, if not directed toward an entirely different concern, to reflect a different set of basic values.

In the case of animal agriculture, for example, there would appear to be two basic approaches from which we might choose in order to achieve sustainability. Both are based upon differing assumptions. On the one hand, we might follow a course of "production technology" and concentrate on developing particular technologies. These, when introduced on a wide scale into the animal agriculture food chain, would ensure that there would be continued advances in the efficiency of food production for man and that animals continue to play a viable role in the food chain. On the other hand, we might follow the course of "stewardship" and "husbandry" and curtail the development of new technologies and their implementation in large-scale farming operations in favour of encouraging the preservation of the smaller (family) farm. While both approaches are concerned with the sustainability of animal agriculture, the former rests upon an assumed confidence in technology which is denied by the latter in its emphasis on the biological and ecological basis of all agriculture.

A further distinction between the two approaches has to do with the respective weight they place on matters of animal well-being. The former regards such matters as being entirely secondary to purely human interests, while the latter, in its regard for the larger questions of the ethical implications of rapid advancements in the development and spread of new technology, recognizes the welfare of animals as a central concern of any viable, sustainable agro-ecosystem.

The goal of the fourth session was to formulate three "Concluding Recommendations" and three "Concluding Questions" to be distributed among all the participants in the conference as a whole. Franklin Loew, the Chair of the workshop, opened the discussion with a brief summary of the three preceding sessions. After referring to the list of issues (given in the above section on "Themes and Issues"), he called particular attention to the difficulty involved in establishing criteria we might employ in our assessment of animal well-being in relationship to food productivity. Following his summary, in my "Rapporteur's Synthesis" I suggested possible guidelines we might follow in our attempt to draw up our recommendations and questions. I noted that in all of our previous discussions, whenever ethical matters had been explicitly dealt with, the workshop participants had adopted an exclusively cost-benefit approach to their analysis, ignoring questions of animal *rights*. The discussion that followed proved to be the most heated of all our sessions, the most controversial topic being precisely the moral status of animals.

Two radically opposing views emerged, with a number of intermediate positions separating them. At the one extreme, some of the participants maintained that the moral status of animals is not an issue, for animals cannot be said to "possess" any rights at all. At the other extreme—represented most forcefully by Frank Hurnik, one of the Coordinators of the workshop—some of the participants argued that concern with the topic of ethical choices in animal husbandry already clearly presupposes that animals must enjoy some moral status, and that the question of animal rights cannot be ignored. A moderate position was represented by those who, while denying that animals were possessed of rights, maintained that their moral status was nevertheless not to be denied. It was at this point in the workshop that fundamental differences among the participants' perception of the problems discussed in our previous three sessions finally emerged most clearly. That these differences were never resolved is apparent in the tone of compromise the reader might discern in the concluding recommendations and questions.

Three Concluding Recommendations

(1) That we formulate a broader definition of the goals of Animal Agriculture in terms of ethics, ecology, equity, and aesthetics.

(2) That the farming, rural, scientific, and urban communities jointly engage in the current discussions regarding the nature and moral status of animals, thereby promoting education and dissemination of information concerning the ethical dimensions of Animal Agriculture.

(3) That Agricultural Research, Technology, and Politics address the issues of increasing population, competition for limited resources, and ecological fragility.

Three Concluding Questions

(1) What, if any, constraints ought to be placed on Animal Agriculture for reasons of animal welfare, environmental considerations, and population considerations?

(2) What role ought Animal Agriculture to play in assuring the quality of human life in a global society?

(3) How are we to proceed in establishing criteria for assessing the quality of animal life?

WORKSHOP 3: The Media, Technology and Ethical Issues

Coordinator: Fred de Vries, Department of Political Studies, University of Guelph

Chair: Peter Kohl, Publisher, The Daily Mercury, Guelph

Rapporteurs: Dennis Murphy, Associate Professor, Communication Studies, Concordia University, Montreal

Workshop Report: The Editors

The media workshop benefitted considerably from the participation of both experts and non-experts by their commonly held view that the use of advanced information technologies have a strong influence upon the users by shaping their perceptions, attitudes, thoughts and values.

The first presentation was by John Meisel, Professor, Political Studies at Queen's University, Kingston on "Innovation in Communication and the Media: Social and Ethical Issues." He argued that "we are what the information we receive makes us." From whatever source: computers, satellite transmissions, video tapes or VCRs, people are inundated with information and this has, in turn, altered the way we go about our daily business from banking to where and how we store information; created a revolution in entertainment habits; and has transformed our cultural life. Even if it is only partly true that we are "what the information we receive makes us," then it follows that people's ethical principles are also shaped, or even profoundly influenced by these same processes.

What then are the ethical principles and responsibilities of those who invent, own, manage, regulate or use these technologies? Being a question of considerable magnitude, only a few of the salient aspects could be discussed. Among them, as pointed out by John Meisel, new and sophisticated technologies are effectively widening the gap within societies and between the industrial and developing worlds. Paradoxically, new technologies have promoted the global village with the storing of information in data banks and the world's press being able to bring information into individual homes around the world almost instantaneously. This serves to undermine parochialism, but at the price of homogeneity which "tends to sap the creative vitality that comes from diversity" (The McDonald's golden arches syndrome). In Meisel's own words, "The advantages of storing information by means of computer technology are such that we can no longer do without it. But means have to be devised to protect individuals from the pitfalls associated with the process" as the new information technology can lead to a considerable invasion of privacy. Data banks contain enough personal information about individuals to be detrimental to the person concerned should this information land in the hands of unauthorized persons. Moreover, access to a file by the RCMP, FBI or CIA for the "national interest" is not reassuring.

Frequent and extensive use of public and private opinion polls are a further manifestation of the "new politics" forged by the information revolution. Do government policies oscillate in reaction to polls, and what effect does this have, in turn, upon the public reaction to what may be policy or simply electoral deception? On the one hand, knowledge of the public mood is important to the democratic process, while on the other, they are a poor substitute for policy in a complex world.

"Compunications," which is the application of computers and the new telecommunications to politics has also made it possible to provide continuous and instantly reported polling while interactive cable services permit an up to date monitoring of plebiscites. Information technologies carry with them ethical implications and concerns. If society does not comprehend the implications and make choices, then technology itself will determine the outcome without reference to the ethical consequences.

On a more philosophical plane, Meisel reflected upon the effects of electronic gadgetry and how it impacts on the individual by substituting electronically induced experience for direct human contact. He feels that it is still too soon to determine the extent to which the human experience is narrowed by electronic inducement but as a result of breakthroughs in telephony, the espousal of "teleshopping" and of interactive cable—these lead to a neglect of social needs at the expense of more traditional encounters. One might equally wonder about the ultimate impact upon a generation that spends more time before a television set than they do in school. The lesson from all this is that society should learn to use technology more discriminately and focus less on its consumer potential and use it more as a means to broaden intellectual and cultural horizons.

The workshop discussion then turned to the examination of the practice and dissemination of ethics by the media and entertained the notion that ethics, as perceived by the industrialized nations, are based less upon traditional "universal" codes of behaviour than on specific interests and principles surrounding such contemporary issues as the environment, gender equity and native rights. This results in competing values of ethical relativity in a world of rapid social change and emergent issues. How then can the media respond? Should they develop a special operational code of ethics? Should they assume a particular responsibility in their conduct and reporting of news? These were questions that reoccurred throughout the workshop deliberations and were tackled by Patrick O'Callaghan, Chair, Canadian Press and visiting professor of journalism at the Ryerson School of Journalism in his presentation on the "Economics of Journalism." He started by saying that the newspaper, "stripped of its lofty aspirations and its often noble intent, is basically a creature of free enterprise dedicated to maximizing profits for its shareholders." Unlike radio and television broadcasters, the newspaper requires no licence. It is independent of government and in fact "fights with its full armoury of editorial bombast against any attempted governmental encroachment into how it conducts its affairs." In fact, newspapers have been described as "money machines" for major fund investors. For a professional money manager, the selling of space for advertising along with circulation determines the financial worthiness of a newspaper. Therefore, a large editorial staff dedicated to quality journalism becomes difficult to justify when 80 per cent of the newspaper's revenues is derived from advertising and 20 per cent from the actual sale price of the paper. Consequently, such revenue producing departments as sports and fashion are less likely to see drastic budget cuts than an editorial department when a newspaper finds itself in financial trouble. O'Callaghan added that "money managers are totally heartless when it comes to pride of quality, [for instance] in non-competitive cities where the only newspaper rules the roost, the contents of news columns can always be pared to bare essentials, without seriously hampering the sale of the newspaper."

But then, no money managers were present at the workshop to counter or defend these allegations.

In the light of such a hard nosed picture of the newspaper world, the belief that newspapers are or should be socially responsible seems to be quite contentious. If the profit motive is so all encompassing, it is also reasonable to question the social responsibility, that is, the ethical criteria and conduct of individual journalists.

Responding to this point of view, Peter Desbarats, Dean of the Graduate School of Journalism at the University of Western Ontario, commented that journalists, "being very sensitive to the problems of definition and enforcement, are profoundly sceptical of codes of ethics." He noted that text books on journalism deal with ethics in a very cursory manner. Based on the principle of freedom of the press, the key operational codes are "getting the story at all costs, to beating the competition, to initiative and enterprise. When codes of ethics are all too often found "in the bottom drawer," expediency becomes the rule. Desbarats states: "The collective wisdom of the craft, in far too many newsrooms, is a mishmash of expedients for avoiding difficult ethical decisions." Younger journalists often learn that, when the chips are down, their superiors quickly forget ethical considerations in their frantic scramble to beat the competition or attract attention. "Yes, we believe in ethical journalism," would be an apt motto for many newsrooms on any given day, "but this story is different."

In effect, journalists today rely primarily on their own sense of personal responsibility and many are better equipped to assess ethical issues than were their predecessors. Nonetheless, they are responsible to human society as a whole. This responsibility, if taken seriously, opens up new ethical dimensions for journalism. The onus, however, does not only reside with journalists but also with the owners, the money managers and the public. For better or worse, ethical standards in journalism correspond closely to the general ethical standards prevalent in society at large. Consequently, greater public awareness and concern with issues such as the environment, human rights, quality of life, and peace and war help ensure treatment of these and like matters in the media. The extent to which they are dealt with in ethical terms, however, leaves much to be desired.

To offer informed opinion and ethical evaluation of these kinds of issues requires a profound knowledge and understanding of ethical questions posed by modern technology—the kind of expertise for which few media corporations are willing to pay. Desbarats illustrates this in his concluding remarks: "If the criterion of success for news media is their ability to prepare their audiences for social change, as the Special Senate Committee on Mass Media stated in 1970, Canadian media institutions, particularly in the private sector, have failed to exploit their potential to prepare all of us for the changes wrought by technology. The current spate of alarming coverage of environmental degradation, after many years of warnings by concerned scientists, illustrates not media sensitivity to technological change but media conservatism and the inability of news media to generate and encourage new approaches to ethical questions posed by modern technology."

Workshop participants felt that the media, which inundates the public with "information" nevertheless have a special responsibility, not only to inform, but to analyze and offer ethical guidance to the complexity and confusion of a troublesome world. This view, particularly, was exemplified by Dennis Murphy, Professor of Communication Studies at Concordia University, Quebec. He related the insistence of an educator, who was an audience member at a conference on news making, to one of the media professionals that "it was his responsibility as news reporter to sift through the daily flow of information and tell him what to think"—a comment presumably inspired by a sense of being overwhelmed by a flood of information from which he is expected to derive his opinions. To expect journalists to be guided by "sound" ethical standards is one thing. But to expect a definitive ethical judgment is quite another matter.

By the same token, the economic, political and social milieus in a democracy each have an inherent set of ethical principles. Among them is the right and necessity to accommodate the expression of many dissimilar, or even contradictory views and opinions as long as they do not violate the basic tenets of democratic practices. Journalists should be acquainted with and respond to the ethical issues surrounding the events they are reporting regardless of the political, economic or social stance they hold.

In this regard, while journalists should recognize their own ethical responsibilities, we must cease to make a distinction between those "inside" and those "outside" the media, as well as between the producers of news, the commentators of news and the audience. The audience, states Murphy, is pivotal to the process. Those who receive what journalists produce are intrinsic parts of the system of public information. They are active components rather than passive recipients. He continues that "while it is true that audience members, for the most part, do not have anything to do with the production of news, etc., it does not follow that we have nothing to do with our responses (and hence responsibility) to that information—quite apart from the nature of the information itself."

There are several implications from this linkage between producer and receiver and the consequence of understanding audience in this way. Firstly, it displaces the traditional notion that the producer and/or owner of the particular medium is alone responsible for content. Secondly, it undermines the belief set forth by ideological critiques of media that human beings are simply products of an ideology whether or not they are involved in any way in "negotiation" with the process. Finally, it recognizes that the audience plays a crucial role in the processing of information whether this be the accepting, rejecting, ignoring or questioning of that information.

This is especially true with the medium of television where what we see and hear can be called a "screen event." The viewer is participant together with the event and the commentator. The information is alive. It evokes reaction and emotion which become "a direct encounter with experience;" a point of view similar to Marshall McLuhan's observation that the medium is the message.

If Murphy's assertions are true observations of reality, where then lays the responsibility for content? We are all part of the process. Nevertheless, this should not obviate the responsibility of media personnel who observe, digest, analyze and transmit information from comprehending the ethical implications of what they do and acting accordingly. The counterpart to this axiom is that the audience are also "actors" in the reporting of events and should also be aware of and respond to the ethical implications of media reports.

While the presentations to the workshop revealed a considerable commonality of views, there were unanswered questions and disagreement on the value of trying to develop ethical codes for the media where issues are so complex and society itself is so divided. There was, however, concurrence on the need for accurate and in-depth reporting. Differences also arose on the desirability of establishing a new world information order that would be designed to overcome the near world monopoly of the Western news media. But a new information order might simply create a new Third World political press monopoly which could be less subject to the principles of a free press than presently exists. It is precisely freedom of the press which is a primary condition upon which other ethical standards are based.

There was considerable discussion of the growing flood of information with concern for the invasion of privacy exacerbated by the advent of new and more sophisticated technologies. The way users and audience utilise and respond to these technologies will continue to raise new ethical issues. No technology is ethically neutral and therefore it is important that society as a whole, and individuals recognize and pay dues to the ethical implications and consequences surrounding information technologies. Unless this happens, ethical principles will remain "at the bottom of the drawer."

Concluding Recommendations

Once all has been said, the media do have an obligation to raise the ethical considerations inherent in the issues and events of the day—ethical considerations which affect how we deal with global matters such as the environment, human rights, quality of life, and peace and war. One way of responding is to ensure that journalists are as well trained in the liberal arts, humanities, and science and technology as they are in the skills of their craft. Equally, the media should provide access for more voices and perspectives in the interest of balance, equity, honesty and integrity.

In the final analysis, there was general agreement that the media does have a moral responsibility to inform the public on the ethical choices confronting them, regardless of the independent rights and privileges of ownership. Societies, and the world at large, are undergoing radical social change. The media are not neutral observers. They have a special role to play in helping their audience understand the transformations underway and in assisting them to make the right kind of choices for the future.

Concluding Questions

New information technologies raise no less critical questions for society than do other technologies. Therefore, we can ask ourselves: What are the responsibilities of the media to ensure traditional values of respect for persons? What notion of knowledge flows from the media which shape our ethical judgements and capabilities to choose? Are journalists adequately informed and educated to understand and report on our more complex world?

WORKSHOP 4: Technology and Ethical Choice in Computers and Information Systems--"From Poetry to Practicalities: Ethical Choices In an Information Age"

Coordinators: Dr. Brian Woodrow, Political Studies, University of Guelph; Dr. John Black, Library, University of Guelph

Chair: Dr. Peter Robinson, Communications Canada, Ottawa

Rapporteurs: Dr. Brian Woodrow, Political Studies, University of Guelph; Dr. John Black, Library, University of Guelph

Rapporteurs: R. Brian Woodrow and John Black, University of Guelph

HE WISHES FOR THE CLOTHS OF HEAVEN

Had I the Heavens' embroidered cloths,
Enwrought with golden and silver light,
The blue and the dim and the dark cloths
Of night and light and the half-light,
I would spread the cloths under your feet:
But I, being poor, have only my dreams;
I have spread my dreams under your feet;
Tread softly because you tread on my dreams.
W.B. YEATS

The Workshop on Communications and Computers ranged widely over its subject area, sometimes touching the poetic and other times the merely practical. The particular issues raised spoke to three key themes: (1) the potential control which communications and computer technologies can exercise over our daily lives; (2) the way in which human activities are being both enriched and ensnared in a variety of global information networks; (3) the growing disparities between the information-rich and the information-poor whether these be defined in socio-economic, regional or North-South terms. The Workshop was chaired by Peter Robinson of Communications Canada—then on the eve of his retirement from the federal public service after many years of dealing extensively with communications and computer issues. He carried out the task with manifest skill and good humour.

Where the discussion and dialogue rose to the level of the poetic, it sometimes became exciting and even profound; where it dealt with more practical matters, it was at least enjoyable and certainly educative. When all was said and done, it was generally agreed that the issues themselves were simply too important to be left to discussion alone. Actions need to be taken, individually as well as collectively, to ensure that communications and computer technologies are designed and used with ethical considerations squarely at the forefront of attention. This was certainly the main conclusion to the Workshop.

This Workshop also faced a basic problem encountered in other workshops—the inability and/or unwillingness to adopt any particular ethical position. Firm in the belief that ethics should be important in a systemic way but concerned about imposing any particular collective view of ethical choice, the participants tended to feel most comfortable talking about the myriad ways in which communications and computer technologies are affecting our lives but found it much more difficult specifying the particular ethical choices which all agreed were there.

A Technological Tour D'Horizon

The Workshop began with a presentation by Arthur Cordell, who has in the past been a major contributor to the Science Council's work on Canada as an information society and who is also currently with Communications Canada. In his talk, he focused on evolving trends in communications and computer technologies and stressed the emergence of the "new media"—hybrids of digital, fibre optic, broadband, satellite and more traditional telecommunications services which hold the potential to be intensely interactive and routinely responsive to user needs. From an ethical stand-point, the introduction and diffusion of these "new media" held at least three important implications:

- ensuring the integrity of the information communicated since these hybrid creations tended to be bound only loosely by already inadequate rules and limits set separately either for communications or for computer activities;

- dealing with the new generation of privacy problems created by the very interactive character of the "new media" themselves which tend to leave their own version of the traditional "paper trail" and which are particularly susceptible to "computer matching;"

- confronting the question of access because the information created or communicated by the "new media" often has considerable economic value and the means and opportunity to create and use them are unevenly distributed and threaten to be even more so in the future.

Almost before Arthur Cordell had concluded, the forty or so workshop participants showed themselves to be very much attuned to the interactive nature of the "new media." There was a barrage of questions, some spawned directly by the presentation and others raised as topics for future discussion within the Workshop. Why should Statistics Canada increasingly charge for the information which it collects? Why should we trust the "new media" any more than the old media of mass communication? How many people even among the participants themselves presently make extensive use of information networks? Isn't there a danger with the "new media" that everyone will present himself or herself as a writer or a poet? Don't the problems of control and abuse of information come more from the private sector than the public sector? Only one lone question dealt directly with the ethical dimension of whether or not the Benthamite principle of the "greatest good for the greatest number" could really serve as the ethic of an information age!

What evolved very quickly after that initial breaching of the wall of reserve was a free and open discussion organized largely—but not monopolistically—around the six papers prepared specifically for the Workshop. As time went on, the blackboard became filled with topics which individuals wanted discussed, whether it be the role of women in an information society, the particular problems of developing countries, or the relationship of communications and computers to the environmental crisis. Some of these were discussed as the opportunity arose. In effect, the Workshop generated its own ethic for allying the technology of keyboarding and photocopying to demands for participation and informed attention.

Privacy and Vulnerability Related to the Use and Abuse of Computers

Two presentations dealt specifically with computer issues, one focusing primarily on the threats to individual privacy occasioned by the collection and potential abuse of computerized information and the other concentrating more on the vulnerability of computer systems to "hacking" and other forms of subversion. Mr. Justice Michael Kirby, formerly head of the Australian Law Reform Commission and currently President of the Court of Appeal of the Supreme Court of NSW, gave the first presentation. This was followed by a presentation by Brian Bawden, a Toronto lawyer and counsel for a newly-formed nonprofit organization called the Foundation for Responsible Computing. The common underlying theme for both presentations was the capability of the law and, specifically, of existing legal principles and rules to cope with the privacy and vulnerability issues. Although allied in applying a similar legal reasoning and exploring many of the same potential solutions, the two presentations diverged on several interesting points.

Mr. Justice Kirby began his presentation by explaining how computers became entwined with the issue of individual privacy during the 1970s when the phenomenon of transborder data flows meant that the jurisdictional ability of governments everywhere came under challenge. Through international agreements such as the OECD Privacy Guidelines as well as through national legislation, regulatory action and court decisions in many countries including Canada, there has been a continuing attempt to regain that effective control. Mr. Justice Kirby suggested that, despite often valiant efforts, our institutions have not always proven able to cope with the ingenuity of our technologies. The task is to establish simple principles for relating technology to ethics and to find ways of adhering to them. In his view, the situation promises, at least in the short term, to get worse before it gets better. What comes to mind is the conflicting issues of confidentiality and protection of public health evident with the AIDS issue which has become linked to computer communications and privacy. Mr. Justice Kirby concluded his remarks with the selection from W.B. Yeats in the prologue to this report—in honour of the fiftieth anniversary of the poet's death—which counsels us to build our individual and collective futures on our dreams rather than our nightmares.

Brian Bawden began his presentation by focusing on a different kind of virus, the so-called "computer virus," which may even have the same tragic human consequences depending on which systems are infested. He detailed several recent cases where major business or public institutions like hospitals or even the U.S. Congress have suffered computer virus problems. He emphasized that computer viruses are not merely a modem form of juvenile delinquency and stressed the need for tougher criminal laws to deal with what is a serious economic threat. He reviewed the inadequate efforts to date at the federal level in Canada and among the U.S. states and looked hopefully to the United Kingdom where a recent Commission on Computer

Abuse has reported with recommendations for tougher criminal penalties. By way of conclusion, he presented the issue as a "dependency/vulnerability dilemma": there is a broad community of interest in the use and deployment of computer and communications technology; deployment of that technology is taking place inexorably and often without sufficient attention either to its use or abuse; there must be a greater recognition of the magnitude of the risk involved from a purely economic standpoint because of the dependency and vulnerability inherent to these technologies.

Needless to say, these two presentations provoked considerable comment and questioning. Chief Justice Kirby faced questions about the weaknesses in the OECD guidelines which he himself had been instrumental in getting adopted, about the responsibilities which should be placed on private corporations and on the qualifications of judges to make technical/moral decisions. Mr. Bawden was also forced to defend his view that computer misuse should be treated as a crime and that information must be treated as a form of property right. One highlight of the discussion came when Vincent di Norcia, a visiting professor of business ethics at the University of Waterloo, took out a credit card and a $10 bill and proceeded to tear up the latter, explaining that the banknote was merely a symbol but that the credit card was much more important because it is embedded with valuable information.

The key issue which emerged for discussion, however, was whether or not technology can be treated as neutral and whether ethical questions are related or unrelated to the ways in which it is used. Isn't information technology subtly changing what we think of as information? Isn't modern society too caught up by the technique associated with communications and computer technologies? What has happened to the more traditional and good quality information disseminated by libraries and universities to the public? If technology is not inherently moral or immoral in itself, doesn't access to technologies of an information age, or the sometimes crass commercial purposes which communications and computer technologies can serve raise ethical issues? Doesn't the problem really trace back to the "socio-technological design" which underlies communications and computer technologies in the same way that it underlies other more obvious technologies such as nuclear power or genetic engineering? This issue of the neutrality or not of communications and computer technologies was one which was to crop up again and again.

The Role of the Mass Media, Globalization of Information Networks, and the Relationship between Information Networks and International Development

These three somewhat disparate issues constituted the agenda for one afternoon session. Robert Mayne, a communications consultant based in Ottawa, dealt with the enhanced power which communications and computer technologies give to the mass media, including both the print and broadcast media. While taking care not to be unduly critical of media workers or any particular media outlets, he raised the issue of ethics and the mass media from two perspectives. The first of these perspectives was in terms of journalistic ethics relating to issues of how media people go about doing their job. Recent lapses of ethical behaviour such as the fabrication of stories or the use of news re-enactments drew obvious attention and the conclusion was drawn that professional codes of conduct can only go part of the way towards promoting and ensuring media ethics. The other perspective of the ethics of the mass media was much broader. Concern was expressed about the standardization and homogenization of reporting style which is directly related to communications and computer technologies. The 20-second television news clip, the fullframe close-up picture, the multi-authored, computer-generated newspaper story, and the tendency towards "pack-journalism" were all presented as evidences of this disconcerting trend. Clearly, the mass media face their own particular ethical dilemmas, only some of which derive from communications and computer technologies.

Brian Woodrow of the Department of Political Studies at the University of Guelph then proceeded to examine the implications for ethical choice of the rapidly ongoing processes of globalization of information and other networks. The world is now girdled with global networks which allow us to converse, pass and retrieve huge quantities of data, and mediate a whole variety of transactions from banking to travel to the delivery of health or educational services.

We live increasingly in an international rather than a national marketplace and one which is organized more and more around the provision and use of services rather than goods. These momentous changes raise important ethical concerns. Four broad examples were explored. First of all, how can the ethical issues relating to the protection of individual privacy be effectively dealt with as transborder data flows become increasingly routine and oldstyle national sovereignty less and less relevant? Second, global economic and political activity takes place now under real-time conditions. There are serious ethical concerns underlying the fact that stock markets are effectively linked together around the world and that news events such as the Tiananmen Square massacre take place and are reported virtually instantaneously. Thirdly, the so-called information society is more and more in a *"pay-per"* rather than a *paper* society, where every bit of information has its economic value. But "doesn't the global village require its own village common?" And finally, it was argued, the processes of globalization portend major changes in societal institutions—"the twilight of hierarchy" as one observer has called it—and ethical choice will be very much affected by these developments.

The last presentation of the afternoon came from Bruno Lanvin of the United Nations Conference on Trade and Development in Geneva. He focused on the development imperative in an age of pervasive information technologies. Developing countries cannot develop without access to and participation in the multiple global networks which are crucial to economic activity and political affairs. We are moving increasingly from an international economy of "make and sell" into one of "joint produce and share." Networks increasingly shape markets and the development imperative requires that the economic inequalities of an earlier stage of development not be replicated in the years to come as a divide between the "information-rich" and the "information-poor." Throughout his presentation and in the questioning which followed, Mr. Lanvin maintained an optimistic perspective, arguing that concern for "the development of developing countries"—as it is referred to in the ongoing Uruguay Round trade negotiations—is not only a matter of ethics but also of good business.

This paper stimulated a diverse range of questions related to the international context of informational and communications technology, particularly as it affects developing nations. The issue of privatization of information (intellectual private property) versus the open dissemination of scientific or research driven communications was raised as a major concern, given the growing barriers (often of a commercial nature) being placed in the way of widespread communication of scientific information. The potential application of information technology to helping resolve the global environmental crisis was also discussed and there were concerns about the ethical implications of possible misuse of vital environmental data (e.g. where one nation has satellite based remote sensing data on a potential environmental problem in another nation and may not choose to share that information).

A recurring theme in this session and elsewhere was the multiplicity of implications of the growing gaps in information technology capacity among the nations of the world who are at such different stages of development.

A Final Presentation, Some Reflections, and the Search for Consensus

The only formal presentation of the morning was given by Graeme Hughes, President of the Information Technology Association of Canada. He spoke largely from a document recently released by his association entitled, "The Enabling Society" which examined the extent to which Canada is not presently taking proper advantage of the opportunities and the challenges afforded by information technology. He spoke to the question of whether the enabling effect of information technology was a myth or a real and substantial trend and presented a variety of evidence to suggest the latter although IT in Canada is still largely underutilized and even then often in a sub-optimal manner. He pointed to a number of Canadian weaknesses: in industrial organization, including management sponsorship and use of IT; in the unevenness brought about by Canada's reliance on niche strategies for IT development; in our human resources situation, including the failure of educational systems to train students adequately to use and develop IT skills; and lastly, in Canada's well-known deficiencies in support for research and development.

The discussion promised to be lively and indeed it was. Mr. Hughes was questioned about industry's failure to engage workers in the process of introducing IT. He was asked whether it was fair to blame universities for failing to train people for industry and business when the role of the university should be education rather than training. He was queried about Canadian corporate culture and its culpability for the country's relative backwardness in the IT field. Marc Belanger of the Canadian Union of Public Employees questioned him extensively about the concept of "enabling technology" itself: enablement for what purposes? merely for the sake of efficiency? who determines those purposes? shouldn't enablement lead to empowerment of individuals? The different understanding on the part of business and other groups of the relationship between ethics and technology became readily apparent.

With all the formal presentations completed and most of the items on the alternate agenda discussed, it was decided that there was a need for reflection. Four participants in the Workshop were asked to make up an impromptu panel to give their impressions and observations on what had transpired over the two days of discussion. Tannis Macbeth Williams, a psychologist from the University of British Columbia, neatly summarized the discussions in five points:

(1) privacy in all ages, including the computer age, is culturally defined;

(2) information inequities, whether they take a North-South, regional or gender form, can be at least partially redressed through a strategy of "leapfrogging;"

(3) monopolies over information, whether on the part of government or private corporations, are inexorably breaking down;

(4) there needs to be more attention and concern about the socio-technological design of communications and computer systems; and finally,

(5) there should be no illusion that even a relatively benign technology can be neutral.

Professor Jimmy Law from the Department of Physics here at Guelph took up the same theme of technology neutrality and expressed concern that people tended to place too much faith in information technology without taking account of the various contexts in which it can be used. Maria Cionni from the Ontario Ministry of Colleges and Universities focused on the gap between the uses to which information technology can be put—in government, business and internationally—and the ability of people to use those technologies to the benefit of all. She stressed the need for critical awareness with regard to human resource development, access to information technologies, sharing of knowledge and, most important of all, the need for long-term commitment on the part of all those involved in the deployment and use of information technology.

Finally, Judy Brace from the Academy for Educational Development, a Washington-based non-profit agency operating in many developing countries, talked about the particular problems of using communications and computer technologies to assist in resolving the educational problems facing developing countries. The world is really a set of "global villages," rather than one single "global village" as Marshall McLuhan suggested, where the twin deficiencies of distance and too few professionals can now be addressed by information technology. What is required as well, however, is greater participation matched to greater access to information.

The only remaining task for the Workshop was to formulate its conclusions and recommendations. Chairperson Peter Robinson opened the floor to suggestions for what should be included in the Workshop report. Soon the blackboard was once again filled with statements, amendments to statements, suggestions for changes in wording, a proposal for a preamble setting out the common understanding of the group, etc. Gradually and quite quickly, he began to shape a consensus on what our conclusions and recommendations should look like; majority rule prevailed where consensus could not be found, and then came the task of taking the jumble of words and phrases and fashioning them into a coherent statement. Appropriately enough, information technology came to the rescue in the form of York University's Sam Lanfranco's laptop computer. Keyboarding away at the back of the room, Sam soon produced a final text with which all participants in the workshop seemed satisfied—*From poetry to practicality—the true range of potentiality and ethical choice in an information age!*

APPENDIX 1

Information Technology both serves and enhances the crucial role of information in human affairs. It is global by nature and demands long-term commitment. In an economy which is increasingly based on joint production and sharing, the notion of property needs to be revisited. Ethical awareness through all means of education is essential. Inaction is an unacceptable decision.

Key Issues Raised

- information technology is not neutral; it requires socio-technological design,
- potential weakening of ethical standards given the economic opportunity and global homogenization of ideas that accompanies technological advancement
- the "new media" is a mix of computer and communications technology

- the integrity of the information communicated and how it could be manipulated
- the impact on individual privacy and use for marketing purposes—the issues of access to information and the unevenness and control which could develop
- computer virus
- volume of transactions on the international networks and the creation of new corporate alliances

Recommendations

(1) OECD guidelines provide a beginning for privacy protection. Information security and protection require urgent consideration.

(2) Informational Technology is not neutral, it requires socio-technological design. All people should be empowered in and through the process of socio-technological design.

(3) Because information technology is a transformative technology, institutional adaptation is necessary. Institutional adaptation (the law, government, international institutions, corporations, media, etc.) requires rules flexible enough to ensure that change converges towards socio-technological design.

(4) Equitable access to information and distribution of the benefits from information technology must be ensured.

(5) Use of information technology to promote awareness of environmental issues and facilitate solutions.

(6) Use of information technology must respect the values of different cultures.

WORKSHOP 5:
Development Ethics in the Age of Pervasive Technology

Coordinator: Dr. Jorge Nef, Department of Political Studies, University of Guelph

Chair: Ivan Head, President, The International Development Research Centre (IDRC), Ottawa; James Mullin, Vice-President, Science and Technology, IDRC, Ottawa; Dr. Nora Cebotarev, Department of Sociology and Anthropology, University of Guelph

Rapporteur: Dr. Jorge Nef, Department of Political Studies, University of Guelph

Introduction

Development, like the Greek god Janus, is a two-faced concept. On the one hand, it refers to a normative ideal loaded with culture-bound values and ethical assumptions. On the other hand, development as well as its opposites (undevelopment, underdevelopment and de-development) refer to actually-existing and empirically verifiable historical processes and comparable structural conditions.

As an idea, development is a transformation of a distinctive Western concept: the notion of progress.[1]

> [This] idea was elaborated at the end of the of the 18th century in the philosophy of the Enlightenment and the French Revolution. Progress in science, technology, the arts and political liberties ... would free all of humanity from ignorance, poverty, lack of education and despotism. People would not only be happy, but due in large part to education, would become enlightened citizens and masters of their destiny.[2]

Progress, in turn, involves the secularization of the Augustinian concept of Divine Providence—a movement from the "City of Man" to the "City of God." History becomes a linear search for perfection. Development becomes not only the unfolding of a superior, whether theocentric or anthropocentric "plan," but also something intrinsically "good" for Humankind: the pursuit of civilization.

Although as a historical process all societies experience a degree of development— as well as possible de-development—the conscious attempt to bring about induced development is relatively new. Its roots are to be found in the policies of economic, technological and military modernization implemented in Wilhelmian Germany and Meiji Japan in the 19th Century, in Lenin's Soviet industrialization, and most importantly, in both the Keynesian anticyclical economic policies of the 1930s and the Marshall Plan for European reconstruction.

The application of induced development strategies to modernize otherwise underdeveloped societies clearly emerged with the rapid process of post-World War II decolonization. More directly, the preoccupation with international development was fuelled by the conflicts of the Cold War. Based on the Marshall Plan experience, Western industrial nations—chiefly the United States—perceived development as an instrument to prevent the spread of communism. It was also a device to prevent a growing tide of anti-Western economic and political nationalism in the Third World.

Development thus became the backbone of a containment strategy: the soft side of counter-insurgency.[3] The North/South idiom constituted the geographical metaphor to encapsulate the multiple concrete tensions between a developed "centre" and its dependent and underdeveloped "periphery." It subordinated the North/South patterns of unequal exchange to the logic of East-West, communism vs. "Free-World" confrontations. Development of the South since that time has been characterized by two fundamental traits:

(a) The process of socioeconomic change does not centre upon the South's development itself, but primarily involves a process, a methodology, and ultimately a technology defined by the North.

(b) The idea of development has been dominated by both the philosophy of Western modernism and by an often implicit Western political ideological framework and foreign policy agenda.

This is not to say that the Soviet Union and its (then) Eastern European partners did not "peddle" their own version of development packages and strategies of non-capitalist development and socialist modernization. They did. If anything, the socialist model, based upon the Stalinist experience, offered to poor and underdeveloped nations a very explicit and faster shortcut to modern society. The socialist road proposed a methodology for transition to an allegedly more rational and equitable order through political mobilization, bureaucratization, central planning, industrialization and nation-building. This is understandable since, despite its questioning of capitalism and imperialism, socialism and its Marxist philosophical foundations are both part of modern Western culture. Its indigenized versions in China, Cuba, Vietnam or in the former Portuguese colonies of Africa, were always predicated as a quantum leap from "the old ways."

The Cold War context coupled with the uncritical acceptance of the tenets of modernism created a developmental paradox. While Western technologies, capital, and values were considered central to the diffusion of development, the cultural fabric of non-Western societies was severely underdeveloped by the very process of modernization. With few—though remarkable—exceptions, both capitalist and socialist modernization packages seem to have failed the Third World. Far from bringing about development, they appear to have contributed to decay.

From a broader perspective, however, questions of international development cannot be limited exclusively to the Third World. What about global development? Are the current practices of modernization conducive to a liveable and sustainable social, economic, political, ecological and psycho-cultural environment for the whole of the human species? The current crisis of actually-existing socialism in Eastern Europe points not only to a severe breakdown of its political and economic systems but to a breakdown of its entire developmental agenda and culture. However, as Arthur Schlessinger Jr. has observed, the crisis of socialism in Eastern Europe should not be construed as the automatic success of Western, and especially American capitalism.[4] Are we really witnessing "The End of History," as Fukuyama[5] implies, or are we rather witnessing the initial symptoms of the history of the end?

The Problem

The problem lies in the extent to which existing theories and practices of development (particularly, though not exclusively those applied to the Third World) can provide for a kind of social change, which is healthy, sustainable, and desirable for the inhabitants of the planet. The central value at stake is survival. This means pursuing what Lasswell has defined as "human dignity"—the maximum shaping and sharing of values: power, knowledge, well-being, wealth, skills, affection, respect, rectitude.

It is here that the intersection of our technological civilization and an ever-increasing ethical void acquires central importance. Where is development going? What are its driving forces? What are the consequences and who will be affected? Are there any alternatives? Most importantly, is there room for choice, or, for that matter, hope?

The Purpose

These questions formed the foundation of the International Development workshop. The core problem addressed was that of survival through sustainable development in light of the existing practices of modernization and technology diffusion and transfer, particularly between developed and under-developed regions of the world. In this we felt that the problem of international development shared a centre stage with both environment, peace, and security as pressing *global issues* par excellence. Such globalism means that these concerns cannot be managed from the conventional state-centric and bilateral perspectives affecting most public policies today. Existing modalities of development based on technological fixes often involve implicit value judgments with dysfunctional consequences for sustained, need-oriented development. They also have planetary effects. The issues we sought to address included:

(1) The degree of access by the Third World to the most appropriate and/or advanced technologies for development.

(2) The manner and extent to which societies determine—or fail to determine—the ethical basis of their own development.

(3) The depth and shape of social change introduced by advanced technologies as well as the mechanisms for technology creation, control, dissemination, application and reproduction.

(4) The role of social technologies in the aforementioned process of technology creation, regulation, dissemination, application and reproduction.

(5) The socioeconomic, political, environmental and ethical consequences of current practices for both the North and the South.

(6) The ethical principles and value choices emerging from present and alternative future development theory and practice.

The Workshop was first and foremost an effort to stimulate critical thinking. We also wanted to encourage discussion on the social innovations needed to increase the benefits and minimize the dangers arising from the current onslaught of technological innovations. The focus was on the social practices and institutions which regulate human behaviour. A fundamental normative issue was raised by Christopher Smart during our early exploratory stages: What new institutional structures are needed to grapple with the ethical choices that stem from pervasive technology in the field of international development?

The Format

In order to operationalize our thesis and its related queries we invited a select group of participants from a list of references provided by both the International Development Research Centre (IDRC) and other individuals with expertise in the field of development. Our terms of reference were largely conditioned by the purpose already outlined as well as by our overall conception of the conference. We were also influenced by the experience of our on-going "South-North" research project with the IDRC. This meant that the International Development workshop was to have a number of characteristics. These included a systemic internationalist and globalist perspective; an attempt to intersect technology (both social and "gadget") with values; an analytical, historical and prospective (future-oriented) intent; an emphasis on linking theory to concrete practices and examples, and a search for gender-balanced representation from both North and South.

The workshop was organized into three sequentially linked panels followed by a mini-plenary. It was conceived as a loosely structured "interactive survey."

The first panel—*modalities and paradigms of development*—dealt with the macro-relationship between culture, values and development. This included general, theoretical-philosophical questions of development as well as historical aspects: "the big picture."

The second panel—*current practices of international development*—examined the role of technology generation and diffusion and the effects and value implications for both the North and the South. This panel was explicitly designed to probe issues of gender, culture, ethnicity and class.

The third panel—*perspectives on the future*—examined both analytical and normative questions of development as they relate to possible historical scenarios.

The mini-plenary was an attempt to integrate and comprehend the issues, queries and prescriptions raised in the previous panels, and to compile, if possible, a brief report to be presented to the Conference's plenary.

Participants were invited to each of the panels as paper-givers, commentators, resource persons or group leaders (chairpersons). A number of rapporteurs were designated to maintain records and keep continuity. Themes for the position-papers were assigned in advance to focus and stimulate discussion from the audience and provide for an interactive process of learning and consensus-building. In addition, the International Development section of the pre-conference publication, *Ethics and Technology* (Toronto: Thompson Educational Publishing, Inc., 1989) was designed to serve as a preliminary thesis for the Workshop. In total, over ten experts were invited in various capacities, including the core participants of the aforementioned South-North project. Although not all worked out as anticipated, three papers were completed by the Conference deadline. The International Development workshop was well attended, with over forty registrants from a variety of backgrounds, enjoying lively and probing discussions.

Analysis of the Main Working Documents and Presentations

The materials distributed included an introductory paper by Mr. Ivan Head, President of the IDRC in Ottawa, "Development, Technology and Ethics," and two prospective treatments on the future of technology. One was "Ethics and Technology in International Development: Perspectives on the Future" by Dr. Ricardo Israel-Zipper, Professor of Political Science at the University of Chile. Dr. Amílcar Herrera, Professor at the Institute of Geosciences of the State University of Campinas, Brazil, presented a comprehensive document on "Risk and Opportunity: The Building of the Future." Formal oral presentations included those of Mr. James Mullin, Vice-President, Science and Technology of the IDRC; Dr. Paul Lin, Department of History, University of British Columbia; Ms. Peggy Antrobus of the University of the West

Indies, Barbados; Ms. Maria Carlota de Souza-Paula (formerly of the University of Brasilia); Dr. Otilia Vainstok of the University of Buenos Aires; Dr. Eleonora Cebotarev, Sociology Department, University of Guelph, and Dr. Mauricio Schoijet of the National Metropolitan University at Xochimilco, Mexico.

(1) Modalities and Paradigms of Development: The Historical Record

The first panel explored the fundamental paradigms of development and their contradictions. In particular it sought to explore the implicit as well as explicit relationships between culture, values, and technology present in the various theories and practices of development. This panel effectively set the stage for the subsequent panels.

Mr. Ivan Head's paper, "Development, Technology and Ethics" acted as an introduction. In this paper Head states that: "More than ever before, scientific advancement has put into our command the power to bring human development to a halt." He notes that this danger is a result of "our baffling inability to place the pursuit of human dignity at the centre of ... development and progress ... as ... a fundamental human process." Head warns us that the current deprivation of the South will inevitably lead to an overall decline of the global quality of life, including that of the developed economies. The search for sustainable growth through Western technologies is no longer the South's problem; it "must also be the goal of those societies which control such technologies."

Head poses two critical questions: "Are the values that we apply to comprehend the role of technology ... based on the pursuit of human dignity?" and "Are the norms [which regulate] ... the theory and practice of development ... responsive to the ethical challenges the world confronts today?"

Head defines development as "the pursuit of human dignity" based upon "fundamental principles of equity, equality, well-being and participation." However, in a modern creed where power, profits, restricted access, and the dogma of efficiency justify human suffering, these values have been pushed aside. Responsible development choices must rest upon the right of self-determination and the practice of self-reliance. This means the recognition that the "options of development available to the Third World ... [arise] ... not only from ... technology diffusion and transfer from the North, but also out of indigenous processes of technology creation in the South."

The paper concludes with an exhortation to meet an ethical challenge and recognize that:

> there may be something fundamentally wrong in the accepted wisdom within which we frame the understanding and responsibilities of our shared future.

> We have become so accustomed to assuming that there is a safe causal link between our technological advancement and development ..., that we seldom wonder about the principles that govern the conduct of humans in the creation, sharing and utilization of knowledge.[6]

Mr. James Mullin, commenting and expanding upon Mr. Head's paper, presented a synthesis of the Western development experiences since the Second World War, with particular emphasis on the effects of these upon the Third World and upon the Western approach towards global development. Mullin recognized that there is no universally accepted definition of either ethics or development, and, in addition, the more conventional notion of technology—centered on material artifacts—is far too limited for an adequate comprehension of its cultural and ideological role. Mullin noted that both development and technologies are eminently political; they are neither class nor gender neutral and entail either explicit or implicit value judgments. Technology is always a form of empowerment; the crucial question is: who is empowered and who is de-powered by technological innovation, and more explicitly by the introduction of "modern" technologies? Technological innovation—and technology in general—must be placed in the context of development strategy and development policies.

In analyzing "what went wrong" and why, James Mullin emphasized the fundamental contradiction between modernization and development as well as the fact that development was primarily conceived as a Western-centered strategy of growth to prevent revolution. The financing, the teleologies, ideologies, and technologies of development have consistently remained culture-bound. Numerous development policies and slogans have been formulated in the last four decades. They range from GNP expansion with trickle-down in the 1950s, to integrated rural development in the 1960s, to "appropriate" technologies, basic human needs (BHN), and human resources development in the 1970s, to structural adjustment and the "survival strategies" in the 1980s. In practice these have shown little concern for the recipients, particularly for the poorest sectors of the Third World, which should have been the primary beneficiaries of the process.

Further commentaries and interventions by Dr. Ricardo Israel, Political Science, University of Chile, Dr. Daniel Goldstein from the Faculty of Biological Sciences, University of Buenos Aires, Dr. Paul Lin, History, University of British Columbia, and various members of the floor, concluded the discussion. Although a working consensus was difficult to achieve, a number of common issues emerged:

(1) Development and its problematic are usually defined from a Northern perspective. Western technology and ideology are superimposed upon Southern problems, needs and circumstances. In this context, it may be possible that further development in the South may mean less overdevelopment in the North.

(2) Conventional definitions of development concentrate narrowly on economic growth. From this perspective, development appears as an issue of transfers—an antiseptic technical exercise. In the process, more fundamental, "subjective" dimensions of human dignity fall by the wayside. Is it necessary for the South to re-enact the North's stages of development, or is the present development situation facing a completely new set of circumstances?

(3) Technology and development must be seen from a more political perspective: who is doing what to whom and for what purpose? For instance, are developed countries really helping the South to develop or are they a major contributing factor to its underdevelopment? What is the role of governments and socioeconomic elites in both the South and in the North?

Likewise, it was recognized that the choice of development policy—and certainly that of development paradigm—affects both the choice of technology and its overall developmental consequences for individuals, nations, and ultimately, for the planet as a whole. It was also recognized that, despite the search for universal principles, technology, development and ethics will inevitably remain culture-bound. This means that, in spite of the hegemony of modernization as a developmental discourse, there is no one single path to development, nor to human dignity other than the Hippocratic prescription: "never do harm to anyone."

(2) Ethics and Technology in the Current Practice of International Development

The panel on current practices sought to look at technology generation, diffusion, and application in specific Third World contexts. As a general guideline the panelists were advised beforehand to concentrate on issues of scale, class, and gender in their case-study presentations. Although no papers were delivered in advance, three topics were covered.

Ms. Peggy Antrobus from the UWI gave a general presentation on issues of gender and development in Third World contexts, concentrating on the West Indies, but with a global analytical perspective. She illustrated the paradoxes of international development in which ready-made solutions are often imposed before a clear understanding of the problem emerges. Ms. María Carlota de Souza-Paula discussed the case of both the pharmaceutical and aero-space industries in Brazil, both instances of high-tech developments in the South. In turn, Dr. Otilia Vainstok gave a general overview of the state of technology in Latin America in an era characterized by a profound economic and social crisis. This crisis has made self-reliant development practically impossible, compounding international trends concerning industrial property and the long-range deleterious effects of a dramatic decline in the quality of university education and research. In fact, despite the return of formal democratic practices throughout the region, technological dependency has deepened.

The search for an alternative model of equitable development requires a revalorization of the role of small and medium enterprises (SMEs) and their capacity for combining new patterns of competitiveness and efficiency with job creation and social equity. A careful study of each country's situation is essential for understanding the socioeconomic, political, cultural and technical conditions for the acquisition, upgrading, transfer and trade of technology by SMEs. These studies would help to elucidate the necessary social conditions for technological innovation and to define appropriate policies for technological development. A comparative analysis of the Brazilian and Argentinean situations described by Ms. de Souza-Paula and Dr. Vainstock suggests that the pervasive developmental weaknesses present in these two countries' experiences are to be found, not necessarily in the technological instruments themselves, or in the lack of innovation per se, but in the nature of "softer" informational and policy parameters. Most importantly, in both cases, the constraints against NIC-like technological "success stories" are to be found in the overall dependent development schemes initiated under authoritarian regimes.

The discussion in the second part of the panel, while addressing some of the questions raised in the presentations (especially Ms. Antrobus' general remarks), concentrated mainly on the themes of the first round of the workshop. Exchanges were particularly heated as participants voiced concerns that the outcome of the workshop—and the Conference as a whole—could have been "stacked" to reach a pre-ordained set of conclusions. Earlier minutes of the first session and summary reports had to be changed to accommodate these concerns.

For this reason, the report of the second session reflected more a general preoccupation with broader ethical and conceptual issues than with the substance of the panel presentations proper. The group recommended expansion of the workshop's main preliminary report. Many of these preliminary conclusions were reflected in the final report.

(3) *The Shape of Things to Come: Perspectives on Our Future*

The third and last panel explored the relationship between ethics, technology, and development by looking into the future. As a sort of prognosis and critical review of international development theory and practice, an emphasis was placed upon both social innovations and institutional structures to grapple with emerging challenges, constraints and opportunities in an age of turbulence. The central thesis-statements were provided by two papers: one by Dr. Amílcar Herrera of the Faculty of Geosciences of the University of Campinas, Brazil, and another by Dr. Ricardo Israel, from the Institute of Political Science of the University of Chile. There was also a more specific presentation by Dr. Mauricio Schoijet of the National Metropolitan University at Xochimilco, Mexico, looking at the connection between nuclear power and Third World development.

Dr. Israel's paper, "Ethics and Technology in International Development: Perspectives on the Future," concentrated on a cultural, as well as political view of technology. To Israel, technology, as part of a cultural system, always implies political alternatives and ethical options. "There is no such thing as a 'neutral' technology" since "its consequences are determined by social and political factors." The functions of a tool or artifact are a consequence of the social environment and its value is related to a given social framework.

He views contemporary society as undergoing an accelerated change of historical proportions. In primitive communities, technology was the simple extension and derivation of community life. In modern society, the production and reproduction of knowledge has been organized and appropriated by large institutions, both public and private. Technology is alienated from society.

Likewise, the process of international development has resulted in an increasing distancing between societies, with the upper echelons of industrialized nations outdistancing the Southern periphery. It has also meant the consolidation of an international political economy of development which has accentuated the weakness and subordination of the South. The key variables here are power and the control of politico-economic decisions.

In the specific case of Latin America, Dr. Israel argues that, despite the fixation with the idea of development in political and technical circles, "the anxiously desired "developed" society never showed up." He traces this developmental failure to a profound crisis of political hegemony in the region, one which continues to the present. Although there is no single model of successful technological development, Latin America has shown a continuous inability to implement consistent scientific and technological policies, and to incorporate these into economic or political plans.

Israel believes that the future remains open. However the future has not been systematically incorporated in our decision-making processes and theories to the same degree as has the past. While the past cannot be changed, the future remains subject to human manipulation and open to study. The best one can do as a social scientist is to predict trends.

Israel envisions three major trends shaping the nature of the unfolding future: The first is the consolidation and spread of a post-industrial society. This poses both a serious threat as well as possible opportunities to Third World countries. Their new reality is a world in which labour and raw materials—which have shaped their political economies—have become less important. The post industrial order also presents a challenge to old views of bureaucratic and political power. Bigger is not necessarily better: "classical organizations, based on hierarchy and controls are challenged, all over the world." Education and information are becoming the most important currencies of this new era. It is not yet clear which system will replace the old division of labour. This presents a challenge to intellectuals: to understand (not merely to describe) these new circumstances at work.

The second trend is the enormous increase in the pace of change. Scientific and technological change is occurring faster than ever before in history. Unlike political revolutions, Dr. Israel sees technological ones as almost irreversible, though cultural-attitudinal changes are much slower and difficult to attain than technological changes.

The third trend involves a fundamental geopolitical shift. While the industrial revolution entailed a movement of power, wealth and innovation from the Mediterranean Sea to the Atlantic, the current geopolitical centre has moved dramatically to the Pacific Rim.

To meet the challenge, Dr. Israel suggests a re-thinking of the relationships between politics, technology, development and ethics. In his view, there is a need to provide for a linkage between the politician who is a generalist, thinking in terms of "problems," and the technological researcher who is a specialist thinking in terms of "solutions." Moreover, he suggests that we recognize that there could not be economic or social development without technological development and that technological dependence will generate political dependence.

Successful countries, in his view, are not imitators. They adapt institutions from other nations, but they do not mimic blindly: "they remain essentially the same without changing their soul." Development and underdevelopment are connected to a society's capacity for using its own brainpower, the "density of information" available and the average "intelligence capability" applied to decision-making.

This also requires an ethical foundation: the recognition that human beings are simultaneously both the objects and the subjects of the technological and the development process itself. No society, developed or underdeveloped, should avoid ethical decisions. Technological development only makes sense in a world which can satisfy basic material needs as well as those for security, knowledge, affection, respect and a sustainable future. An economic boom does not transform a society into a developed one. In the final analysis "development is [not only] the attempt of man to control nature ... [but also] ... the attempt to increase the possibilities of social and political freedoms for the largest possible number of individuals."

Dr. Amílcar Herrera's paper, "Risk and Opportunity: The Building of the Future" explored the role technology plays in global social options. He based his research on two premises: that we are undergoing a world crisis, or process of transformation, and that the social impact of technologies is contingent upon the nature of the socioeconomic strategies adopted. For Herrera, the present crisis lies in the style or philosophy of development based on indiscriminate economic growth and an accelerated process of global impoverishment. Irrational consumption and the ecological impact of poverty affect the nature of present underdevelopment trends, characterized by increasing international inequality both in quantitative and qualitative terms.

Conventional development strategies have conceived the attainment of prosperity without major socioeconomic reforms. As a world recession unfolded in the 1970s and as the failure of modernization schemes became apparent, a new conception of the Third World "problem" emerged in the West: The South was perceived as a threat to the material progress of the North. The dialogue between the two blocks became increasingly more difficult. This is particularly dramatic with regard to threats to the ecosystem. "Unless an environment policy at the planetary level can be implemented—and this is impossible with the present division of the world—there is little chance of avoiding a global ecological collapse in a not too distant future."

Dr. Herrera asserts that the present crisis is one which is founded on the very nature of modern man. In his view, the tendencial scenario is not viable: "Western civilization has become dysfunctional, in the sense that it is no longer able to give adequate responses to the problems generated by its own evolution." Herrera suggests that the prevention of global catastrophe lies in an alternative view of development. This possible future society will be one in which environment and natural resources become the central determining element. Herrera sees sustainability as a possible goal where the provision of an austere material life is accepted. This conception runs counter to the conventional Western attitude of indefinite growth of consumption. Instead, it bases development upon time devoted to creative activities eventually leading to the elimination of the social division of labour.

This alternative social scenario—based upon Dr. Herrera's previous work on possible futures carried on at the Bariloche Foundation[7]—involves a style of development featuring four major principles: egalitarianism, participation, autonomy (not autarchy) and compatibility with the physical environment.

The attainment of this scenario would require global cooperation between North and South. However a fundamental dilemma emerges when the possible transition to this new style of development is studied at length. In terms of technological and material conditions, the North is in a favourable position to achieve change, while the South is in a far better position to accept austerity, since even such austerity would entail a quantum leap from their present situation. Northern acceptance of the new austere society would, in contrast, mean a profound cultural change: distinct Western notions such as progress, nationalism and superiority would be eliminated. This dilemma could only be solved if a high degree of conscientization emerged (particularly in the North), that is, the recognition that "in the crisis of survival confronted by mankind, there are no separate solutions for the North or for the South."

Professor Herrera is not pessimistic about such an occurrence. He believes that a paradigmatic change is already evolving among sectors of Western political decision-makers as well as among certain groups in the population such as today's youth, scientists and intellectuals, and grassroots ecological, peace, and feminist movements. The "very possibilities of building the proposed society depends on the ethical options adopted in the period of transition." Technological choice, in this context will have to be subordinated to ethical and normative considerations.

A new cluster of mutually-articulated innovations will configure the technological "wave" of this new global paradigm. This cluster is already with us. The central element in it is micro-electronics with fundamental implications in two leading fields: automation in the workplace and information in the realm of participation. The impact of these appears to be strongest in the organization of production, the labour process and in the social division of labour than in the general profile of the productive system; that is, in the very basis of industrial society.

Dr. Herrera foresees that as automation advances, the central role of wages will decrease, and most significant forms of authority in the workplace will be obliterated. The importance of human activity will be greatly reduced. Social marginality, until recently a characteristic of underdevelopment, is already appearing in the developed world. A dualistic stratification—a "South Africanization" of social relationships—is likely to occur. This new nature of unemployment in "advanced countries cannot be solved without a complete questioning of the relationship between technology, employment and work." The only solution is the reduction of working time and the distribution of remaining necessary work among the entire population.

In this society, new socially productive activities will have to be created: informal education, community organization, preservation of the environment, among others. Likewise, a new set of principles will have to be instituted such as the right to a useful task in society and the right to have access to intellectually creative work. This means a redefinition of work back to its original meaning as the liberation of the creative human potential.

The right to participate in all social decisions will be affected by the new technologies. Participation must become an end in itself, above and beyond the limited electoral mechanisms of the present. These decisions will refer not only to the "political" space of elected officials, but to the community and workplace as well. Information here will likely play a crucial role, but its beneficial effects will be conditioned to its close determination through the participation process itself.

North/South cooperation in science and technology is an ethical option which is a cornerstone of the proposed model. Common prescriptions for technological development in Third World countries see the latter concentrating their R&D efforts almost exclusively in basic needs. The new approach seeks to concentrate R&D efforts in the technological areas which are crucial for entering the new society. Research in new technologies would prevent the maintenance of a world divided between first and second class countries. The proposed strategy concentrates more on income redistribution, combined with existing basic needs technologies as a vehicle for providing a better quality of life. The determination of R&D priorities is central in achieving a degree of technological autonomy sufficient to prevent the creation in the Third World of deformed copies of advanced societies. These priorities should be based on socioeconomic goals. The main "problem is not to close the technological gap ..., but to gradually reduce it as a function of the demand of the socioeconomic strategy."

Dr. Herrera articulates his teleology as a world based upon solidarity, austerity in material consumption, and continuously increasing free time devoted to creative activities. He not only sees this as possible, but as the only option which could ensure the survival of mankind. He sees a reduction in human aggressiveness as an essential cultural mutation in accomplishing this sustainable scenario. Cultural mutations, unlike biological ones are those upon which the human species can have a degree of control and use to confront a challenge or a crisis. Man is a social and cultural animal, one whose spiritual achievements—the search for meaning, beauty and knowledge— are vastly more important than its material creations. The transmission and accumulation of knowledge, as functions of the mind, require freedom of choice. Without the possibility of free choice no true knowledge is possible. "The adventure of *Homo Sapiens* is essentially the adventure of freedom; it contains the seeds of self-destruction but it also contains the promise of unending progress and self-realization."

The misery and deprivation of most of humanity are not the unavoidable consequences of an incomplete control of the physical environment, but of the irrational use of the scientific and technological instruments at our disposal. For the first time in history, humanity has the knowledge necessary to fulfil its material needs. This offers an opportunity for the liberation of the human race. The emergence of a new global cultural synthesis through cross-fertilization, rather than the old view of the Westernization of the world, will be an essential ingredient to reach this goal. Instead of the distorted understanding of civilization as the product of one single "superior" culture, a cultural synthesis will assert the consciousness that we are the heirs of the entire past of humankind.

Conclusions and Recommendations

The discussion that followed the presentations was extremely lively and dynamic. Participants expressed their various points of view, some voiced their frustrations with time constraints, the format of the conference, the very large number of participants and the inability to have the opportunity to develop some of the ideas expressed.

In general, some form of consensus was reached on the critical points sketched at the end of the second panel, though fears of biased reporting and "pre-cooked" "pro-technology" conclusions were ardently voiced by some members of the floor. A minority position also emerged, represented by what could be labelled a "pragmatic," engineering view of development. In this view, development is an objective and universal process characterized by its rationality in which scientific knowledge and human effort are applied through technological instruments, irrespective of ideological intent. Although the dynamics may mean social cost and personal sacrifice, the ultimate effect would be human progress.

The majority position could be summarized as follows:

(1) Development is an ethical, moral and philosophical issue as well as a practical one. It involves the affirmation of human dignity and of human potential. Without this understanding there is the danger of making development a "technical" exercise occurring in a moral vacuum. Even minimum development must incorporate basic human rights; these rights are both material and moral rights at the heart of which is life itself.

(2) Power is the main *instrumental* drive in development. Without political resolve, and most importantly, without the empowerment and effective participation of those affected by development the substance of development cannot be realized.

(3) Experience shows that tactics and strategies of development are controversial. Political questioning of who makes the decisions and for whose benefit, are constantly posed and must be addressed.

(4) Technology is a means to development, not an end in itself. Although it is important in solving concrete problems, it is nevertheless, like all tools, subject to human control.

(5) Efficiency, profitability and political expediency have become in practice the immoral substitute for ethical choices in development. They constitute both the prime directive and the overriding command in modern culture.

(6) The ideology of economic growth which heretofore has dominated development strategies must be subordinated to bring human dignity to the centre of development.

(7) Development is a global phenomenon. It is also a complex phenomenon conditioned by a variety of historical and specific cultural experiences. It affects the people in the South and in the North (as well as in the East and West).

(8) Development has been a Western, gender-specific phenomenon conditioned by time, space, and experience. International development, to be truly comprehensive, must incorporate a multiplicity of perspectives encompassing the totality of the human experience and in

particular the other half of the human experience: a feminist perspective.

(9) The actors involved in development bring with them the values of their experience. Four general categories of such actors, or stakeholders, can be identified: (a) decision-makers, i.e. politicians and CEO's who control money and power; (b) scientific and academic communities which control symbols and knowledge; (c) practitioners who command specific skills and, (d) the public at large.

To conclude the workshop, three main resolutions were presented to the Conference plenary:

(1) Development requires the application of technology. However, technology in itself will not produce development by and for the people unless it is guided by ethical choices.

(2) These choices entail the constitution and operationalization of development paradigms which recognize the importance of humanness in development, as well as the necessary relationship between humans and their environments.

(3) A contribution of this conference towards such a paradigmatic shift could be the inclusion of an ethical focus in the agenda of the United Nations' Fourth Development Decade.

REFERENCES

[1] See Helio Jaguaribe, *Economic and Political Development. A Theoretical Approach and a Brazilian Cast-Study*, (Boston: Harvard University Press, 1968), pp. 1-7.

[2] Jean-Francois Lyotard, "Ticket to New Decor," in *Harpers Magazine,* June 1989, pp. 26-27, excerpted from his article by the same title in *Copyright*, No. 1, 1989.

[3] See J. Nef and O.P. Dwivedi, "Development Theory and Administration: A Fence Around an Empty Lot?", *Indian Journal of Public Administration.*

[4] Arthur Schlessinger, Jr., interview with *The Journal*, CBC-TV, February 23, 1990.

[5] See Francis Fukuyama, "The End of History?", *The National Interest*, No. 16 (Summer, 1989).

[6] Ivan L. Head, "Development, Technology and Ethics," Notes for remarks prepared for Ivan L. Head, President, International Development Research Centre, World Conference on Ethical Choices in an Age of Pervasive Technology, October, 1989, p.7.

[7] See Amílcar Herrera, et al., *Catastrophe or New Society? A Latin American Working Model,* (Ottawa: IDRC, 1976), passim. This work was based on the "Technological Perspective for Latin America Project" (TPLA), sponsored jointly by the UN and the IDRC. The basic thesis of the book questions the Club of Rome emphasis on the physical limits to growth by arguing that the fundamental limits to development (the latter defined in terms of quality of life) are social and political in nature.

WORKSHOP 6: Technology and Ethical Choice in Education

Coordinators: Drs. Clive Beck, Margrit Eichler, Madan Handa, Jack Miller, Edmund Sullivan and Alan Thomas, Ontario Institute for Studies in Education, Toronto; Jokelee Vanderkop, University of Guelph

Chair: Dr. Edmund Sullivan

Rapporteur: Dr. Jack Miller

This workshop was developed by professors at the Ontario Institute for Studies in Education who have a special interest in values and technology. The workshop focused on themes developed in several papers.

The workshop began with a paper on "The Obsolescence of Students, Teachers, and Other Human Beings" presented by David Bella, a Professor of Civil Engineering at Oregon State University. This paper was presented in two forms. The first was a dialogue between Bella and a "stranger" about the role of computers. The dialogue raised questions about what computers can do in relation to what teachers do. The stranger argues that computers can do almost anything a person can do and thus, could very quickly make teachers and students obsolete. The stranger in his summary comments says:

> It seems to me that higher education now gives its high priority toward training people who can make and manage new machines to do the tasks that the old machines couldn't do. Humans are in a race to see if they can find some task to do before some new machine makes them obsolete. The unskilled faced this race first, then skilled workers. Now, with advanced computers, educated people are feeling the pinch of computer-driven obsolescence. Finally, the educational system itself may become automated. Why shouldn't human teachers and students become obsolete just as other workers have become obsolete? Aren't the same arguments for automation valid? And isn't an "ideal" outcome of this "rational" trend a completely computerized teacher-student system? Isn't this what education is preparing people to do? Hasn't teaching and learning already been defined in such a way as to define such an outcome as "ideal"? The evaluation standards have already been established! All that needs to be worked out is the increased ratio of silicon to carbon-based components. I'm not talking about the future! The "ideals" are now being pursued!

The dialogue provoked discussion about such issues as what is knowledge and how should knowledge be transmitted? When does knowledge become propaganda? Another issue arose concerning the real purpose of education and the role of the teacher in relation to those purposes.

The second part of Professor Bella's presentation took the form of a story. The story focused on capsules that fit over a person's head and provide a simulated environment for whatever that person desires. The story encouraged the participants to reflect on the effects of simulated learning environments. Bella's talk produced intense discussion around issues related to the use of computers and artificial intelligence. Bella's talk also raised the issue of the technological imperative or the idea that technology sets the agenda for human choice and even determines the resulting decisions. Bella himself argued for the importance of caring and involvement in education. Bella states:

> Teacher and students form a community and together they participate in a history within which they care about what they say and accept. Because they care, they are called to seek out knowledge that is worthy of trust and respect. Thus, facts, as you say, are drawn into the course and critically examined because people care about what they learn. Such a course should be exciting, there should be enthusiasm, because people are discovering things that they really care about. Then, the history that such educated people live out will produce statements and experts worthy of trust. Then, caring people will have trustworthy knowledge that they can draw upon to challenge the repeated statements arising from power, manipulation, fear, and habit.
>
> However, the presentation and acceptance of facts and techniques to get facts becomes an end in itself. Then "caring about" becomes irrelevant or even detrimental given demands for efficiency, order, and evaluation. Common knowledge of the second kind is not nurtured. Trust becomes a meaningless term. The efficiency of presentation and acceptance of facts, common knowledge of the first kind, becomes paramount. Students cram to get the facts and throw them back regardless of whether they care about them or not. When the educational system ceases to be a caring and trustworthy community and instead becomes a collection of people rushing to complete their assignments, then it is not at all unreasonable to say, "let's replace the system with computers." When one finds a lack of enthusiasm and excitement, when there is no time to "care about," when efficiency, order, evaluation, and productivity become the dominant norms, then the reasons for not replacing humans with computers have already departed. Then, "education" has become a way of manipulating minds. Education ceases to be a way to help people care about what is said and done; it fails to prepare them to live out a more trustworthy history within a complex technological world. Then, a shift from a carbon-based educational system to a silicon-based system may indeed be the "reasonable" thing to do.

Mary Evelyn Tucker, Professor of Religion at Bucknell University, presented the next paper entitled "Educating for the Ecological Age: Earth Literacy and the Technological Trance." Tucker outlined our environmental crisis focusing particularly on the power of technology to accelerate the depletion of nature. She also discussed how the response of the educational community has been muted or even become "ostrich-like." According to Tucker, "teachers and students are caught in the technological trance of the industrial bubble." In response to this problem Tucker argues for cultivating "earth literacy" which focuses on the need for sustainable development, intermediate technologies and alternative energy sources.

Central to earth literacy is the movement from "an anthropocentric view of dominion and stewardship over nature to an anthropocosmic one of reciprocity and respect." Tucker argues that this movement is part of a new cosmological paradigm. This new paradigm focuses on how the earth is 4.5 billion years old and how we can now marvel at the earth from pictures taken from the moon. This new cosmology will require "imaginative meditations, poems, paintings, dances, dramas and stories before we can reorient ourselves to a universe which is much larger, more complex, and more mysterious than we had previously realized." The concept of earth literacy is based on the notion that the earth itself is the primary educator as it is the "primary healer, law giver, and producer of life." Earth literacy would encourage students to listen to the voices of the earth. Hearing the voices of the earth means that we attune ourselves to nature and to the needs of other species.

Tucker's paper provoked a discussion that focused on the role of science in relation to this new cosmology. The view emerged that science without mystery and reverence will only lead to further alienation from the planet.

The theme of development was pursued in the next paper presented by Professor Gustave Esteva, Division of Educational Policy Studies, Pennsylvania State University. In his paper entitled, "Stop to Technology Transfer; On Appropriate Technologies and Development Education," Esteva called for the end of development in the Third World as it is currently conducted. According to Esteva, development often means following experts so that you become something you are not. In brief, development leads to the degradation of livelihood. Esteva drew from his experience in Mexico and talked about how a "bankrupt technology" has begun to collapse and this has encouraged people in the villages to communicate again at a more human level. For Esteva technology must be a tool, not something that begins to determine who we are. In short, technology must reflect our moral convictions and political will rather than the reverse which has so often been the case in the Third World. Esteva's thoughts had a strong impact on the group as seen in the final recommendations.

Esteva's paper was followed by Jalna Hanmer's paper on "Reproductive Technologies and Ethical Choice." Hanmer is a Senior Lecturer in Social Work and Coordinator of Women's Studies at the University of Bradford in England. Hanmer began her paper by focusing on current reproductive technologies. For example, she discussed "insemination by donor (AID) and in vitro fertilization, or genetic continuity through egg or embryo transfer, embryo, egg, and semen freezing and storage, embryo experimentation, so-called surrogacy, and potential practices such as the creation of transgenetic species, cloning, sex selection and sex predetermination." The contradiction within all these technologies is the claim to return women to their natural nature through artificial means. Reproductive technology, of course, is connected to science which according to Hanmer, is connected to a certain set of power relations. Hanmer claims, "The increased medical and scientific intervention into the processes of conception, pregnancy and birth has the consequence of denaturalizing motherhood while naturalizing fatherhood through the increased ideological importance placed on the male genetic contribution." Reproductive technologies have forced us to examine what is natural, what rights are actually involved and how these rights are expressed. Hanmer claims that the personhood of women must be reasserted so that they can control their reproductive processes to secure an equal status in relation to men. This involves a "fundamental reordering of knowledge, an epistemology in which woman is subject, her body whole, in one piece with growing cells that will become child."

The last two papers were on "Spiritual Education in a Technological World" and were presented by Madan Handa and John Miller, Professors at O.I.S.E. Professor Handa identified scientific materialism as the major problem in our age and the need for a new paradigm based on several principles. The new paradigm is based on oneness rather than the prevailing scientific materialism. Spirituality is also central to this new world view and particularly the relation of the individual to the Cosmic. This new world view recognizes the oneness of the human family of all life on earth of which human life is an organic part. This new paradigm includes a vision of a peaceful world order that transcends present day divisions of the nation state and focuses on social justice, human rights, ecological order, and communitarian and participatory social structures. The movement to this new world order will have to be implemented by peaceful means and a network of communities organized around global values of peace, ecology and spirituality. Finally, this new cosmic paradigm must be lived as a way of being in our everyday lives.

Finally, John Miller focused on fragmentation as a problem underlying many of our world problems and the fact that technology is used within that context of separation. Spiritual education would counter the problem of alienation by focusing on "connectedness." The paradigm of connectedness is noted in ecology and sub-atomic physics as well as in the mystical strain of the major faiths. Spiritual education would allow students to explore and make connections in a variety of areas. Some of the connections that could be explored included the linkage between linear thinking and intuition, body and mind, various subjects in the curriculum, and school and community. Spiritual education would also explore the connections with Self and with the Earth. Miller also discussed the role of the teacher and encouraged teachers to engage in various forms of inner work (e.g. meditation) as a vehicle for facilitating spiritual education.

Definition: The technological imperative means that if something can be invented it is invented, if it is invented it must be used, if it is used we conform.

Conclusions

(1) Education must cease to support the Technological Imperative.

(2) Moral discourse must come first, political process must come second, and technical means, third. The Technological Imperative reverses this order.

(3) The Technological Imperative reduces education to the efficient transfer of information from "experts" to "non-experts." We object. We support active learning that promotes the ability to select and interpret knowledge.

(4) Education must support the ability to make ethical choices by avoiding the dual pitfalls of fragmentation through overspecialization, "departmentalism," and the division of labour, on the one hand, and the false generalizations and abstractions that eliminate distinctions of race, gender, culture, etc., on the other.

(5) The power to set the agenda of education must be shifted from bureaucracies and allowed to remain with the constituencies affected by the educational process.

(6) To educate for the long-range survival of life on the planet and to deal with our present ecological crisis, "Earth Literacy" which connects the human to the environment of the planet, the social order, the body, and the inner life, is essential to orient curriculum and educational policy.

WORKSHOP 7: Technology and Ethical Choice in Forms of Energy

Coordinator: Dr. William James, School of Engineering, University of Guelph

Chair: Dean Iain Campbell, Physical Science, University of Guelph

Rapporteur: Dr. Fred Knelman, Knelman Consulting Services, Vancouver

Workshop Report: Dr. Fred Knelman and Dr. Henry Wiseman

On a worldwide basis the multiform production and use of energy is one of the most critical contributing factors to industrial growth, increasing food production and improved quality of life.

But it is not all a happy picture. The monumental production and disproportionate use of energy in the industrial, as contrasted with the developing world, reflects an equally disproportionate standard of living. There is also indisputable evidence that the unrestrained production and use of some forms of energy are the cause of excessive pollution, resource depletion, ecological damage, deterioration of the ozone layer and the greenhouse effect. Although there is some dispute about the data and the extrapolation of future effects, there is none about the gravity of the physical consequences and ethical implications. Furthermore, these matters are compounded by a considerable divergence of interests and points of view among those who control, produce and consume the energy.

What ethical principles should guide national energy policies and who should ensure their implementation? These are formidable questions, especially when raised at a conference on ethics and technology which attempted to analyze the many fundamental interrelations, or lack thereof, between ethics and technology. This was certainly the case in the Energy Workshop, though substantial differences were also evident in other workshops.

Yet, while acknowledging these differences—at times heatedly expressed in the Energy Workshop—there was at least a minimum consensus on the following:

- The evident and expanding need for energy;
- The overwhelmingly disproportionate use of energy in the industrialized world as compared with the developing world;
- The need to stabilize demand in the industrialized world through conservation and more efficient use;
- The evident requirements for more energy production in the developing world to provide basic and equitable availability for all sectors of the population as well as for industrial development.
- present uses of traditional forms of energy are wasteful and detrimental to the survival of the planet.

The central disagreements in the workshop revolved around the following questions:

- What is the most available benign and appropriate source of energy—nuclear, fossil, hydro or solar? (This underlined almost all of the workshop proceedings.)
- Can the same ethical questions be put to the developing world, which lacks adequate energy sources and production, as to the industrial world which has access to seemingly abundant sources of energy?
- What are the appropriate energy sources and technologies for the developing world? Should they be restricted in the use of fossil fuels because of global ecological damage and the greenhouse effects when fossil fuels are their only or primary sources of energy?
- Where changes in resource use are necessary for environmental reasons, who should make the decisions, who should bear the cost? Should there be a democratization of energy policy-making?
- Are the present corporate, governmental and institutional structures capable of comprehending and making the necessary changes?
- Will the affluent of the world be willing to reduce their consumption of energy? If so by whom and how will the choices be made?
- Are the required changes so fundamental in nature that the essential cultural values and commensurate systemic structures are unable to undertake the transformation? If they are not, then what other choices are there?

The manner in which these questions were addressed depended partly on individual perspectives, ethical criteria, and interpretation of the data. Some expressed the view that too many workshop participants appeared to represent establishment views and hence were incapable of an open, unbiased and penetrating analysis. These critics themselves were criticized for misreading the data and insisting upon a rapid, radical and impossible restructuring of societal values and institutions to accommodate lower energy requirements from benign sources.

The failure of a meaningful dialogue between these two solitudes was a loss for all those involved. On the one hand, scientists, technologists and engineers, the "keepers of the flame" were almost exclusively concerned with technical means related to efficacy and efficiency. This absorbing concern was selective, being applied to the dominant existing or currently available energy sources. This connection, it was argued, was not accidental. The "technical" group was made of stakeholders (and stockholders) in these chosen means, having both vested and invested interests, which made them almost opaque to the profound ethical implications and impacts of their preferred means. At best, the opponents charged, they made simplistic and positive correlations between their chosen means and broadly desired ends. Any existing problems connected to these technologies were allegedly reduced to improper use or improper management or improper application, the technical means themselves being neutral and ultimately infallible. Modern technology, whether in energy, agriculture or medicine, was touted by these technological optimists as the solution to the most urgent problems we face—social inequities, conflict and environmental degradation. This group purported to be aware of all the ramifications of the various sources of energy and their ethical implications.

On the other side of the two cultures were the philosophers, social or "soft" scientists and social critics. They were concerned with the relations between ends and means, with the structural and systemic contexts in which science and technology were developed and disseminated and therefore with those means which were appropriate for particular ends. In fact, this group tended to see modern technology (and the group that developed and managed it) more as the problem than the solution, having led the world to the point where we have invented multiple means to our own end.

In the view of the rapporteur to the Energy Workshop, it would appear that insufficient thought was given to the selection of workshop participants in order to achieve some balance. In particular, the energy workshop had a skewed distribution of papers as between a large number of expert "hard" scientists collectively supporting a single energy option—nuclear power—and, on the other side, by "soft" scientists and social critics, generally without any technical expertise.

No energy expert was invited, either capable of critiquing the nuclear option or able to present alternative energy options and paths. This was very surprising since the great majority of independent energy experts chose the conservation and efficiency (C and E) option as the best choice in the short-to medium-term future, from both an economic and environmental point of view.

Energy is highly correlated with both the quantity and quality of life. Yet, it presents a paradoxical situation. The "good news" is that a certain lower threshold of energy is essential for life-support to supply the goods and services necessary for survival. The "bad news" is that a higher threshold of consumption threatens the delivery and availability of environmental goods and services, thus threatening survival itself. According to one point of view, the ideal energy policy is to steer a course between limits (i.e. at consumption levels) which optimize the quantity-quality mix. More than any other human activity, the production and consumption of energy impacts on the environment. Therefore, energy policy choices can be the means of managing (or mismanaging) the level of environmental degradation. The policies that yield the highest returns, economically and ecologically, and above all permit the purchase of that most valuable of all commodities—time—are conservation and efficiency. With this purchased time we can match the learning curves for various alternative energy forms with the social and environmental needs of the future.

A central focus of debate in the workshop, as noted earlier, was about the choice of energy paths—nuclear, fossil, hydro, solar and conservation. The first three have built in deleterious consequences: the disposition of spent fuel and the danger of a nuclear calamity as per Chernobyl, the danger of nuclear arms proliferation and war (a matter hard to calculate and predict), as well as pollution and the greenhouse effect from fossil fuels, and ecological disruption from hydro. By contrast, can "cleaner" solar technologies command the necessary confidence and investment to make it a viable alternative? If the answer is negative could adequate conservation techniques be adopted to buy time until solar or more safe nuclear technologies can be developed? Here is where the polarization between the energy experts, on the one hand, and the social philosophers or "soft" scientists, on the other, is most intense.

According to the global energy demand estimated by Chauncey Starr, energy demand, driven by modest annual increases of the two major forces of global population growth and of GNP per capita, would result in annual energy use in 2060 of more than 4 times the total global use in 1986 if present trends continue, and more than 2 times with extreme efficiency in energy use by means of full conservation. As Starr argues:

> The global energy demand projected to the year 2060 is likely to be so large that only a massive expansion of non-fossil sources could slow the annual increase in CO_2 emissions globally. Even with a full conservation effort to use energy effi-

ciently, total energy use will roughly double, driven by global population and economic growth. Electricity demand is likely to increase more than four times, and its supply will obviously require an expansion globally of all sources. Nuclear power is one of the few non-fossil sources that can make a substantial contribution.

Yet with the evident massive devastation caused by Chernobyl and the yet unfound and/or undecided means for the safe disposal of nuclear wastes, and fears of nuclear arms proliferation, what choices are there? According to the "soft" science side of the conundrum a massive conservation and efficiency program would not only purchase the time required to complete the R & D on alternative energy options, but would also enable us to seek solutions to the most serious of problems associated with nuclear power—reactor safety, waste management and storage, and proliferation, both vertical and horizontal. It appears eminently unethical to proceed with a rapid expansion of nuclear power while these unresolved problems exist. The cleavage here was whether the most urgent global problems were a consequence of existing social structures and systems or whether existing structures and systems, if not the best of all possible worlds, required only modest modifications. On the other side, the view was expressed that these problems were directly the consequences of existing sociopolitical structures and systems and what was required was a radical restructuring, if there was to be any hope of solving the major global problems.

Of course the debate included arguments on feasibility with the "hard path" group largely downgrading the solar option. The other side, in turn, drew attention to the radical bias in current funding between dominant supply options and solar, with the latter receiving a very small fraction of R & D support. From this point of view it is clear that the debate on energy futures is not merely a technical argument about data or between advocates of "hard" or "soft paths." It is perhaps even more a debate about politics, economics, culture, ethics and equity. In fact, energy choices are pregnant with values, particularly those which are concerned with the longer term future. The U.N. report of the World Commission on Environment and Development (WCED), *Our Common Future*, correctly cites energy centre-stage in the issue of sustainability.

There was, nonetheless, general agreement among workshop participants on ultimate objectives: an adequate world wide provision of energy with social equity and justice and environmental protection. The sharpest debate was reserved for the discussion of what were appropriate technical means to achieve these desired ends. In most ways, the three areas of division—structure, process and means—were highly integrated within each of the opposing groups. Those who supported existing structures and processes also supported the current major focus on energy supply options while downgrading, or at least expressing less confidence, in the virtues of demand management, conservation and efficiency and "soft energy paths." "Appropriate" for them meant greater reliability, fission and fusion and the inevitable electrification of the world, operated by giant utilities with centralized structures. Appropriate energy for the other side had its appropriateness defined by a restructured society, much more decentralized, much more open and democratic, with large elements of cultural, thermodynamic and human appropriateness. This ultimately would be a solar future, a future regarded from the perspective of current technologies, levels of investment and associated radical, social and economic transformation as somewhat improbable in the foreseeable future.

The debate carries on, but so does the threat of the "greenhouse effect" resulting from the very significant worldwide production increases of "greenhouse gases," such as CO_2 and CFCs. In this respect it was noted that successive Canadian governments had expressed deep concern and proclaimed remedial policies on these matters, such as expressed by Prime Minister Mulroney who made the following statement at the end of the Conference of June 1988, "The Changing Atmosphere" sponsored by the Canadian government:

> In no area is the link between our economic activity and environmental degradation more evident or more troubling than in the area of energy policy. Canada is committed to applying the principles of sustainable development to our energy future.

Regrettably, expressions of good intentions have not produced the necessary results. Canadian expenditures or Energy Efficiency and Diversity Initiatives (EEDI) have in fact been declining, while investment in fossil fuel and nuclear energy production is on the increase, such as the investment projected for the Oslo oilsands which, it is claimed, would emit into the atmosphere 220,000,000 tonnes of CO_2, almost twice the Canadian output of 1985.

Not surprisingly, those who spoke for the developing world were not so caught up in the issue of energy source. The developing world, for the most part, does not have adequate indigenous sources of energy, from whatever source, nor the luxury, if it can be so-called, of having financial and other resources to choose an optimum path for the future. Nor have they, at least until recently, been the cause of energy related environmental damage and greenhouse effects. After all, the industrialized sector with, 20 per cent of the world's population, consumes 80 per cent of the world's energy production and commensurate output of environmental damage and greenhouse effects.

For most of the Third World, other than for the oil producing nations, the most serious issues are the high cost of energy, the lack of national sources and technologies and dependence upon the industrialized world for both. The result in *both* the oil producing and non-oil producing nations of the Third World has all too often been that these countries have been induced to replicate the energy programs of the North at high cost without commensurate benefit. On the one hand, scarcity and cost have stifled development, while on the other, massive energy infrastructure requirements account for almost 50 per cent of the severe debt crisis of developing countries. Furthermore, the pattern of energy development which has taken place in the Third World has favoured urban development, whereas the greater proportion of people in developing countries live in the rural areas. The fundamental need is for low cost and equitable availability of energy to all segments of the population. The needs and population distribution of Third World countries is almost the mirror image of the developed world where most people live in cities. Yet the energy programs "offered" to developing countries are based on the paradigm of the developed world. This has all too often been the case where models of Western industrialization have been applied to the Third World.

Appropriate technologies are always and necessarily a subject of concern in any discussion of Third World development, especially when it comes to energy. It was forcefully pointed out in this regard that applied technologies can have a radical effect on the culture, social structure and economy of the users. For example, solar cookers, though efficient and benign, cannot be used by the peasants cooking the evening meal. Nor can the peasant population afford them. And what of the work related dislocations that affect women whose traditional roles and work patterns are seriously disrupted by the introduction of a technology as seemingly simple as a solar cooker?

Many such examples of the application or misapplication of new technologies to the needs of the developing world were cited as having unanticipated and deleterious consequences. The obvious implications call for a more radical approach to energy decision-making; to invoke the recipient population directly in assessing their own energy needs and forms of production. But such a simple proposal runs counter to generally large-scale monopoly control of energy production and distribution. Some in the workshop argued strongly the incompatibility of profit maximization and broad social well-being. All this underlay the need for greater democratic participation in the decision-making process and equity of access to energy.

At the very minimum, most participants believed that the decision-making process should be open and accessible, and with essential information being available for all concerned. Several ideas were expressed about the possibility of developing quantifiable criteria to assess the essential elements of energy production, health, environmental and social and financial impacts. In this regard, a representative of Ontario Hydro presented, by way of example, the corporation's current emphasis on an ambitious program to place demand management conservation and on-site presentation ahead of centralized distributive supply options.

Virtually everyone in the workshop agreed that energy is a central factor in its influence on all human activities, social systems and ethics. Sciences, ethics, economics, the environment, society and culture are all interrelated. None of these factors can be fully understood or appreciated in isolation from the other. In effect this represents the accomplishment as well as the difficulties encountered by the workshop.

Recommendations

The recommendations proposed by the workshop participants were abundant. There was a sound suggestion for an open democratic forum to develop energy policy, to strengthen workers'/citizens' roles in determining an ethical basis for energy policy by financial, legal, and other support, including the subsidization of solar (or renewable) energy, and the rewarding of critical perspectives on energy. Science education of energy was considered to be seriously lacking and thus steps must be taken to provide information to all citizens. A serious reconsideration of our energy policy, particularly the transfer of energy technology to the Third World must be addressed. Finally, it was suggested that the close relationship between energy and the environment, and in particular, the role of fossil fuel-based energy systems in the "greenhouse effect," leads to the necessity of new policies and decisions of national and international abatement while serving legitimate energy needs. The workshop also urged the conservation of fossil fuels for purposes of chemical production.

WORKSHOP 8: Technology and Ethical Choices in the Environment

Coordinators: Ron Kelly, Arboretum, University of Guelph; Henry Kock, Arboretum, University of Guelph

Chair: Beatrice Olivastri, National Survival Institute, Ottawa

Rapporteur: Jane Dougan, Rockwood, Ontario

Session 1

Over the next three days, ethical choices and technology with respect to the environment were discussed. Our deliberations would, it was hoped, culminate in the articulation of three key questions and three recommendations for future action.

Beatrice Olivastri, Workshop Chair (Environmental Consultant) welcomed participants to the opening session of the Workshop, and introduced the Honourable Charles Caccia, Liberal MP for Davenport and Member of the Opposition, House of Commons, Ottawa. Mr. Caccia spoke about *Sustainability: Economy vs. Environment.* He pondered the question of ethics in politics and noted that the question could be addressed from numerous vantage points. One could consider, for example, the ethics of how we relate to nature; of how we set priorities in nature or in political life; of how we pursue security; of power; of how we live off the land. While each could be the focus of considerable discussion in its own right, Mr. Caccia spoke particularly about how government works with respect to the environment and presented some new ideas for how it could work in the future. In short, the current administrative and economic structure of government in Canada can be viewed as contributing towards environmental degradation rather than sustainability. For example, the Department of the Environment is merely one part of a large institution, in competition with other departments. A better balance might be created if the environment was seen as a central issue pervading all other considerations, rather than as an isolated, peripheral entity. Similarly, one can either have an economy separate from environmental considerations (as it is at present) or an economy based upon environmental considerations. In the present economic structure, most environmental costs are externalized. The environmental consequences are therefore to a large extent left for either nature itself or, eventually, the public purse to absorb and rehabilitate. Pollution should be prevented before it happens, rather than cleaned up afterwards. The Brundtland Report *Our Common Future* proposed the integration of economic and environmental planning. If we had a "Brundtland" economy, in which the environmental costs of production were internalized, this would provide initial motivation for ensuring that resources are used efficiently and that we have strong well-enforced environmental regulations. Goods and services would cost more initially, but pollution would be reduced and in the long-term we would have more assurance of an environmentally sustainable future.

Mr. Caccia wondered whether a generally acceptable definition of the term "sustainable development" can be arrived at, and suggested that we might better try to establish a set of principles by which environmentally sustainable development could be attained. These would include: (1) concentration on long-term political horizons instead of on short-term political gain, (2) an emphasis on environmentally-clean economic growth, (3) internalization of the costs of production, and (4) making the user pay in both the private and public sectors (e.g. municipalities charging more for sewer and water). In our use of natural resources, we should concentrate on living off the interest rather than depleting the capital. We must concentrate on an educated consumer to lead the marketplace.

In the discussion, it was evident that the participants were far from being a bland homogenous mass: a wide diversity of viewpoints, ages and cultural groups was represented, with deeply-held and sometimes disparate views about environmental priorities, and the correct path to be taken.

As might be expected in a conference that by its very title brought ethical considerations to the forefront, much discussion centred on the disparate values espoused by various sectors of society. This ranged from consideration of the various ways religion teaches us to relate to nature, to the question of whether the pursuit of scientific knowledge and the technology that comes from it are in themselves as objective as they often claim. Like all else, scientific knowledge is a product of human thought, and prone to the same frailties and influences as all other spheres of human activity.

Similarly, governmental decisions are determined more by political suitability than by ethical considerations. Each chapter of "Our Common Future" could be seen as a blueprint for remedial action in achieving sustainable development. In the Hague in March 1989, 22 political leaders from some of the most powerful countries in the world publicly espoused the concept of sustainable development, but how does one encourage the necessary political will to move from such small beginnings to deeply-entrenched convictions? We must acknowledge that environmental sustainability is going to cost many of us something, whether in terms of taxes or convenience. This will lead to social and political upheaval, and where are we going to find the politicians who have either the moral authority or the will to be the catalysts for change of this nature? And what of the economic values that filter down to each one of us—for example, is development a prerequisite for a meaningful life?

There were also concerns with the underlying homocentric values of the Brundtland Report; i.e. it relates to natural processes primarily as they benefit our own species, with little consideration of each part of the ecosystem as being intrinsically valuable, regardless of its use as a "human resource." On the same theme, a participant from the Amazonian rain forest pointed out the misunderstanding that often arises as a result of the predominance of European languages (especially English) as a means for environmental discussions. The values inherent in many European words pay unwitting homage to a legacy of greed and corruption that is contrary to the values espoused by many of the world's aboriginal peoples; e.g. "salary" (a derivative of the word "salt," in itself a finite resource turned by language to a commercial end).

Some discussion revolved around the question of extracting payment for environmental degradation. How should any associated taxes be applied? All taxes affect the material quality of life and if the greater percentage of the world's people are to achieve a higher standard of living, then those in the developed world are going to have to accept a lower standard. The onus is on the North, rather than the South, to bear the brunt of environmental costs. The environmental costs of our demands must be spread throughout society; the user cannot absorb the total amount.

Dr. S. Ercman (Legal Directorate, Council of Europe, Strasbourg, France), complemented Mr. Caccia on addressing the concept of user's fees, and traced the historical development of environmental departments and directorates in Europe since the late 1960s. In many European countries, for example, there have been user charges for sewage and water maintenance since the mid–1970s. At least one participant called for energy policies to be addressed on an international basis, e.g. a UN Energy Agency or similar international body.

There was general concern with the now-ubiquitous phrase "sustainable development." While it was recognized that we could struggle for years to come up with a mutually acceptable definition, there was apprehension that the pre-eminence of this phrase may blind us from pursuing more radical solutions or addressing environmental problems at a deeper level. One participant noted wryly that this had become in some instances a gimmick phrase to justify highly questionable undertakings. Charles Caccia pointed out that the developers got the noun "development" while the environmentalists had to content themselves with the adjective "sustainable;" he had tried to even the balance by adding the word "environmentally" at the beginning of the phrase. Another concern was that "sustainable" is a somewhat ambiguous concept: it is relative to what—to the preservation of the biosphere more or less as it is now? And if so, is that enough? With regard to "development"—whose idea of development? On the other hand, this is a compromise phrase and as such it is a useful political starting point for negotiation, until a better term can be found and agreed upon. This was the idea behind trying to develop a set of principles for sustainable development: if we could get agreement from various sectors as to what these criteria were, that in itself would be a tremendous breakthrough. The idea of "sustainable development" is useful primarily as a vehicle for consulting and sharing at one particular level, and should be seen as a stepping stone in a tiered approach towards achieving international environmental discussions. It is not the ultimate goal, but only a means of achieving a greater end. One participant proposed that it is really a question of who benefits from the *status quo*, that is, the existing economic system. How are we to bridge the ideological gap between those who believe that new principles for environmental change are vitally necessary, and those who don't think that environmental degradation will affect them?

There is in the developed world an inherent polarization between economic and environmental interests that must be addressed. Radical changes are needed to the structure of industry and to political decision-making. There was some scepticism about whether all sectors of society would be willing to address the necessary scope of change, but society has been prepared to accept tremendous upheavals before in times of war or perceived threat, and the current environmental threats are somewhat analogous to an assault on our own (and other species') environmental survival.

Session 2

Stuart Coles (Toronto Community Theologian, Social Planning Council of Metro Toronto) began the morning session by addressing *The Ethical Filter*. He appealed to the group to consider how to make the faith communities aware of the very earthly urgencies that this conference was covering. The importance of this gathering lay not so much in the knowledge we acquired but in what action we took when the conference was over. He echoed Dr. Alexander King's address of the previous evening that spoke of the three phases inherent in environmental considerations: the comprehensive, holistic dimension; the "civilization" that we build upon the natural world; and the essential spirit that lies inside each one of us. Somehow we must have the integrity to draw these together, and to remember that what we are and what the environment is are interdependent. For better or worse, we are all part of the action, and there is therefore no escaping our accountability.

This reopens the entrancing possibility that we are all part of one universe, one reality, as the native people of this and other lands have long recognized. Mr. Coles commented on the increasing recognition of the importance and environmental-sensitivity of the North American aboriginal faith community. Many of us are struggling under the deadly doctrine of a society founded upon an ethic of increased consumerism, and Mr. Coles produced numerous newspaper clippings to support his claim. He concluded his address, however, with the optimistic reminder that individual actions could indeed make a difference.

Discussion began with support for the idea of a spiritual re-evaluation, but the concern was raised as to whether we could return to the old mythologies in this technological era. Mr. Coles responded that we might look on this as analogous to a tree: new leaves may flourish, but they depend upon the existing roots for nourishment. In the same way, the old mythologies still have much to teach us as a foundation for new beliefs and values to lead us through this spiritually bereft age.

Another query concerned the separation from nature inherent in urban society. Urban and rural life must be reconnected; e.g. the urban energies of Toronto could be said to be "killing" the rural economy for at least 100 kilometres in each direction. A high school student wondered what students could do besides taking part in recycling programmes, to which Mr. Coles responded that the very idea of "waste" should be an obscenity in today's education. Instead of wondering how to distribute waste, we should learn how to stop producing waste that the world cannot even find space to bury, much less afford. Today's students should be taught to become stewards and caretakers of the earth rather than wastrels. On the note of the educational challenges that await us all, Beatrice Olivastri introduced the next speaker: Mr. Tom Savage, (Chair and President, ITT Canada Ltd., Toronto) who would address *The Responsibility of Industry.*

Mr. Savage began by quoting the philosophy of Pogo: "I have seen the enemy, and they are us." He introduced himself as one businessman bringing his perception of the responsibility of industry and the role business must play, both in the national and international debate, and in the implementation of the changes and practice, processes, cultural norms and indeed ethics that will be necessary. He proposed that his essential message was: "Raising the levels of environmental awareness and consequently developing constituencies for change is a noble pursuit, but the creation of fear with unsupported and confrontational rhetoric is counterproductive. The result is polarization of an issue that demands partnership for effective solutions." In essence, then, in pursuit of a common environmental goal, industry and other segments of society can no longer afford to deal with the issues at play in an isolated or adversarial manner, but must learn to work together. It should be remembered, however, that lasting amalgamations can only be built on a basis of credibility and mutual respect. There is no time to do otherwise; sincerely held but conflicting ethical views must not become an insurmountable hurdle to environmental progress. The stakes are too high; i.e. the destiny of this planet and the nature of human life on it will be determined by the decisions that we take together, nationally and internationally, in the next few years.

Mr. Savage identified industrial and economic development together with rapid population growth as the main contributors to the present environmental dilemma. Admittedly, past business decisions were often based on greed and lack of information. However, there is a new and growing environmental awareness throughout the worldwide business community. This is fuelled by a combination of altruism and practicality—a response to public pressure, and the realization that it makes sound economic sense. Coincidentally, last year ITT hosted two major meetings that brought together their senior executives throughout the world: one was on the theme of the environment, the other on ethics.

Mr. Savage identified five key areas in which the business community could respond: (1) business has a social responsibility to inform the public, employers and shareholders what it is doing about the environment, including related costs. (2) Environmental responsibility calls for dynamic rather than static commitment, above and beyond existing laws and regulations, and must promote research and development. (3) Environmental responsibility is not an add-on, but an integrated systemic part of business planning and production. (4) Cost benefit analyses and environmental audits must become standard integrated operating procedures. (5) Business has to cooperate in these endeavours with government, labour and all relevant non-governmental organizations. He concluded by quoting a definition of ethics attributed to a journalistic acquaintance of his: "ethics is the difference between doing what one has a right to do and doing the right thing." This attitude must be inculcated into all our decisions as a society, whether business-based or otherwise.

Dan McDermott (Greenpeace Foundation, Toronto) spoke on *"Corporate Responsibilities in the Age of Environmental Degradation."* He reminded participants briefly of the bleak state of the environment at present, and asserted that the impact of technology on the global ecosystem has been, on the whole, a negative one. The main thrust of his address was on the underlying theme of ethical choice, particularly as it related to the business community. He spoke of the past unwillingness of corporations to accept environmental responsibility, not because they were callous but because of the ultimate dilemma of business: it must make a profit to survive. Until recently, it was difficult to justify the costs of pollution control in terms of tangible benefit to the investor. The recent greening of the political and business arena, however, is due primarily to the strength of public demand for widespread environmental responsibility. The public has demonstrated its support and willingness to take action to "protect and repair" the environment and to shoulder some of the costs; e.g. there was public understanding rather than outcry when Ontario Hydro recently announced that adoption of "scrubber technology" that would necessitate an increase in electricity rates. The public expects similar environmentally responsible action from the business sector and politicians in general.

He presented a critical analysis of the concept of "sustainable development" as an environmental panacea. The promise implicit in this phrase—that if we are careful with the way we use the world's resources, we can still have unlimited growth—is a false one. Many of the resources on which the world economy depends are finite; therefore, growth cannot expand endlessly. History, however, teaches us that long-term goals are usually sacrificed to short-term successes. Therefore, when the crunch comes, it is likely that the "sustainable" end of the equation will be sacrificed at the altar of "development." In short, we cannot expect the marketplace to take on the necessary depth of commitment to solve environmental problems—it is against its very nature. Despite the political and business communities' recent apparent embrace of an environmental ethic, little meaningful change has been achieved, beyond the level of a public relations exercise. Rather, it is the public that are the real environmentalists. The adoption of an environmental ethic, whether at the individual or the corporate level, means behaving in a manner that will not advance the deterioration of the global biosphere. Mr. McDermott contended that any other mode of behaviour was not merely unethical: it was suicidal.

Charles Caccia returned to the morning session to address *"The Role of Leadership in Government."* In a concise discussion, he examined the process and substance of government. He compared the balance of power and the role of government to a triangle in which the media and the public are at the top two sides, and the government (elected and non-elected officials) at the apex. A burning question was whether money (= lobbying) is at the top of the triangle, or inside. Advocacy has a vital role to play in the political process. The political process can be compared to a carrot and a stick: the "carrots" are incentives—tax write-offs, credits and subsidies; the "stick" is punishment—regulations, means of enforcement and penalties. To get environmental action, you need very strong sticks! Both the process and substance of governmental action can be driven by ideology. The exercise of pressure on government, whether from the public or the media, is a vital factor in ensuring an efficient system. He touched on substantive balances between whether, for example, (i) policy in particular cases deregulates, or regulates more strongly, (ii) the environment and the economy should be separated, or integrated, (iii) energy should concentrate on mega-products or efficiency, and (iv) the costs of production should be internalized or externalized. The role of government is complex and sophisticated. Mr. Caccia concluded with a motto that owed its origins to the Toronto subway system: "Politicians are like disposable diapers—it may take 70 years before you can make them environmentally friendly." He hoped that we would make every effort to reduce this span of time.

Fiona Nelson (Ontario National Schools Trustee, Toronto) aired some stirring views on the *"Responsibility of Education."* Many of her views succinctly complemented earlier opinions that had been expressed, both from the speaker's podium and from the floor. Essentially, she believes that the importance of education lies in giving people the necessary skills and knowledge that can lead them to living both appropriate and ethical lives. Knowledge in itself does not lead to improved behaviour: it is the actions that result from what you have learned that are important. Education must teach people how to formulate the questions that need to be asked, and to make sure that they then pursue the answers. This echoed the earlier comments of Mr. Coles, in that the true test of the success of this conference would lie in the actions we took when we had left and gone home.

Mr. Savage had suggested, through Pogo, that we were the enemy; Ms. Nelson quoted Philip Berrigan in suggesting that "we are not all guilty, but we are all responsible." She suggested that there are no real geographic separations in the world; there are only lines drawn on a map. The air and water we foul goes to other places; the resources we waste deprive other parts of the world.

Dan McDermott had spoken of the essential conflict between profit (i.e. development) and environmental sustainability. Charles Caccia had given us some potent words about the role of government. Ms. Nelson reminded us that, in Paul Ehrlich's words, "nature always bats last." She commented further, echoing Martin Luther King, "legislation cannot train the heart, but it can restrain the heartless." To return to her original thesis, perhaps the true value of education lay in producing strong people, in the sense of people who knew what needed to be done, and how it could be accomplished. With such strength at the backbone of our society, we might not have to rely on strong laws, which in the end are only as effective as their means of enforcement.

The virtues of the past (e.g. prudence, tolerance, faith) cannot be taken to the bank, and so they have been replaced by the motivations of the present. What were once vices are now virtues. The basis of much of our advertising is dependent upon greed, envy, lust and gluttony. The "Gross" National Product is aptly named because it is hindered, rather than helped, by a self sufficient, conserver society. Therefore we need a different criterion by which to measure economic health.

Ms. Nelson also commented on a theme that had been raised earlier: the responsibility of language. A true understanding of the proper use of language is critical. With it, the truth can be discovered; without it, the truth can be very effectively obscured. Finally, she noted that there cannot be different sets of ethics for business, for politics and for society at large. Everyone has to subscribe to the same moral principles or it simply won't work. Furthermore, adherence to this common moral code must permeate everything we do.

In group discussion, concern was expressed with the role of the media, particularly television, in creating a false sinful mythology, that was driving us towards an ecological precipice. Fiona Nelson agreed, and commented that television is an especially powerful and dangerous medium because it tends to equate action with news, and insists that the viewer surrender to it. This is unlike the print medium, which allows you the luxury of reviewing and analyzing what you have just absorbed. Dan McDermott pointed out that the media depends upon advertising to pay its bills; therefore, it is usually in the business of promoting consumerism. Mr. Savage reiterated his earlier comment that the problem lay perhaps not so much in the essence of the media as in how it is used; e.g. to promote fear and foster counterproductive rhetoric. Further, our insatiable demand for up to the minute reporting means that television does not usually have the time to sort out the underlying facts and present a true perspective. Charles Caccia commented that we might as well accept the fact that television is a potent technology that we are all going to have to live with, and so the best defense might be to learn how to manipulate it from the environmental perspective. In some cases, and properly used, one picture can indeed be worth a thousand words.

One participant agreed that there shouldn't be more than one ethic for society, but suggested that this already exists: i.e. economic growth as a common ideal. Traditionally, education has to a large extent existed to inculcate the ethics of a society, but he wondered what the response will be if and when schools begin to teach a new environmentally responsible ethic that challenges existing principles? Fiona Nelson replied that she had recently attended a meeting where industrialists had made exactly the opposite complaint, i.e. that the school system was failing to teach the work ethic and foster a spirit of competition. Schools have to reflect society to a certain extent, but perhaps society has already moved towards environmentalism and away from the growth ethic espoused by many supposed political and industrial leaders.

Another theme was raised: how can the developed world tell developing countries that they cannot use fossil fuels to industrialize, when it may be a question of survival for them? Tom Savage agreed that this was indeed a paradox, to which he did not have a simple answer. It was a moral question for the consideration of society at large. He lamented the fact that while much money is spent on legislation to reduce emissions, little is directed towards finding better ways to burn fossil fuels or on renewable fuel technology. Fiona Nelson again suggested that perhaps we were not asking the right questions. Most Third World countries lie quite close to the equator. Perhaps the question should not be how to export our wasteful technology to other countries, but how to provide the resources and development needed for them to discover the technologies most appropriate to their own particular needs, such as tidal, wind and solar energy. Dan McDermott commented that we do not have the luxury of another several hundred years to change our ingrained wasteful behaviour patterns. We may have less than one decade to avoid massive global destruction. He agreed with Ms. Nelson, but thought that an additional question should be: what is Canada doing domestically to reduce its own energy consumption? Tremendous breakthroughs are happening in renewable energy research, yet the federal government has cut most spending in this area. About a decade ago, the Harvard Business School produced a book entitled "Energy Futures" that suggested that the true solution lay in finding sources of renewable energy (apart from nuclear). It proposed that a real commitment to energy conservation alone could solve the energy problem until about the middle of the next century. A participant from the Third World agreed that there was no need to transfer the industrial world's energy technology and its inherent problems to other countries. There exist indigenous systems of energy use that are sensitive to local conditions, but neither First nor Third World governments invest in their development. Furthermore, the onus for energy conservation is on the developed world, which uses the vast majority of the world's non-renewable energy reserves, rather than on developing countries, which at present cannot even afford the luxury of reducing the minimal level of fossil fuels that they use. If the U.S.A. alone reduced its energy consumption by 30 per cent it would make a tremendous difference to global warming and allow Third World consumption a marginal increase.

A philosopher in attendance agreed with the importance of collaboration and cooperation between various sectors for the greater good, but commented that in a crisis, confrontational analysis could have a valid and essential role to play in ensuring that the right questions were asked. Mr. Savage responded that he was concerned essentially with the validity of the data presented and of the rationale behind a confrontational approach. Issues must be brought to the fore, but that does not excuse the unnecessary fostering of fear or false information by either party. He fully supports the right of any environmental group to bring issues to the public attention, but this should be done on a base of factual data presented in a responsible way. At one level, cost benefit analysis comes down essentially to this: if a product cannot be changed to meet environmental concerns, then there is no choice but to take it off the market. Charles Caccia suggested that cost-benefit analysis is essentially a conflict between the short-term and long-term. The Love Canal, for example, would not have happened if the chemical company involved had done a long-term Cost Benefit Analysis (CBA). Historically, most corporations that withdraw products from the market are more concerned with avoiding negative publicity than they are with the eventual effects on the environment. Cost Benefit Analysis is a useful exercise, but it can also be manipulated. If one looks ahead no more than 4 years, then it is quite likely that the go-ahead to releasing a new product may be given. On the other hand, if a true long-term CBA was the rule rather than the exception, examining eventual effects on a variety of public sector interests such as ground-water and human health, then there are numerous products that would never have been put on the market.

There was some frustration that we were not yet asking the right question in this conference: namely, what is the root cause of the environmental problem? Instead, we had largely concentrated on work symptoms and results. It was suggested that the root cause lay with the value system inherent in modern science and technology, which is concerned with control, manipulation, and dominance. We need new mythologies or belief systems to replace our rampant western rationalistic consciousness; these might be found in some of the non-confrontational eastern religions and philosophies. While there is an immediate problem that needs to be addressed, the answer over the long-term surely lies with replacing our present one-dimensional consciousness. Fiona Nelson agreed, and suggested that some of these concerns were already being addressed in the nurturing, feminist perspective. She echoed earlier discussion by suggesting that the idea of value-free science is a lie, and formulated a powerful question that she felt was not being asked often enough with regard to scientific and technological discoveries: Just because a thing can be done, should it? Tom Savage echoed Fiona's sentiments, but tempered them by admitting that he cannot accept that all technology is inherently bad; rather, he feels the problem is the exponential growth of technology, so that our technological competence has outpaced our ability to change societal norms and expectations, and even our ability to monitor the impact of these technologies.

A European participant expressed similar frustration, but from a different stance: he wondered when the group was going to tackle the question of what is meant by ethics. He hoped that we would sit down and propose a commonly accepted understanding for the ethical handling of the environment, particularly by business. Tom Savage responded that to some extent this was already happening, at least in many prominent Canadian industries. A major industrial organization of which he is a member, for example, is already developing a set of environmental principles for their member companies. One of the difficulties, however, that they are facing in producing this code is that numerous diverse industries had already or were in the midst of developing their own environmental codes of behaviour when it would be more beneficial if all of them collaborated on a joint set of guidelines. Charles Caccia wondered whether business could be asked to have an ethic if its overall motive was to make profit? Can science have an ethical motivation if it is driven continuously by the desire to explore the unknown, to push further into what we can see and what we can not yet see, and then utilize it? He does not have the answers, but agreed that the purpose of this conference in part was to suggest what these might be. We might equally question whether there is an ethic in politics at any given time. Efforts are made, but basically what counts is the next election, getting votes and it is therefore an exercise in power. Has a party emerged that is willing to go into the next election standing on a principle that will result in certain defeat, but nevertheless choosing to be an ally of integrity rather than a slave to public opinion?

The following presentation was by Chief Harvey Longboat (Iroquois Confederate Chief, Assistant Superintendent of Traditional Educational Programmes at Six Nations Reservation, Brantford) about *"Responsibilities to the Earth."* What he hoped to convey was an explanation of the attitudes that native people have developed to guide their lives, and what these might have to offer to us. From the very start of his presentation, Chief Longboat underscored the essential spirituality and humility of Canada's indigenous people. According to his culture, whenever people gathered together, much as we were doing this morning, they began with a prayer to remind them that their deliberations would be made in the presence of the Creator. This serves, among other things, as a constant reminder of the traditional interplay and interdependence between humanity and the rest of the natural world. He offered a translation of this prayer, which gave thanks to the Creator, in turn for one another, for Mother Earth and all that she provides, for the wind and the heavens, for thunder and lightning, the sun and the moon, for the four guardian angels and for his messenger Handsome

Lake, and finally for the Creator himself, who sees that we have everything that we need. Chief Longboat gave examples of how some of these traditional beliefs have been reinforced by present day scientific discoveries. Common sense has long told his people what many others have forgotten, and what we are now rediscovering: all of nature is interdependent, and the destruction of any part of the cycle in some way lessens each of us. An educated person, to Chief Longboat, is one who thinks with the head and the heart. If you have a good mind and you use it, and if you care for everyone, then you have strength. The older members of his society, many of whom never had formal schooling, are the most educated. Little is written down; it is an oral tradition. A knowledge of a people's history is essential to understanding the future. The creation myth, for example, cannot be proven, but is nevertheless believed.

> After the world was formed, the Creator moulded the body of a man from the earth, and breathed into it to give it life. The earth is our mother, the air our father; therefore, as we destroy these, we destroy ourselves.

They are a fluid people, and survivors who adjust very quickly. The coming of the non-Indian had a devastating effect on native society. In about 1700, the Creator caused an Indian by the name of Handsome Lake to go into a trance so that he could send a message to his people. This message set down ethics governing their way of life, to ensure that the native culture survived. It also included some predictions that are startling in light of our modern technological discoveries. People would see something moving along the earth and in the air, with nothing pulling it; though attractive, these things would cause them a lot of grief. The trees would begin to die from the top; corn would grow only three or four feet, and then there would be no more corn. The water will become so infested that people will not be able to drink it, and eventually it will burn. The earth will one day become too warm for the partridge to nest on the ground, so they will be forced to nest in the trees. Older women and younger girls will begin to have babies. A hole will appear in a net around the atmosphere of the earth; one of the four angels will try to patch it. At first, he will be successful but eventually will fail. As we near the end of the earth, no babies will be born and the earth will burn. This time, no one will escape.

According to these predictions, we have about 85 years left.

The perspective of the native people in both North and South America can be summed up in one word: *respect*—for the earth, for all creatures who share it with us, and for one another. We must be losing this respect, or we would not treat either our home or each other in the ways that we are. His only answer to the problems that now confront us is that we have to somehow change our attitudes. We must look at our environment through new eyes, and remember that the only laws that last are the laws of nature.

To begin discussion following Chief Longboat's presentation, Charlotte Waterlow, (World Federalists, U.K. and U.S.A.), suggested that one word that had not been used in discussions so far was love. She sympathised with Chief Longboat's concerns, and proposed that the concept of world brotherhood and sisterhood should be an ethical norm. It is her belief that if the world's environment is to be preserved and nurtured, we need to support the proposals put forward by statespersons for the United Nations Security Council, for a United Nations Environment Fund through which the "rich" countries could help the poor, and the powers of the International Court of Justice could be extended to deal with environmental matters. Harvey Longboat responded that he thought of brotherhood as analogous to a forest in which numerous different species of trees coexist and flourish. Similarly, our collective power comes from an understanding of each other's strengths and weaknesses. He emphasized, however, that we cannot go backwards; we have no choice but to use the technology that exists. If we can decide what we want to use it for, and if we can determine what our destiny should be, then its use can be controlled and turned towards the common good.

The question was raised as to how the native people can reconcile the traditional philosophies that Chief Longboat had just espoused with many of the realities of life in the 1990s. For example, the need for food now had to be considered along with the necessity for conservation and preservation of endangered species. Chief Longboat acknowledged that, while native people have adopted many non-native customs, there was still a strong attempt to practice conservation and take only what was needed. He had no easy answers for how to reconcile such dilemmas. They cannot go back to the past; he had tried, but realized that you could not make a society alone. Like most indigenous people, he was aware that we do not own the land; if it belongs to anyone, it belongs to the next seven generations that will come after us.

This presentation reminded one participant that what is missing from the non-native culture is concern for the well-being of the whole, rather than the individual. Perhaps social mechanisms need to be created whereby the individual will can be channelled for a collective purpose. The inherent selfishness of much of our culture means that we get the government, and the industrial products, we deserve. Chief Longboat agreed that we are indeed all in this together, and if we are content to buy the products that industry supplies, then we must accept a good part of the responsibility.

Session 3

Professor Vernon Thomas (Department of Zoology, University of Guelph) began the afternoon session with discussions of *"The Ecological Web."* His attitude towards technology can be summed up in one word: ambivalence. His interest lies in establishing criteria to evaluate technology, which we can then use in the ethical choices we make. If, as he believes, ecology is a web, then everything in it—the living, the dead, plants, animals—is connected. No one part is isolated, it functions as a whole. Unfortunately, the science that we use to analyze the environment, and the technology that springs from it, has abandoned its origins in the natural sciences and become little more than a fragmented starburst. Analysis has taken precedence over synthesis. On this and many other university campuses, for example, the sub-disciplines work in physical and intellectual isolation from each other, and the result is indifference and ignorance.

We have to a great extent forgotten the second law of thermodynamics, which fundamentally stated means that you can never get more out than you put in. There are limiting factors in all ecosystems. A lot of our technology is designed for use at some future point, but unfortunately we have not held scientists accountable either for their actions or their promises, particularly in developing technologies that have proven injurious to the environment.

We must be synthetic in the sense of being aware of the combination of all the elements in the natural and in the social sciences. Ecologists should explore the economic and the social world as well as the physical world. The success of future environmentalists will lie in their ability to diversify, rather than in specialization. Analysis is a valuable tool, but it is a holistic understanding that ultimately will provide the basis for solving the problems that confront us.

Two important features of any ecosystem are productivity and persistence. Without a balance between these two fundamental aspects, you cannot have a sustainable whole. Instead, we have concentrated on expanding the former at the expense of the latter. All ecosystems, in fact, can be complemented by the technologies that we have taken such trouble to devise. Environment can be our ally in production, but instead, we have attempted to find technological substitutes. We concentrate on synthetic nitrogen instead of crop rotation to provide soil fertility; we spend vast sums of money to remove natural water bodies from the Canadian prairies and then lament the drought that ensues. Hedgerows are human artifacts that have nevertheless made phenomenal contributions to agricultural production—moderating water flow, providing alternate habitats for insects that may consume species we consider to be pests, and as repositories of genetic diversity. Many otherwise educated people see forests as little more than plywood on the root, lumber in waiting. They fail to recognize the alternative functions forests provide; e.g. in hydrological cycling, in the carbon-dioxide/oxygen equation. We are animals, and as such waste is a necessary and inevitable by-product of existence. We may flush it away, but it comes back to haunt us. The question rather is how we can use technology to minimize its impact on the viability of the ecosystem? How can we recognize the technologies that are productive; i.e. those that complement environmental productivity and persistence? These are the technologies that we might ethically choose not only to preserve, but to expand. We need to examine the problems that confront us in a way that will allow us to detect solutions.

Why are we choosing to build Skydomes rather than developing environmentally-sympathetic technologies? How can we overcome the existing disparity between the economy and the environment? Somehow we must foster an active interplay between the two very much related systems. It is time to start reinvesting in the environment. We must recognize that we live in a technological era, but there are types of technology that can bolster both the integrity and the persistence of the natural world. The best ethical criterion for their identification is to ask if they complement productivity, enhance persistence, and minimize our environmental impact. If so, we must back them both with our mouths and with our money.

Dr. S. Ercman (Legal Directorate, Council of Europe) addressed the question of *"Technology and the Environment: Legal Implications."* She supported Professor Thomas's defence of environmentally-friendly technology, and added that technology's usefulness can also lie in its preventative and monitoring capabilities. Dr. Ercman addressed the legal complexities of state responsibility, civil responsibility, compensation for damage and access to information with regard to environmental matters. She spoke in particular of recent environmental policy developments by the Council of Europe, European Economic Communities, OECD, and the Economic Commission for Europe. It is ironic that it is precisely because of recent major environmental accidents that people throughout the world have become intensely aware of the need for adopting policies concerning environmental protection and the prevention of pollution. The failure of the state and private enterprise in this regard quickly became apparent after an appalling decade of damage beginning with the dioxin release in Seveso, Italy (1976) and culminating with Chernobyl and Basile (1986). On examination, the international European community (through the Council of Europe) decided that remedial action was needed both nationally and internationally in two main areas: (1) reform of the present concept of international liability, including civil responsibility regimes and setting up methods for compensation, and (2) improved public access to information, both about pollution and potential human and environmental losses. The focus for reform internationally (directed by such organizations as the UN/ECE, OECD, EEC and the Council of Europe) has focused on five main principles:

    (1) preventing accidents caused by certain hazardous activities and the introduction of dangerous substances,

    (2) imposing a strict liability regime on the operator (public or private) under whose control such activity is performed,

    (3) providing adequate compensation for damage, including the cost of reasonable measures to prevent or minimize damage and for reinstatement of the environment,

    (4) developing adequate emergency plans to mitigate the consequences of accidents in the future, and

    (5) improving public access to information.

Dr. Ercman also addressed the questions of liability and compensation that were the focus of intergovernmental discussion, particularly by the Council of Europe. A Committee of Experts and its Working Party have been working since 1987 to draft rules on compensation for damage caused to the environment. She briefly reviewed some of the environmentally-relevant topics that were now or had recently been on the table for discussion by the European communities, particularly with regard to freshwater and sea water, chemicals (including the 1988 Vienna Convention for the protection of the ozone layer), major accident hazards (a directive which has been completely revised and brought up to date since the accident at Seveso), and a proposal on a directive on civil liability for damages caused by waste. The latter, a direct consequence of the Sandoz accident, is based on the "polluter pays" principle and is envisaged as having a preventive effect as well as securing compensation for victims. The United Nations and the Economic Commission for Europe (ECE) have adopted a Draft Code of Conduct on Accidental Pollution of Transboundary Inland Waters. These guidelines emphasize the importance of appropriate national and international rules concerning responsibility, liability and compensation for damage caused by accidental pollution. In March 1989 the OECD adopted an International Agreement on the Control of Transfrontier Movements of Hazardous Waste. This trend towards establishing a legal means of enforcement to ensure adequate liability and compensation for environmental damages that do occur has been followed by actions taken in some individual European countries; e.g. the Federal Republic of Germany, Greece, Italy, Sweden. All of these actions underscore the fact that in Europe there is significant awareness that there is an urgent need for legislation to safeguard the environment, both at the national and the international level.

Ms. Beatrice Olivastri thanked Professor Thomas and Dr. Ercman for their contributions. In particular, with respect to Dr. Ercman's topic, she contrasted the European response with the recently released Auditor-General's report, which more or less announces that Canada simply cannot afford a major environmental accident, such as an earthquake. Let us hope that Mother Earth reads the Auditor General's report and is willing to cooperate.

Professor Thomas responded to a question on whether or not he supported the theory of sustainable growth by confessing his scepticism that we could continue to have development in the sense that we currently perceive it. If we could achieve a ceiling on population levels, then perhaps we could have the basis for some sort of sustainable society, particularly if we are speaking of growth with respect to economic change (such as the greater participation of service industries) as opposed to the growth of consumerism. With regard to environmental preservation, there are ways in which people can interact with the environment that would allow it to change and persist without being subject to destruction. Who controls the technological decisions that are made—hopefully, it will be an informed public.

To a great extent the choice is ours in the direction society takes and the priorities its sets: we can write letters to politicians and the press, we can make statements in front of City Hall and the media, we can influence the voting.

The issue of ethics and technological choice led into a brief discussion of the use of genetically-manipulated and patented forms of life, whether plant or otherwise. Professor Thomas asserted that it is not geneticists but the environment that ultimately determines which forms of life prosper and which fall by the wayside. Our control is not as ultimate as we sometimes like to pretend. Furthermore, we should examine why we develop some new strains, particularly in the agricultural field; often the countries that would most benefit from these manipulated hybrids cannot afford to pay for the patent to acquire them.

Dr. Ercman was asked to comment on the legislation governing transboundary pollution between the U.S. and Canada. While she had studied in the U.S., she had not concentrated on environmental law, and was more familiar with existing European legislation. International law is based upon customary law, not written law, which holds that, for example, in cases of air pollution, the country which pollutes should pay. Neighbourly relations hold that one country should not pollute another, and if a disturbance ensues, then the instigator must be responsible. A distinction was made between some common legislative terms: Accords, Agreements and Memorandums of Intent are "gentlemanly agreements" to collaborate, with no legislative teeth; Treaties, on the other hand, are legally binding.

While discussing legalities, it was commented that an imbalance usually exists in environmental disputes because the perpetrator (e.g. a large industry or company) usually is better able than the claimant (e.g. the public) to afford sustained, superior legal counsel. There should be a means whereby funds can be provided to enable the public to adequately challenge polluters in court. Under Class Actions, for example, a case can be surrendered to interested parties (such as Greenpeace) to bring before the courts. The lack of international action on acid rain was noted.

Some participants felt that discussion had moved away from the key question of discovering the root of the problem, and was instead getting caught up in technicalities. Humanity's response to the environment involves an ethical and spiritual dimension that cannot be measured in terms of economics and legal jurisprudence. The true value of wilderness areas such as Antarctica surpasses narrow questions of legal ownership and economics. Dr. Ercman agreed, and commented that environmental ethics concern the values which govern social behaviour. These should also provide the basis for environmental law and resulting Codes of Conduct. Law and ethics are related; ideally, law is based upon ethical values. New legal systems should be developed to meet urgent needs regarding defining the respective duties and rights of the state, industry and individuals. It was argued that truly relevant environmental questions cannot be answered in economic terms. Dr. Ercman responded by putting forward the example of the governmental response to a chemical fire at Sandoz, which had resulted in pollution of the Rhine and the death of millions of fish. Ethical pressure led to immediate proposals by the Swiss government that victims be fully compensated. A workshop participant responded that he wondered how one compensates a dead fish.

The session then split into two groups to prepare for the final workshop report. How do we ask the right questions, both here and afterwards? And assuming we can do this, then what are we going to do? One group was to debate controversies and how to ask the right questions; the other group was to ascertain how we could move forward and come up with recommendations. We would meet together the next morning to agree on the content of our final workshop report.

Final Session

When the group gathered together for its final meeting on Saturday morning, many ideas and questions were articulated before consensus was reached on which three recommendations and questions should be submitted to the conference as a whole. There was disagreement over whether the invoking of an environmental ethic should consider the present generation—those alive today—or be geared towards the seven generations as yet unborn, articulated in Chief Longboat's presentation. Some pointed out that the needs of the future can only come from a secure base laid upon the demands of the present; others argued that environmental deliberations must bear in mind succeeding generations. The workshop recognized and endorsed the existing IUCN/UNEP World Charter for Nature. There was agreement with the participant who felt that a key underlying principle was that "respect for the ecosystem is the beginning of wisdom." Finally, painstakingly, with each word carefully considered, the workshop set down the required concluding questions and recommendations, based upon the sub-group discussions of the previous afternoon.

Three Concluding Questions

(1) How do we change from an ethic centred on humanity to one centred on the ecosystem?

(2) Why is there not more investment of all available resources to employ appropriate technology to contribute to the healing and revitalization of the environment?

(3) What are we to do when we leave this conference to challenge each one of us to participate in alleviating the environmental crisis?

Three Concluding Recommendations

(1) To initiate a massive campaign on issues related to ecology and technology, leading to the acquisition of skills, and enabling an integrated, wise, action-oriented response by people of all ages and at all levels of responsibility. This will incorporate a variety of resources ranging from the print (e.g. text books) to the visual media.

(2) To redirect priorities in research through the establishment of a technological assessment body to focus on criteria setting, to readdress the question of "environmentally friendly," to tap and supply increased resources to document indigenous knowledge, and to promote research and development on alternative and renewable energy.

(3) Legislation at the national and international level should be developed, making use of existing charters to provide for strict liability for environmental damage, including compensation for restoration of the environment and measures for enforcement. This legislation shall include an environmental Bill of Rights and Responsibilities. We urge

the Canadian government to immediately take all necessary steps to initiate national and international negotiations on this matter.

Summary Expressions

In preparing this report, the Rapporteur and Workshop Co-ordinators felt that the underlying theme of the workshop was a need for urgent action and for change in every sphere of society. For each one of us, this means a need for re-evaluation of the ethics that govern our spiritual beliefs, our ideas of what makes life meaningful, the technological and industrial choices reflected in the purchases we make and the politicians we elect. The impact of human activity on this earth is far-reaching, and the scope of present technology has intensified this impact to an unprecedented extent. We must make substantial changes within the next ten years, if we are to sustain both our survival and a state of environmental equilibrium on this planet. Our consumptive demands are leading to resource extraction beyond sustainable limits; 80 per cent of the world's resources are consumed by 20 per cent of the world's population. In so doing, we are poisoning the fundamental skin of life—the air, water and soil—that supports our own and all other species. We are stripping the forests and turning the land into desert.

The workshop attempted to determine the route that change should take. What is the way? Can we continue with a political, economic and individual value system, that sees the environment as peripheral to economics and is largely motivated by considerations of GNP and short-term profit for the few at the long-term cost of the many? How can we shift in focus from the ego-centric to the eco-centric, i.e. from an ethic centred on ourselves to one centred literally on this planet, our home (ecology being from the Greek *oikos* or house), so that environmental considerations become fundamental to the decisions made and the actions taken by all sectors of society? What are the moral and ethical criteria that should be adopted to achieve environmental justice? How can we implement an Environmental Bill of Rights? Because a given technology exists, should it be used?

Because a particular scientific goal is possible, should it be pursued?

Only by holding respect for the earth and life as central tenets of all our deliberations can we make the appropriate choices, and hold ourselves accountable both to the world today and to the generations that will follow. We must not forget that our most important, primary ethical relationship is with the environment that sustains us.

Education can play a major role in giving people the strength and the wisdom to ask the questions that will lead to change and help us to determine what is really important. We must draw on all of our human resources, spiritual wisdoms, and appropriate technologies to chart a new course for the enrichment of life on this planet. This will require a reallocation of money, resources and priorities from consumptive to conservationist strategies. There is an urgent need for government, media, universities, the corporate sector and each and everyone of us to play a role in bringing about the changes that are necessary.

Within this workshop, there was a surprising degree of unanimity of purpose with respect to environmental responsibility from the various representatives of industry, politics, the faith communities, the educators, the environmentalists and the academics. This in itself is heartening. The challenges are formidable, but they present a tremendous opportunity for each of us to become involved in a very worthwhile mission: the continuance of life on this planet. The stakes are high, but the rewards for a job well done will be tremendous.

WORKSHOP 9: Technology and Ethical Choice in the Human Health Sciences

Coordinators: Katherine Arkay, Science Council of Canada, Ottawa; Cara Westcott, Baycrest Centre for Geriatric Care, Ottawa; John Phillips, Department of Molecular Biology and Genetics, University of Guelph

Chair: Justice Horace Krever, Ontario Supreme Court, Toronto

Rapporteurs: Katherine Arkay and Cara Westcott

Section 1. *The Workshop Overview*

The objective of the Health Workshop was to make recommendations for better integration of ethics into health and health-care related decision-making (particularly with reference to development and delivery of medical technologies). This objective was approached through a series of presentations which focused on specific health technology related ethical issues and conflicts.

Day 1 of the Workshop consisted of an opening discussion by the Chairman, Justice Horace Krever (Ontario Supreme Court), and the health panel, followed by 5 presentations covering: to what extent (and how) science and technology should be controlled; some lessons to be learned from historical applications and attitudes towards medical technologies; the role of medical technologies in developing countries; ethical issues associated with genetic technologies and transplantation technologies.

Each presentation dealt with a topic which merits at least several conferences to do the subject a modicum of justice. Our objective was not to provide a feverish minuscule summary of each complex topic. The panel and the audience worked valiantly (and surprisingly successfully) to use the specific topics to highlight the need for a process for dealing with the ethical issues, and to make related recommendations.

Each presentation served as the focal point for both panel discussion and audience participation. The discussion periods were used not only to elaborate on the points introduced in the presentations, but also as a jumping-off spot for related (and occasionally unrelated but important) issues.

The morning of Day 2, Sir Kenneth Stewart summarized the main themes from the presentations and discussions. The remaining time was spent developing workshop recommendations to take to the Conference plenary.

In addition to the panel members allotted specific speaking time and topics there were two roving panel members: Ms. Joan Watson (Joan Watson Enterprises Ltd., Toronto) and Dr. Maurice MacGregor (Conseil d'evaluation des technologies de la santé, Montreal) who were invaluable in the discussions and specifically served to keep the issues of technology assessment, health policy decisions and public participation in our minds.

Justice Krever opened the Workshop by pointing out, with some graphic examples, that despite advances in dealing with the ethics issues associated with health technologies, concerns, misunderstandings and problems remain. In setting the stage for the Workshop the panel members noted the importance of considering the following: ethos as well as ethics; multidisciplinary approaches to ethics issues; national and international priorities and needs (including implications for the Third World); good decision-making and mechanisms for public participation; social and cultural context and implications; resource allocation; awareness and education; determining the common good; effective technology development assessment. These issues identified early in the workshop arose again and again in the presentations and discussions, providing strong themes and leading to the Workshop recommendations.

The presentations and discussions reiterated and built on the same themes. For the purposes of these proceedings the presentations and related discussions are summarized briefly in Section 2. A summary of some issues, needs and recommendations distilled from the individual presentations/discussions follows in Section 3. The major Workshop recommendations and questions taken to the plenary are shown in Section 4.

Section 2. *Presentations and Discussions*

Use and Control of Science (David Roy)

Dr. David Roy (Centre for Bioethics, Montreal) addressed aspects of how, and at what stage, science and technology should be controlled. Dr. Roy noted that there are different philosophies and approaches to technology. There is a risk that the "white-western" approach to technology will result in our hitching ourselves indiscriminately to technology and going wherever that may lead us. However, it should be possible to use health technologies carefully and with intellectual mastery; to choose directions, objectives, and applications.

The point was made that technology builds on science and research. Steering of research into "productive" and safe directions is easier said than done. It is not always obvious what research will lead to most useful (let alone problem free) applications. If excessive bureaucratic control is imposed, important research of future benefit may not proceed. For example: Salk's polio vaccine was the result of decades of basic research to identify the 3 distinct polio viruses, identify their antigens, and culture the tissues.

Another problem area identified was the relationship between the general human and scientific communities in decisions regarding the directions of scientific research and innovation. At what stage should the general community (public) become involved?

As an example, in the 1950s and 60s research on genes and recombinant DNA was conducted quietly, without public awareness or debate. Strong bureaucratic control would have slowed down the early recombinant DNA research. As a consequence we would, now, be in a worse position to understand AIDS.

In the case of recombinant DNA research the researchers themselves identified the need for care, restraint and protocols. The recommendations proposed by the scientists at the 1972 Assilomar conference were subsequently translated into National Institute of Health guidelines. This example shows that scientists can and should regulate their activity. But is such self-regulation sufficient?

Effective public participation in shaping the course of scientific advance, and related technological innovation are dependent on 3 conditions:

- public access to, and understanding of, scientific information;
- public access to, and understanding of, information which links scientific discoveries to applications, effects, individual and common good;
- effective technology assessment procedures to evaluate the impact of the scientific and technology development.

Can these conditions be met in time for effective public participation? Or will public involvement always be a little too late? Is too late better than too early? The answers involve trade-offs.

Discussion

Discussion focused on the objectives of health technologies; on how the scientific community should relate to the general community; and on how public good is determined.

Historical Perspectives (Steven Martin)

Social, cultural and intellectual beliefs and values are reflected in the development, delivery and adoption of health technologies.

Using the stethoscope, "machines" and obstetric anaesthetic as examples, Dr. Steven Martin (Albert Einstein College of Medicine, New York) provided a historical perspective of forces shaping decisions on health technology.

Dr. Martin pointed out that the stethoscope, a useful diagnostic tool (but essentially only a hollow tube) was invented in France and introduced into medical practice as recently as the 1800s. Earlier the concept of health and disease was based on the humoral theory, which made physical examination unnecessary. Physical examination was not only considered unnecessary, it was viewed with disdain. The medical hierarchy was also relevant; until the 19th century surgeons were of low (uninfluential) status. After the French revolution the gap between physicians and surgeons narrowed and the Paris model of medicine emerged. This model reflected social and cultural changes of the time, and accommodated physical examination and diagnostic technology.

The changing attitudes to obstetrical anaesthetic provided an example of how public will and attitudes affect health policy, and also showed how public tastes in technologies can change.

Increased use of machines has caused a shift from subjective to technical evidence, and has changed the physician-patient relationship. Use of technology can leave more time for patient contact, or can be an obstacle between patient and physician. More technology and specialization are leading to fragmentation of patient care. Ironically, new, high technology communications systems may help overcome fragmentation of care (caused by technology) and reinforce the central role of the family physician.

Discussion

Discussion focused on the role of technology and on how technologies are changing the physician/patient relationship. There was also considerable discussion on the need for both effective technology assessment, and communication among scientists, health care providers, the public and patients.

Developing Countries (Cecile De Sweemer)

Dr. Cecile De Sweemer (International Development Research Centre, Dakar) spoke on ethical issues in developing countries and global responsibilities. Dr. De Sweemer reminded us that the developing countries represent 2/3 of the world's population, have significantly higher mortality and morbidity rates, and often devote more attention and money to burial than to health care. You need faith to deal with death but hope to deal with disease.

Little money is available for disease prevention. Local remedies often compound common problems. For example, cow urine, an accepted treatment of convulsions in young children, leads to low blood sugar and actually increases convulsions. Overall, the process of delivering better health education to mothers is little developed.

Different priorities are needed to get better effect out of health dollars spent. For example, 80% of physicians are located (and disproportionate health resources are spent) in urban areas, while 80% of the population is in rural areas.

Ethics which predominate:
- do not do harm (unless victim can be blamed)
- clear autonomy of the healer/ health worker.
- solidarity of extended family (most pronounced at death).
- protect patient from alienation from family and society.

Dr. De Sweemer identified a number of service delivery, resource allocation (international to local), health and social policy issues. Of particular note, social policies and international economic policies impact on disease prevention and treatment in developing countries; international policies are leading to reduced resources available for health and education.

Specific needs include: better equity in health care outcome (needs of women and children exceed those of middle aged males); ensuring autonomy of the community and family; consensus based on dialogue; and societal rather than legal enforcement.

Discussion

The discussion focused on global ethics, the effects of international and national policies and actions on health in developing countries, and on how we can really help.

Some beneficial interventions are technically very simple. In India $2./person applied to oral rehydration for diarrhoea, female malnutrition, vaccinations, etc. cut mortality in half.

However the socio-cultural problems are complex. Effective intervention on a large scale becomes difficult because of vested interests. Internationally the trends to capitalistic market freedom, and freedom of countries to develop their own capacities are conflicting and can block choices, opportunities and distribution of resources.

It was noted that international corporations play a relevant role in many ways. For example marketing strategies in developing countries can undermine local products and be detrimental to health (e.g. milk and baby food products).

Genetic Health Care Technologies (Charles Scriver)

Dr. Charles Scriver (Montreal Children's Hospital Research Institute) discussed issues raised in the current Science Council of Canada project on the role of genetic technologies in Canadian health care. It is now understood that genes play a significant role in disease or susceptibility to disease. Increasingly, we have technologies to identify susceptible individuals and to help prevent, treat or avoid genetic disease.

These technologies are of particular relevance to developed countries now, and will have increasing applications in developing countries.

In Canada individuals use genetic technologies as another component of health care, to prevent, treat and avoid some genetic diseases. Prenatal diagnosis is used (voluntarily) by families (at risk for producing children with serious diseases) to have healthy children. We are proceeding, cautiously, with the development and delivery of genetic health care technologies.

The genetic technologies provide a good example of issues and problems associated with bringing new technology into the health care system, and of the need to identify and address related ethical issues. Their implementation also provides an example of the need for dialogue, with public participation, and the need for educating citizens to understand the issues and take part in decision-making.

There are many ethical issues associated with genetic research, technologies, service delivery and information. While some relevant policies and guidelines are in place, there are issues where more direction/policies are needed.

Genetic knowledge and technologies have benefits and costs (financial and other). The technologies are considered good if they benefit individuals and are of individual choice. There are still some problems to be dealt with. For example:

- Overall, the current ability to predict genetic disease or risk exceeds the ability to prevent or treat such disease.
- Genetic information could potentially be used to exclude individuals from employment or insurance opportunities.
- Emphasis on avoidance technologies could result in less research on disease prevention and treatment.
- The technologies could be used in a paternalistic or eugenic way.
- Should we take dollars away from acute care today, for more disease prevention?

There is a need for a formal mechanism (an advisory body?) to review the evolution of genetic technologies and applications with specific attention to the related ethical issues.

Discussion

Discussion was wide ranging and touched on: the long-term effects of gene therapy; testing for late-onset disorders (e.g Huntington Disease); discovery of non-paternity; test accuracy; confidentiality of genetic information; and eugenics.

The discussions, and the current Canadian approach to genetic technologies and services, confirm the importance of integrating ethical considerations into all areas including research, service delivery, and use of information.

The genetic technologies also demonstrate the importance of effective guidelines, and evolution of policies to deal with issues which will emerge as the technologies and health services develop.

It was noted that there is a kind of suppression of past eugenic abuses. It may not be necessary to review Nazi abuses each time the eugenics topic arises, but it is wrong to block discussion of eugenics, its history and implications. Ignoring the issue prevents intelligent discussion and policy decisions.

The way genetics is applied today is not (and should not be) based on improving the species. But individual decisions on prenatal diagnosis and pregnancy termination do imply an opinion on the overall quality of life. Does the application of prenatal diagnostic technologies present an ethical "slippery slope?" Is there an ethical difference between using the technology to avoid the birth of a child with Down's syndrome, or for sex selection (for non-health related reasons)? A difficult area but decisions and policies should be possible.

It was noted that prenatal diagnosis and pregnancy termination are only one aspect. The technologies also have the potential to prevent and treat many important diseases such as cancers and heart disease. In addition to availability of genetic technologies, there should be a strong commitment to social and health care support for people with disabilities.

Genetic technologies offer choices. To make wise choices we need more research, more health care options, better dialogue and information, effective technology assessment, an informed public, and good guidelines for use of genetic technologies and information.

Transplantation Technologies (John Dossetor)

Dr. John Dossetor (Bioethics Project, University of Alberta) was initially involved in transplantation as a surgeon. Dealing with the many important ethical issues led to his current involvement in bioethics (an example of the slippery slope?).

Transplantation is primarily a technology for developed countries (this itself is an ethical issue) but is of increasing relevance to developing countries as they apply the health care technologies, or are considered as sources for organ donors.

Issues discussed included definition of death, organ ownership, allocation of resources, and developing country issues.

- Definition of death is pivotal because transplantation is largely from dead people. In several countries "brain death" has come to be equated with death. How did this equation develop? The media played a large role in gaining acceptance for the concept.
- Who owns organs? Ownership is clear when in the original host, or when transplanted. But interim (in between bodies) ownership remains unclear and needs resolution.
- Who has authority to allocate organs, and how should such allocation be determined?
- What factors determine allocation of limited resources between competing transplantation programs, or for that matter between transplantation and other health care programs (e.g disease prevention)? It was noted that the media and lobby groups play an important role in influencing public opinion and health policy.
- There are several issues particularly relevant to developing countries. For example, kidney transplants in India are mostly from living family members or from poor individuals willing to sell a kidney. India is in the process of developing policies and guidelines, ethically acceptable to Indian society, to entrench benefits for donors (rewarded gifting).
- Other relevant issues include use of fetal tissue and tissue from aborted fetuses, and the ethical implications of breeding primates for use as donors.

Discussion

Discussion focused on public will, the difficulty in allocating scarce resources, the ethics of selling organs, and the role of the media.

Transplantation technologies are a good example of issues associated with resource allocation, and of the evolution of technology. Originally there was fierce competition to deliver transplantation programs. Now there is better control over quality of transplantation programs. Some transplantation technologies (kidney and heart) have become standard therapy.

In Canada it is considered unethical (and indeed illegal) to buy and sell human organs. Our policy is gift based. However, imposing our gift based views on developing countries may be paternalistic and prevent true opportunity and choice for individuals. Perhaps instead of condemning commerce in organs we should concentrate on ensuring that relevant policies are just, and on clarifying the responsibility of organ recipients to donors (e.g social contract, access to medical services).

While commerce and rewarded gifting intra-nationally are being considered by individual countries, there is strong international opinion that commerce in organs between countries should be prohibited, at least until all countries have the opportunity to determine their will and establish policies and protocols.

Nationally and internationally we need registries of organs as well as a process (and criteria) for allocation of organs. The primary decision regarding allocation of organs should be based on medical criteria (#1 criterion is tissue matching).

The print and electronic media have great impact on acceptance of transplantation technologies, and availability of resources; they can also help raise consciousness of public regarding the importance of donating organs. It was also pointed out that the media can give a very personal face to individual needs for transplantation and can result in unrealistic expectations and skewing of resource allocation. Will the media consider the need for livers for children more important than advising the public of the significance of osteoporosis? What are the responsibilities of the media regarding public education?

Finally it was noted that despite all the publicity on transplantation and the scarcity of organs, people generally do not get around to signing their donor cards. Physicians often hesitate to raise the issue with next of kin.

Section 3: *Summary of Points on some Special Issues*

Control of Research and Technology Development

Research, basic and applied, is required to understand causes and process of disease, develop solutions, assess technologies and outcomes. There was no agreement on the extent to which basic research should be controlled, or the public involved in related decisions. There was agreement that application of research as health care technology should only proceed if technical benefit has been demonstrated and if there is clear public good, and public will. It was recognized that differentiating between basic and applied research is not always easy.

Overall, constraints on basic research are not seen as the answer to health technology problems. Research should proceed, with decisions made on a topic specific basis.

Meanwhile we need to ensure that scientists integrate ethical considerations into research planning and the establishment of checks and balances; and that the public are ready and able to participate in the ethical and technical debate on health issues.

Directing research to the most "promising" areas was recognized as difficult. Who can predict (effectively) where the best results in terms of public good will come from?

Role of Technology

Health, well-being and quality of life are not primarily medical issues although medicine and technology have a role to play. Health policy has broad social, cultural, economic, and technological components. Health technologies must be considered in terms of overall health objectives and patient needs. The right machines and technologies in the right context are good, but should only be used where they result in better health or health care.

Better health is one clear objective of health technologies. Technology should be integrated into truly holistic health delivery. The requisite technologies will vary with the issue and the community. Achieving better health through disease prevention and health maintenance often involves lower versus high technology.

Technology should be the servant not the master. Dialogue and decisions are needed to set objectives and guidelines for application of medical technology. In setting objectives we need to work both from universal objectives and principles through to objectives for specific issue, and vice versa.

Some goals (succinctly summarized by Joan Watson):

- technology should be used primarily to enhance the health of individuals;
- the growing body of knowledge and technology should be integrated into health care in an appropriate and ethical way.
- technologies should be used in a way which accommodates participation and decision-making by the patient.

Role of Ethics

Technology is an expression of values and is not ethically neutral. We are interested in the process by which society responds to health issues and integrates ethics into all deliberations regarding technology objectives, research, development, assessment and delivery. Integration of ethics is achieved in a number of ways. Many professions have an ethics code which is a self-regulated part of professional practice. Many health technology issues reflect universal human ethics as well as specific social and cultural values.

Some major ethical conflicts relate to specific cultural differences and priorities, and differences between collective and individual good.

The ways of determining common good vary. In Ontario the Premier's Health Council advises the Premier on health issues, and helps set policies. Policy recommendations are not always implemented (because of conflicting priorities and demands) but at least information is available. Better information may lead to better decisions.

To develop good health policies we need scientists with an ethical view, enlightened bureaucrats and politicians, and good public participation. We need informed buyers and users of health technologies. There is a need for public involvement and response to public concerns. In Canada the public concern that conventional health care systems are limited, and that there is a need for another model, is affecting health policy.

Effective public involvement requires appropriate mechanisms, and informed participants. Strong lobby groups help in developing policy and in drawing attention to issues. For example, policy setting for occupational health issues is effective because mechanisms and informed participants are available.

The role of ethics is critical in the process of establishing laws. First we need to clarify our values, objectives and policies on specific issues. Then laws can be developed as required. The law should identify limits within which most people can live comfortably. We also need to accept that for some issues (e.g. abortion) it is difficult to develop widely acceptable policies (let alone achieve consensus). We must ensure that majority opinion does not override minority opinion; ongoing dialogue is needed.

Resource Allocation

Resource allocation is relevant to health research, technology development and service delivery, and involves ethics on issues ranging from global policy to individual patient care.

How should health resources be allocated? There are difficult trade-offs. Research is expensive. Would the money be better spent directly on prevention and treatment of disease? In addition to delivering current technology to meet health care needs, it remains important to allocate resources for research to arrive at better disease prevention and treatment.

High technology, generally focused on acute-care, plays an important role but is just a part of achieving health and reducing the burden of disease. Resources are also needed for disease prevention.

As examples, resources are needed to develop and deliver technologies to successfully bring low birth weight babies to adulthood; resources are also needed to improve maternal nutrition and reduce the incidence of low birth weight.

Similarly in the 1950s money was needed to purchase respirators for polio victims. Resources were also needed to develop better respirators, and to develop and deliver effective immunization (to reduce the need for respirators).

Honest dialogue and careful resource allocation are important. We need to carefully consider the options, and what we are capable of doing. As an important step we also need to clarify our objectives. Preventing death? preventing disease? ensuring health? improving the quality of life?

Some additional points:

- Health dollars should be allocated to where they are most needed and most cost effective, rather than to areas considered more important because of status of either types of technology or of recipients of the technology.
- Since health technologies have global implications it is important to address global distribution of wealth and its effects on health.
- At the level of patient care, we should not be wasteful. Nor should we make physicians into budgetary officers.

Dialogue

Dialogue among informed participants is critical to health technology/health care decisions, to the development of ethical views, and the determination of common good. Health issues must be addressed by a full range of participants: communities, patients, health care providers, educators, lawyers, ethicists, bureaucrats, politicians etc.

Dialogue has to be organized otherwise it won't happen. However, care is required to ensure that the ongoing dialogue on health issues does not become limited to a health elite, capable of understanding the terminology. Success in establishing dialogue is possible as in the case of the Oregon Health Care Parliament.

There are many problems. In many countries there are constituents who have little voice in defining the common good or affecting policy (e.g, women and children in many developing and developed countries). And how do you get representative public participation in countries which are not democracies?

Even with good dialogue and information, choices are required, and many of the choices are difficult. The debate is often a case of good versus better.

Education

Education is a key to effective participation in decision-making. Better methods of developing informed participants (scientists, politicians, bureaucrats and the public) are critical to good health care decisions at all levels, individual to international. Both formal (school) and ongoing education should encompass ethical as well as technical issues. Attention should be paid to global and developing country issues.

Education is a lifelong process. Technologies and issues evolve. Formal education systems and the media have important roles to play in preparing the involved parties to deal with health issues. Schools should prepare individuals to continue to learn and deal with issues. Although the media have a certain responsibility to inform, it is not really in the public service business. Other means of educating the public are also needed.

Scientists have a responsibility to facilitate media comprehension of issues. Useful approaches would include development of better communications skills and roles on the part of scientific associations and professional bodies; and development of a national data base of experts available for the media to consult.

Developing Countries

There are some fundamental differences in health issues, status and priorities between developing and developed countries. Technology has a role in addressing health problems and priorities in developing countries, although at present, the solutions to many major health problems still lie elsewhere.

International and national economic and social policy affect health prevention and promotion. In many cases current policies, and the underlying economic crisis, are leading to decreased resources for health and education. Cecile Sweemer noted that the International Monetary Fund (IMF) treats health as a luxury consumer good and is requiring countries to reduce their debt through reduced social programs including health programs.

We should recognize global responsibilities and the need for global ethics and justice. While addressing global concerns and problems we must respect local and cultural needs and wishes.

Global issues include resource distribution and ownership, and responsibility for meeting the basic needs of people.

While it is possible to help developing countries, international "help" can also cause harm. We should not step back from trying to help, we should just do a better job of it. A new formula is required. We have to empty our heads of predetermined notions on what form the help should take. Community needs should be identified and serve as the basis for developing solutions.

It was recognized that some simple technologies and modest health care resources, effectively targeted and delivered, could significantly reduce the burden of disease in developing countries.

Technology Assessment

There is an urgent need for effective technology assessment to assist in decisions regarding which technologies to keep and adopt. (Note: traditional technologies should not be exempt from assessment.) The criteria for evaluating technologies require clarification.

We must also assess technologies effectively, and provide unbiased, scientifically credible, understandable information to assist in making technology related decisions. Information transfer and communication are critical to social and personal decisions regarding use of health technology.

Section 4: *Major Recommendations and Questions*

The troupe reassembled (day 2) to develop major questions and recommendations for the conference plenary. Sir Kenneth Stuart (Welcome Tropical Institute, London, Great Britain) started the process by providing a summary (grab-bag) of major points culled from the presentations. Major issues included:

- Health technology issues require decisions at numerous levels, international, national, regional, individual. Difficult choices have to be made. There is a critical need for effective decision-making processes which integrate ethics considerations.
- Health technologies should be developed, assessed and used in the context of cultural and socio-economic goals and needs. Technology provides tools but requires context; the focus should remain on the needs of the person/family/culture.
- There is a need for effective dialogue on health goals and priorities. Dialogue must involve, and be comprehensible to all relevant parties (e.g public, scientists, health care providers, politicians).
- Processes/mechanisms are required to establish goals, set priorities and allocate limited resources. The mechanisms must involve all relevant parties.
- There is a need to establish objectives, boundaries and priorities for development and application of technologies. The boundaries must accommodate the range of acceptable values (per culture).
- For effective improvements in health of individuals *globally* we require global solutions which transcend current compartmentalization of disciplines (e.g, science, medicine, environment, economics) and national interests. Disparities in health status between developed and developing countries, and between different socio-economic groups must be addressed.
- Control of technology applications is important but advancement of science (basic and applied research) is necessary to address health problems. Ethical considerations should be integrated into all aspects of research and technology development (e.g, protocols, funding).
- There is a need for effective technology assessment processes and practices (which incorporate ethics considerations).
- There is a need for better *education* on technical and ethical issues to assist participants in the decision-making process. Education should involve all parties: public (through schooling and media), scientists, politicians.

- Science is a moving (evolving) target; accommodating, preparing for, and directing change is critical.

The subsequent discussion focused on whether there is a point where cultural ethics might have to give way to universal values and the importance of recognizing global versus parochial needs and responsibilities.

All roads led to the need for better dialogue and education in determining the role for technology (with due consideration to ethical issues).

At this stage Drs. Dossetor and Roy, with the remainder of the panel and audience in enthusiastic pursuit, wrested the following major recommendations and questions from the foregoing work. John Dossetor was awarded the Workshop commemorative sheepbell for this yeoman service.

Three Concluding Recommendations

(1) All health research and technology reflect values; therefore ethics considerations must be incorporated at all levels of research, basic and applied.

(2) It is ethically mandatory that all nations develop a world-wide perspective for health care and ensure that their national and international policies, programs and activities support improved health by addressing regional and local needs.

(3) It is ethically mandatory to establish mechanisms for interdisciplinary and public discussion, at a grassroots level, within each community. To this end, we recommend the establishment of a Canadian forum for innovative public education on Science and Technology. This forum will foster the continuing and systematic mutual education of media communicators, scientists, health care providers and planners, political representatives, and citizens.

Three Concluding Questions

(1) Are there *universal* ethics? If so, how are they reconciled with specific cultural ethics?

(2) How can technologies be used to narrow the differences in human health between developed and developing countries?

(3) In allocating health resources, how do we resolve the sometimes conflicting needs of individuals versus the collective, and short-term versus long-term needs?

WORKSHOP 10:
Technology, Industrial Development and Government Policy

Coordinators: Dr. Saul Silverman, Silverman Consulting Services Ltd., Kanata, Ont.; Dr. Victor Ujimoto, Department of Sociology and Anthropology, University of Guelph; Dr. James M. Gilmour, Director of Policy Analysis, Science Council of Canada, Ottawa

Chair: Dr. Hugh Wynne-Edwards, formerly of Alcan Aluminium Ltd.

Rapporteur: Dr. Saul Silverman

Introduction

The Industry and Technology Policy workshop focused on major issues linking Canadian and global industry-technology concerns. Rather than focusing narrowly on a box called "industry," we found ourselves exploring the widest issues—environment, sharing of participation and responsibility (at home and globally), the prospects of a "peace dividend" and what to do with it, and many others—in the perspective of where industry was at the present time and how it might evolve.

In retrospect, our key question became: "How can we take practical initiatives to deal with major issues so that industry can become more responsible, in the context of market competition and changing values, for constructive innovation and use of technologies in support of development that is sustainable, democratic, and accountable?" Put in this way, the workshop was tidy and abstract. In actual fact, our proceedings were messy, concrete, challenging and full of specific divergences. Very open discussion laid out where people were coming from; the development, by our chairperson, of a series of issue frameworks provided a dynamic for cooperatively sorting out some converging themes.

This report cannot recreate the richness of our group's coming together. We will try an overview, first by reprinting the final documentation that the workshop participants agreed to bring forward; then by providing some background to the workshop's conclusions. This background summary is in three parts: how some major thematic guidelines evolved; an abstract of the presentations by our resource people; and some discussion highlights.

Orientations: An Emerging Framework for Action

In general, the workshop reflected two basic assumptions. One was that the industry and technology context is global. Considering it in less than a global perspective would not address today's realities. The second premise was that market competitive pressures had to be recognized and fully used in any new departures (perhaps by trying to make constructive environmental use of technology more profitable, while linking the costs of pollution more directly to polluters). While there was some questioning whether market forces went far enough, there was little support for older notions of governmental action. There was much more interest in roundtables and forums to represent varied stakeholders and mobilize their strengths. This line of discussion led to the recommendation of a Canadian "Commission on Renewal." (Whether this indicates a repudiation of government, or a desire to re-invent government, is a moot point.)

Galbraith's speech to the initial plenary session of the conference served to help focus our concerns. If we could begin to think in terms of redeployment of resources from military to other purposes, what sort of redirection of industry and technology would be compatible with this? To which major issues and priorities? And, if these were our priorities under conditions of such redeployment, would they serve us as guidelines to our general consideration? As we explored this, some specific priorities came into focus (see below, "Discussion Highlights"). We also came to realize that redeployment of resources involved not simply redirection of financing, but also of skills, existing and new technologies, organization, energies, and even ideology. This was reflected, in part, in the proposal of a "Global Marshall Plan."

While convergence emerged around specific issues, the element in the discussion that seemed most elusive was the effort to probe for an ethical position that could be recognized as both practical and easily generalized. It seemed harder to articulate a common framework of values than to recognize a need to seek values that could be shared. Thus, while problems and issues could be clarified and acted upon, a formal ethics was seen as a "gap" in our current understanding. This was reflected in our questions (as distinct from recommendations), with the questions focusing on major processes (linking ethics and social decision-making) that had to be discovered or invented.

On the borderline between ethics and group psychology, there was discomfort with differences between talk and action, with the idea that the rich were preaching about environment from a comfortable position, and that we had benefited from a "let it rip" period of development and were belated converts to a philosophy of restraint. A major, continuing concern was that Canada not simply preach morality to others, but adopt practical positions and take on tasks, at home and internationally, that demonstrate that Canadians put themselves on the line. This, too, was incorporated in the recommendations in various ways.

In the course of discussion, a list of operating concepts emerged, labelled "change-makers," that accompanied the group's selection of issues. In the end, they were reflected directly or indirectly in the recommendations. (Numbers do not reflect priorities).

(1) A commission on renewal.

(2) Pressure for "closure of systems" to promote the internalizing of costs.

(3) Effective linkage among risks, costs and benefits.

(4) Changing rules to make "clean" technologies economic and "dirty" technologies uneconomic.

(5) Education for science, technology and society interaction-awareness.

(6) Democratization of risk decision-making (i.e. those who take risks should have a fuller share in making decisions).

(7) Institutionalization of the social justice process.

(8) Competitiveness through entrepreneurship.

Background Presentations (Resource Speakers)

Initial presentations on the nature of contemporary industry and technology were made by James Wessinger, Vice-President for Marketing Services of the Ontario International Corporation, on behalf of Gordon Gow, President of the Ontario government agency, and by Laurent Thibault, President of the Canadian Manufacturers Association. Wessinger emphasized three themes: the need to separate what is possible from what is desirable; limits on the powers of government—they are not as all-pervasive as we may think they are or, perhaps, should be; and the ambiguous position of developed countries talking about ethics of development today. Since we in the industrial world have already ravaged forests and other resources as part of our own history of development, we are in a position to alienate other parts of the world when we insist on strict criteria for economic development. Dealing with current problems requires participation of all of the world, including areas that may feel that we are talking about environment just when their needs for development have become most pressing. This instigated the view that we should concentrate on examples that put the onus on the Western world rather than generalize about ethics for the Third World.

Laurent Thibault presented an overview of technology derived, in part, from Peter Drucker: technological innovation consists of "all new applications of knowledge to human work"—products (complex or simple); tools and production methods; creation of new raw materials (e.g. plastics or ceramics); organizations and systems. The most important technology is entrepreneurial management itself—entrepreneurialism as skills is a social technology. For the true entrepreneur, change is less risky than more of the same.

Environment, as an issue, is a symptom of other developments and changes in the industrial economy and society. The erosion of traditional industries, since the oil shock of the 1970s, has been characterized by downsizing. In North America, what picked up the slack was not high technology (this contributed to quality, but not to quantity—only one eighth of jobs in 1988) but rather, according to Drucker, the emergence of the entrepreneurial economy. Entrepreneurial innovations are not necessarily, or even largely, scientific inventions. Many innovations are social innovations in the business environment, such as McDonald's close monitoring of customer behaviour to design and re-design products and process. "Middle-tech" entrepreneurs—chains of donut bakers, speciality printing shops, etc., become typical of an innovating service economy. Their lesson is that self-renewal for societies is not in more planning and government, not in a "romantic notion of high tech," but in innovating entrepreneurship and in letting obsolete approaches die out.

In response to Thibault, there was some discussion of market economics. Can the market respond to the full range of needs? Is the main problem really over-bureaucratization and control? Is a new bureaucracy to be found in the international transfer mechanisms of contemporary finance?

David Nitkin, President of EthicScan, helped focus discussion on how decisions and behaviour could be assessed. His review of corporate ethics, monitoring and assessment activities (drawn from the work of EthicScan which monitors and compares activity of firms across Canada), was preceded by his comments on the various levels at which significant industrial and technological decisions are taken: the decisions by individual business as regards products and production processes; industry associations and similar groupings which take, or strongly influence, many environmentally significant decisions; intergroup decisions—note the recent emergence of provincial and national roundtables.

In general, Nitkin suggests that greater emphasis on "stakeholder decisions" may be becoming the "Canadian way." There is some response to public concerns. For example, the Canadian Chemical Producers' Association has come up with a quality approach to danger management which is beginning to be adopted and applied by various groups around the globe to situations other than chemical spills. Nitkin notes that this was an initiative by an industry association—a response led by 4 or 5 visionaries who reviewed public opinion polls, saw how poorly the chemical industry was regarded, and thought that something proactive should be done by the industry itself. Within industry, ethics and competition in markets can sometimes reinforce each other. Businesses exist to serve society; they find markets by meeting needs. If you don't do that, your competitors will. The question for management then becomes: are you proactive or are you reactive?

Thus, reviewing ethics in industry is essentially a process; not a quick answer that you get from some place and impose on a situation. The various stages of the process involve a stakeholder analysis. This includes everybody who has a vested interest in the decision; integrating goals with scanning of the corporate environment and behaviour at all levels; and trying to close the gap between values and behaviour.

When we relate corporate behaviour to values, we need to define three domains that are often co-mingled: law (conforming to what society requires and has the capability to enforce), morality (conforming to the behaviour that is accepted in the society at the time), and ethics (striving for "good" behaviour). The last may be harder to define. Nitkin suggests what he calls the "four do's:" respect life; respect property; respect truth; respect rights."

The next group of speakers (Fred Pomeroy, President of the Communications Workers of Canada; Calvin Sandborn, Staff Counsel of the West Coast Environmental Law Association; and Des Adam, Mayor of Kanata) addressed questions of stakeholders' interest. Each found flaws and limitations in the process as it exists today.

Fred Pomeroy built his presentation around concepts of rights and the need for a "technology bill of rights" that, among other things, would extend participation by labour in the design and operating of the workplace. He colour-codes the rights that we have and need: the traditional "blue" rights (i.e. individual rights such as freedom of speech, due process); collective and affirmative "red" rights (i.e. labour's fight to achieve and strengthen rights to organize and bargain); the emerging ecological, interactive "green" rights. The latter will be difficult to achieve, and should include the right to refuse work assignments which pollute or which feed into military activities.

In the technology sector, as represented by communications workers' activities, specific problems needing to be addressed fall into three categories: physical-neurological stress (need for better ergonomics and social design of technology, and of the work process); social-psychological stress (lack of privacy and close, intrusive, monitoring of activity); job insecurities (plant layoffs and technology changes, downgrading of skill levels to achieve a lower-cost workforce that is more interchangeable among tasks in machine-dominated environments).

In the era of technological change, workers and unions do not really participate in workplace design. The reason for this, says Pomeroy, is that "we're not invited to the party, and we haven't yet gathered the strength to gate crash." Thus, a key stakeholder is left out—or kept out—of the process affecting technological conditions. "Little wonder that the union movement in Canada isn't 'responsible' in the policy debate around tech change when no responsibilities are assigned or even imagined by the key economic actors: business and government." The "right to manage" is enshrined in collective agreements; the right to participate in workplace design is an essential right in the era of technology and ecology, and has yet to be gained.

Calvin Sandborn dealt with stakeholders' interests under the heading, "The Democratization of Risk Decisions." In a just society, those who face the risk from a technology should have a voice. In the regulatory process, for example, it should be equal to those who benefit. This does not happen. In support of this theme, Sandborn's thesis emphasized the impact of environmental poisons, past and present, as products of economic activity that impact those who have little say in decision-making. He developed a general model as to why public interests are diffused or tend to be overcome by those with vested interests in promoting "harmful" technologies and presented specific criticisms and suggestions for change of the current Canadian situation.

The historic case was an initial prohibition, in the 1920s, of leaded additive to gasoline, based on health hazards known at the time. Permanent policy was under study by the U.S. Surgeon-General. Although the ban on lead was supported by experts (including editorial opinion in the American Medical Association Journal), the ban lasted barely a year. Pressure was applied at the political level that influenced the final editing of recommendations so as to reinstate lead additives, with some cautions as to procedures to be adopted to limit hazards in the manufacturing process. In effect, over a half century of additional lead hazards occurred in general public health leading to subtle forms of neurological damage, and in particular, to levels of lead in the bloodstream that the U.S. Centres for Disease Control have recently found to be "of serious concern in young children."

Analogous recent cases stressed by Sandborn are the risks from pesticides faced particularly by farm workers. Historically, Canadian farm workers have been excluded both from helping to shape pesticide regulatory policy and from full protection, or full compensatory benefits, as regards the health impacts of pesticides. In the 1980s, however, there has been some correction of the Workers' Compensation restrictions in some of the provincial jurisdictions.

To correct this inequity requires major changes in public policy. Sandborn emphasizes (1) that those at risk be fully represented in groups that study problems, influence decisions and help make regulations; (2) that funding for advocacy groups and expert resources be available so that those at risk can compete with the economic interests on a level playing field in the balance of influences on decision-making; (3) that specific mechanisms and funding procedures be put in place to reflect these criteria for fairness; and (4) that at all levels of government, environmental ministries have the final say—even over other government ministries or policies—in any decision-making that has substantial environmental impacts.

Des Adam, Mayor of Kanata, Ontario, looked at these issues from the perspective of an elected official in a high technology centre. Some key questions, in his opinion, are "How clean are the so-called "clean" industries? How can we deal with problems of wastes and water supply? Who is going to pay for the environment? "

Recent reports of chemical pollution in the Great Lakes and problems in the Ottawa River emphasize the significance of measures like MISA (the Municipal Industrial Strategy for Abatement) passed by Ontario in September 1988.

Municipalities have shareholders—the taxpayers and voters—who look at the bottom line. If we are to continue, how are we to proceed? Do we lower the level of service or do we raise the tax base? One way of raising the tax base is to attract industries. The challenge is to attract industries that are not environmentally harmful. The problem is whether we have enough control.

In Ottawa-Carleton, the municipalities have no real power over wastes. The regional government deals with the water and waste problem. The only real lever the municipalities have to potentially screen industries coming in is initial site-plan approval; but in Adam's experience, unless your zoning is very restrictive, you cannot keep an industry out. In effect, the pressure in this area is coming down increasingly to the municipal level, but the power and resources to act are the most limited at that level.

Fred Belaire, chief economic advisor to Atomic Energy of Canada Ltd., dealt with changing values and the need for "closed systems" technology to help deal with risk. In the September 1990 special issue of *Scientific American* (September 1989), William C. Clark offers a framework for looking at value change and global technology. We have to ask two kinds of questions: What kind of planet do we want? What kind of planet can we get? To be able to answer these questions, we have to know how values change in the decision-making process. The relationship between Values-Science and Technology-Economics is one in which we have to get *all* of them right. But to say that is the equivalent of posing a three-body problem in mathematics, for which, so far, there is no general solution. To paraphrase Keynes: if we wait for the perfect solution, we'll all be dead as a species.

Rather, we have to work things out by approximations and to recognize where we have knowledge and where there are gaps. We know the economic costs of production and markets, but we are largely ignorant of the full costs of the environmental absorption problem, and of how to deal with it. This absorption problem is key. Belaire cites a National Academy of Engineering report, *Technology and Environment*, which notes that pressure for closure of systems now stems more from concern about the environment as a receptacle for wastes than from issues of scarcity of resources. Both resources and environment, to some extent, are functions of technology, and technology can be used to promote and effect closure of systems.

Closed systems technology is an area where AECL has had a lot of experience. Some key needs are to define reasonable safety standards, to identify and quantify the hazards, to acquire methods or technologies for controlling hazards to the accepted standards, and to have working systems (monitoring and regulation) to ensure that standards have been met. Currently, in its own areas of responsibility, AECL invests about $50 million a year in environmental science and technology, aiming to translate a scientific know-how into tangible applications so as to effect closure of nuclear systems. The frameworks, information and knowledge developed because of the need for care in the nuclear energy option may have broader application as the world looks for other "closed systems."

A final panel consisted of the workshop coordinators and sponsor's representative, James Gilmour of the Science Council. He focused on questioning the substantive and process aspects of technological change. We were talking of ethics in terms of the alleged progress in dealing with poverty in the industrial countries versus the problems of the Third World countries. Were we in fact that sure that we had really made the progress we claimed in the distribution of the benefits of technology in terms of "real" progress? Looking at the international development of science and technology, were we sure that we—in the historically advanced West—were really on top of technological development processes, and had a message to give the world as regards the ethics of technological progress in the future? The problem was not just ethics, it was keeping sufficiently in tune with technical and social progress to be able to back ethics with substantive contributions.

Victor Ujimoto, Professor of Sociology and Anthropology at Guelph, stressed some earlier points: that technology is a combination of resources and knowledge (including organization) to meet needs. He would add to these concepts that have been generally accepted in the workshop that technology is affected by social values, and in particular, by the difference in values among various societies. A key variable will be whether society is motivated to pull together and has a tradition of doing so. In Japan, it is a foregone conclusion that people must work as a group. In North America, the dominant values imply working as an individual. Paralleling this is whether the style of thinking in the culture is really encouraging a grasp of the problems and opportunities adequate to today's challenge. In this connection, Ujimoto reminds us of Theobald's writings in the 1950s: the stress should be on systemic thinking (unifying fields), in contrast to linear thinking (segregating topics).

Saul Silverman cited a number of examples of historical change and value shifts, including the 18th century period of Revolutions, the 19th century rise of abolitionism in the U.S., and the 19th century shift from the Tokugawa shogunate to the beginnings of modernization in Japan. In each case, change took place for a long period under the surface, while things seemed as they "always had been." The entire period of the shift from disdain for abolitionism (even in the North) to legitimation of social protest and creation of new political forces leading to civil war and the legal emancipation of slaves took place in the U.S. over a period of as little as 30 years. But the climatic shift to new values and accepted ways of doing things appears to take place very suddenly; it registers quickly, and only in the aftermath of historical reconstruction are the events tied to the seeding of change. This pattern seems so general that it can serve both as a warning and as an encouragement to the effort to re-examine values, and to work for constructive change in the world, hopefully through non-violent and cooperative means.

Discussion Highlights

In the course of discussion, a number of key issues were identified that became part of the process of formulating the overall group position. These issues, which were linked to the "changemaker" processes cited earlier, are as follows: (they do not reflect an order of priority):

(1) Employer-employee power sharing

(2) Fulfilling employment

(3) Health care and caring

(4) Consumer choice/power

(5) Environment

(6) Third World development

(7) Innovation

(8) Research

Most of these issues are reflected directly in the synopsis, recommendations and questions that were the final contribution of the workshop to the Conference. Others, however, were subsumed in more general recommendations. For example, Third World development was reflected in the recommendation of a global Marshall plan to redeploy resources. A few further comments are required to complete our effort to present a picture of the workshop.

There can be little doubt that, both directly and as an element of other concerns, the environment became a major focus of discussions. In this regard, a convergence of views occurred between a number of thrusts. Some participants, notably Alek Olsen and Michel Giguere, emphasized the need to push ahead on dealing with specifics to protect scarce environmental resources and on dealing with particular major problems like the ozone layer and acid rain. Others focused on processes for problem identification and solution. Thus, Fred Belaire and Lee Doran both advanced ideas for permanent commissions—even, perhaps, with "wartime powers"—to deal with major environmental and other problems of renewal.

There was also growing support for the concept of developing systems and technology for physical closure of industrial systems (closed loops for wastes and reprocessing), and for reinforcing this by economic adjustments that would affect the balance of profit and loss between environmental technology innovators and polluters. The recommendations tended to use both the specific problem agenda and overall process approaches to reflect the groups's industry/environment concerns.

The question of relating this to Third World needs, and to equities of cost-benefit burdens and opportunities between Rich and Poor, was emphasized by a number of participants. It was a continuing concern of the chairperson, Hugh Wynne-Edwards, and was also emphasized by Desmond Egan. Egan linked the need to encourage Third World participation in environmentally appropriate technology (leap-frogging traditional industrial processes) by making this a part of a major global development effort, including the transfer of knowledge and technology. Similarly, on the domestic front, it was noted that industries and individual companies were at varying levels in their appreciation of the problems of transition, and in their ability or willingness to innovate. James Gilmour suggested that programs would be required to assist industries to adopt environmentally sound science and technology. It could not be expected to come about spontaneously or to lie wholly within the economic capabilities of individual firms.

Discussion tended to oscillate between specific issue areas and the prospect of generalized applicable ethics. While there was probable convergence around the notion that value consensus was likely to continue to be a pursuit rather than an achievement, and that an "ethical gap" was likely to continue (at least as regards practical implementation of overall formal systems of ethics that meshed with piecemeal or systemic problem-solving), there were particular efforts to suggest where an ethical focus could lie. Thus, in suggesting some priority for resource recycling to life-enhancing research, especially in the health-care area, David Nitkin suggested that an accompanying ethic could be condensed in terms of enhancing the value of life and trying to compress the incidence of mortality. In an analogous way, the concept of enhancing human dignity was tied to specific economic priorities in a number of ways. First, as regards the notions of fairness for those who were impacted by technology but had little say in decision-making; second, as an ethical value associated with a priority for creating meaningful work and work environments including a sufficient quantity of jobs, but also quality of jobs to reinforce human worth and respect.

The issue of meaningful work was not fully resolved and raised one of the continuing dichotomies of the workshop. While the global view was recognized by all participants, and dominated much of the time, the issue of jobs at home, of poverty versus dignity, and of the relationship between job export internationally and Canada's own economic ethics simmered throughout, without real resolution. This probably contributed to a general willingness to see that recommendations focused on a strong bonding of domestic and international problems, rather than assuming that one or another focus should predominate.

A final theme of discussion was the role of education. Here a major contribution was made by Trudy Knight who described experiences in education in the area of science-technology-society linkages. The recommendations reflect her persuasive analysis (encompassing general education as well as specific education for two groups: politicians and public officials; media people) that unless there are major changes in available education in this area, the underpinnings of understanding and public support for programs recommended by this workshop and this conference, will be lacking.

Conclusion

The workshop was successful in raising issues, though it certainly had to leave most issues unresolved. More questions were taken away by participants than answers. Nevertheless, the feeling at the end of the process was a good one, and there was support for the notion (as expressed later in the concluding plenary discussions) that the recommendations and questions of various workshops had cleared some of the underbrush and could serve as a basis for the work of continuing networks.

If answers are to be found, they will require rousing ourselves from drift and moving beyond good will to good action. If the conference title suggests a sense of being overwhelmed by pervasive technology, it also suggests the possibility of choice and responsibility. In a sense, then, the work of coming together in this and similar workshops, to explore and debate issues, to suggest processes and priorities, represents one small series of steps—but a useful beginning—towards accepting the challenge to change.

Synopsis

In addition to formally approving three concluding recommendations and three questions, our group endorsed a final summary of central concerns.

Central Dilemma—Haves/Have Nots

Focus of Decision—International Commons:

- Environment
- Market competition
- Science and technology
- Education and "know-how"

Critical Gap—"Relevant" ethical framework for decision-making.

Objectives and Goals:

- Democratization of decision-making
- Closure of systems to internalize responsibilities
- Dignity of work
- Education

Money and Resources—"Swords into Ploughshares" (Galbraith's speech to the opening plenary of the Conference).

Three Concluding Recommendations

(1) Canada should lead by example. We should pioneer an ongoing search for shared values. To cap this process, an ongoing *Commission on Renewal*—ecological, social and institutional—should be established.

(2) Ethical choice in industry and technology should centre on taking responsibility for what we are doing and on being assessed in a framework of ethical accountability. This involves "closure of systems," e.g., that wastes be absorbed and recycled by industries creating them (water intakes downstream from sewer outfall).

(3) Canada's political leaders should launch concrete actions at home to start major cleanup of our environment, planned, with a defined time-limit for specific actions to be achieved and with specific resources to do the job. Our government should use every international forum to bring abut a new "Marshall Plan," financed by developed countries, to rejuvenate the global environment, redirect military expenditures and related industrial resources, and to use industrial skills for global economic and social innovation in the common good.

Three Concluding Questions

(1) What are the ethical imperatives of the international commons, and how do we apply these nationally and locally?

(2) How do we democratize and devolve decision-making (in industry, society, and globally) without dissipating accountability?

(3) How can we create educational objectives and systems so that a process of public learning that educates for awareness of science and technology, and social interactions becomes the underpinning for ethical choice in industry and elsewhere?

WORKSHOP 11: Technology and Ethical Choice in Labour Relations

Coordinators: Daphne Taylor, University of Guelph; Kevin Hayes, Canadian Labour Congress, Ottawa

Chair: Dr. Elaine Bernard, Executive Director, Trade Union Program, Harvard University, Cambridge, Massachusetts

Rapporteurs: Kevin Hayes, Canadian Labour Congress; Heather Crisp, Solicitor, Toronto City Hall, Toronto

Workshop Report: Jokelee Vanderkop

Workshop Paper: James M. Ham, Canadian Institute for Advanced Research, "A Review of the Issues: The Role of Government Policy and Education".

Session 1

The workshop purported to take an historical and demographic overview of changes within the labour force owing to technological advances and to look at the changes which have occurred in attitudes toward work, leisure, reward and gratification due to changing technologies. This was followed by an examination of the current issues, problems and concerns which face unionized employees, non-union employees and management. The objective of the workshop was to identify and understand these considerations and determine the appropriate role of government policy, education and unions in addressing these concerns.

Edmund F. Byrne, School of Liberal Arts, Department of Philosophy, Indiana University, Indianapolis, opened the workshop deliberations with his presentation on "Definitions and Preliminary Considerations." He defines ethical choice as any choice that is consistent with ethical standards, however it is arrived at. He describes technologies as being both "hard" and "soft" in that they are not only machines but organizational arrangements as well.

His presentation addresses five main questions: (1) When is a choice ethical? (2) Is it permissible in theory (as distinguished from practice) to segregate ethical considerations that arise in a decision-making process? (3) When are choices involving labour-impacting technologies ethical? (4) What arguments can be put forward to show that the ethical aspects of workplace technology belong front and centre on our public policy agenda? (5) How might the ethics of decisions about labour-saving technologies be placed on the agenda of policy-makers who prefer to limit their attention to purely economic or political considerations?

For the first question, he argues that a choice is ethical when its consequences are on balance more beneficial than harmful and involve no serious affront to basic human dignity. For the second question he points out that the decision-making process can be divided into various dimensions ranging from the psychological, social and economic to the ethical. In reality, however, the world is not divided up in this academic manner and no decisions can be made without ethical implications. The third question sends forth a stream of further questions such as: Under what circumstances should a new technology be adopted? What provisions should be made for those affected and by whom? Should maximum profit or only profitability be a determining consideration? What importance, if any, should be given to the investment of workers in their workplace? In responding to point three, he stresses the fact that all of these questions involve political and economic considerations but that neither politics nor economics can be exempt from the exigencies of ethics. This has unfortunately been the case in both socialist countries and in market economies. In answer to question four Byrne provides several examples from history to show that policies implemented without regard for "good ethics" have turned out to be "bad economics and bad politics" whether we look at the USSR and the collectivization of Kulak farms, China's population control program or mercantilism and laissez-faire practices in the UK and the Americas. For question five, Byrne advocates ethical universality in institutions as a way of counterbalancing the individualism which dominates public policy and corporate practices.

Session one served to raise issues as highlighted in Dr. Byrne's presentation but did not reach any conclusions.

Session 2

Session two raised five specific issues highlighted by Keith Newton, Senior Project Director, Visions of Canada in the Year 2000, Economic Council of Canada, in his presentation entitled, "Changes within the Labour Force due to Technological Advances" and by Daniel Benedict, CERLAC, Political Studies, York University in his presentation on "The Human Dimension." They were: (1) What is meant by the "flexible workforce?" Is saying that workers must be flexible fixing responsibility unfairly?; (2) Who should be educating workers and how should this be done?; (3) Why are political and other structures not adopting to workplace realities?; (4) What is the management prerogative versus worker participation and the democratization of workplace decision-making?; (5) What is the role of the non-unionized or unpaid worker?

Main Conclusions

The main conclusions were that technological change involves more than machines and includes organizational structure. Moreover, technological changes, even at the level of machines, come with their own bias. It is therefore necessary that human-centred ethics, rather than simply economic-centred ethics be considered in decisions affecting workers and their community.

Session 3

In session three, Fred Pomeroy, President of the Communications and Electrical Workers of Canada, Ottawa, stressed in his "Perspectives from Union Labour" that labour is not opposed to the introduction of new technologies but rather it is opposed to *how* they are introduced. Often new technologies only fulfil short-term corporate objectives and immediate financial gain and profit for those who own and control the technology. The implementation of new technologies has created a surge in job displacement and turned many full-time jobs into part-time jobs thus reducing the purchasing power of workers. The wealth and economic growth that is derived from new technologies is not directed so much to the creation of new jobs as it is to financing corporate takeovers. Moreover, those jobs that are created tend to be limited and repetitive. Many of the former skills are integrated in the functioning of the equipment, thus taking away from the human factor. This in turn reduces the full potential of the technology. The only recourse that workers have to stem this tide and keep up with changes in the workplace is through the use of collective agreements by modernizing contract language. Public attitudes to technological change also need to be changed and communicated to the public at large and to government.

Heather Menzies, adjunct professor at Carleton University in the Department of Canadian Studies, takes the discussion one step further in her presentation on "Perspectives from Non-Union Labour." She examines the polarization of post-industrial society into the working rich and working poor, those who control technology and those who are controlled by it and takes up the argument for the "unorganized." By this she refers to those whose interests are not represented by any specific organizational structure. These are (1) the children of the middle class, employed at the margins of the economy and holding what she calls "turnstile" or "Mcjobs;" (2) the middle class, and (3) the homemakers.

The division of labour leads toward a two-tiered pattern of highly paid, highly skilled executive professionals and those who hold "turnstile" or "Mcjobs." It is particularly the first group, the children of the post-war middle class who mostly end up in this precarious form of employment. Their jobs are usually part-time, not full year, or under short-term contract. Peoples skills, income and involvement with the job are no different when they leave than when they started. Moreover, they are "costlessly replaceable" because it is the software of the system which controls the knowledge, thinking and skills.

Menzies sees an erosion of the second group, the middle class, as society becomes more polarized with decision-making power and related information being controlled from the centre. Although the middle class still considers itself in control, there is a restructuring and downsizing taking place within this group. She states that "managerial control has been shifted into the centre of the now-integrated decision-making management-information systems of restructured corporations" which results in the middle class being "hollowed out quantitatively and qualitatively."

Homemakers too are affected. Technology has a vast impact on our personal or family values and traditions whether we tune into the news or "fast-forward meal preparation" with food processors and microwave ovens.

For Menzies, it is not a case of making doomsday predictions since, as she says, "we're all instruments of technological rationality." She warns, however, that we cannot assume that we are in control. Individuals, including the unorganized and organized workforce can too easily be "assimilated through total immersion in the technological context, and no longer be able to think of appropriate uses of technology except as expressions of technical values such as faster, cheaper or more technically efficient if they do not take control. Technological choices need to be negotiated if people are to control technology rather than be controlled by it.

A presentation on "Perspectives from Management" by Wendy Tupling-Guest, Labour Relations Officer, Canada Post Corporation, Vancouver discussed the concerns of management and employer in terms of efficiency and the requirement to remain competitive along with, in this case, the ability of management in Canada Post to remain receptive to technological change. She presents a strong, controversial position and raises three questions.

The first question is: What are the concerns of management and employers? In response, she argues, quoting David Stewart-Patterson, technological change and updating by Canada Post is not meant to displace jobs, but would in fact help "win back lost business and attract new business, and that would mean it could not only keep safe its existing jobs but go out and hire more postal workers." Also, it would take the drudgery out of the work and make it a safer, cleaner and more pleasant job. She stresses that Canada Post is now a business whose primary concern is "establishing, maintaining and expanding the business" to counter competition from its rivals. Consequently, to be successful and efficient, factors such as profitability and productivity need to go hand in hand with efficiency and competitiveness while balancing labour and capital.

The second question is "What is the attitude of management and employers to new technologies?" Here one can answer that the necessity of new technologies is not in dispute. In fact, not only is technological change accepted as a given, so is there the realization that the way business is conducted must be altered accordingly along with a readiness to change one's career or profession.

The third question asked what the employer position was toward employee concerns? Tupling-Guest says that a survey of the literature on this subject indicates that opposition to technological change is expectantly strong and vigorously expressed. This is particularly due to the fact that people find changes in their routine disruptive while there is a tendency to believe that technological change will require greater effort and threaten job security. By the same token, a survey conducted by Decima Research in 1985 showed that nearly 90 per cent of those who had been affected by technological change had benefitted personally from the use of technology. An Ontario Task Force on Employment and New Technology stated that the adoption of technology should not be impeded but rather it is necessary to "implement the technological change in ways which effectively and fairly deal with the legitimate interests of all affected parties ... ." A concern expressed by David Robertson and Jeff Wareham in a booklet entitled *Tech Change in the Auto Industry: CAW Technology Project* was that the effect of new technology would lead to "deskilling" and shift the balance of power within the workplace to the centre. Although certain minimum standards in collective agreements have been mandated in labour legislation, the Canadian government has not adequately addressed this problem. Tupling-Guest points out that in Canada, "the employer finds itself to be one party in an adversarial relationship, one which appears to lack the trust and confidence in the other party's ability or at least willingness to make responsible decisions affecting the future viability of the firm." What is necessary is an emphasis on co-determination between employers and employees as a means of setting out policies on wages, job protection and the regulating and securing of work conditions. She rephrases the question of "how does technological change impact on labour relations?" to "How does the climate of labour relations impact on the implementation of technological change?" In response, she cites Harold Dunstan who argues that it is not technological change which is the problem but rather general operating change. This becomes a question of whether the union should have any say in making operating decisions for a company when it may not be willing to make those tougher decisions which could effect the operating future of the firm. It becomes a matter of the effects of technological change on economic security for both the firm and the employee.

In closing, Tupling-Guest argues that employers must be responsible to their employees but she believes that employers should not be "obliged to retrain workers who can no longer fulfil their part of the contract, which is to exchange their labour for payment, when technology ... is the cause for it." This burden would lessen competitiveness. An economic rationale, however, would require that employees do retrain and reskill in order to keep up with technological change, and this, she argues, "ought to be one of the priorities of government in planning education curricula."

Main Issues

Some of the main issues that came out of this session were that: (1) the critical ethical issue underpinning technological change and the human factor is the distribution of power and its exercise; (2) people as workers, consumers and women, as a separate interest group, are stakeholders. Issues of ownership, therefore, need to be redefined; (3) Stakeholders need to be given the power to negotiate technological change; (4) there needs to be a reassessment in the division of process and the division of labour (i.e. skilling); (5) there has to be a rethinking of the decisions about technology itself which now excludes the concerns of the general public. At present, the main concern centres around business survival.

Main Conclusions

The main conclusions reiterated what has been pointed out in other workshops that technology is not value-neutral. Stakeholders have rights which need to be considered or work will continue to be defined in a master/servant relationship. The word "ethical" in business and labour relations must therefore encompass justice, participation, equity and fairness.

Session 4

The final session and wrap-up of the workshop concluded that the technology of work cannot be divorced from its social environmental context. The context for discussing technology is the human condition as experienced by men, women and children. All are stakeholders.

Technology was defined as the complete set of arrangements, practices and institutions through which human purposes are accomplished. Technology in context is never value-neutral. Everyone shares the responsibility for its design and use, and for its impact on individuals, on social relationships and on institutions.

Finally, institutions, as they are now structured, are a fundamental barrier to the empowerment essential to ensure the participation of all people in the design and use of technology to meet human needs. Systems design is not just an engineering speciality; it is a human mandate. Therefore, it is recommended that individuals and institutions develop the will to design and use technology to meet human needs.

In conclusion, James Ham of the Canadian Institute for Advanced Research in Toronto wrote a summary paper of the workshop, "A Review of the Issues: The Role of Government Policy and Education."

"A Review of the Issues: The Role of Government Policy and Education."

The Human Condition

At root we are discussing the human condition which, in mythical terms, follows from the eating of the apple from the tree of knowledge of good and evil in the Garden of Eden.

We cannot deny our capacity as homo sapiens to discover through the sciences and our capability as homo faber to ingeniously contrive technologies. No one has suggested that we be neo-Luddites.

The Division of Labour

The division of labour is rooted deeply in human experience. It was explicitly present in the making of Chinese bronze pieces, and in modern life, is associated with the fragmentation of processes and procedures.

The Centrality of Power

In the city states of Greece, the Roman Republic, the Chinese Empire, the Feudal States of the Medieval World, in the Islamic World, and in modern nation states, the procession and exercise of power is at the core of lived experience. In Western democracies, the dominant centres of power are in corporations and governments.

Associated with the locus of power in any society there is always that which is sacred. The sacred embedded in the locus of power in our society is money.

Characteristics of the Ethical

In our secularized, pluralistic society, it is not clear that there is a mutually agreed ground for moral discourse within which we can agree on the essence of the ethical. We use words such as fair, equitable, just and participatory. These words have no meaning except as used between persons. They are not "I" centred but rather are "us" centred. They imply respect and concern for personal dignity and fulfilment.

The Meaning of Technology

Technology is concerned with the dimensions of the world that we contrive for ourselves from cities to satellites, to machines, to corporations. Technology includes systems, processes, procedures, organizations and institutions.

Technology as contrivance is shaped by human intent and purposes and is therefore not something that in and of itself is neutral and becomes good or evil only through use or abuse. The expression of purpose is inherent in the contriving.

Ethics for Whom?

We are concerned with the ethics of the encounter with technology of persons, families, neighbourhoods, communities, corporations, governments, societies, as well as with the ethics of the consequences of such encounters.

The Worker's Encounter

The worker encounters technology as machine and as organization through the act of accepting employment which is historically characterized by a contract of relationship in the form of master-servant. The work experience is characteristically subject to prescriptive control.

While the division of labour has the potential to be in the nature of shared but distinctive tasks, it has, in the face of the automatizing of machines, processes and procedures of modern technology, become highly depersonalizing and deskilling for very many workers who have come to tend rather than to control the technology.

Displacement from particular forms of work is a personally radical consequence of ongoing technological change for many persons. The sequence of employments associated with volatile technological change fragments the experience of many workers and denies them the natural justice of cumulating seniority and pension benefits as the fair fruits of their commitment.

Informative technologies based in computer controlled systems are perceived to have the characteristic of enabling the concentration of control ever more centrally within the power structure of management. The great majority of workers have little if any opportunity to participate in, or even to be reasonably informed about technological change, the consequence of which may be personally catastrophic. The absence of the reality of sharing in the way things work is a personally stressful circumstance.

Society's Encounter

Societies have always been transformed in structure by technological change. The innovation of the iron plough and the three-field system of crop rotation in the early Middle Ages in Medieval Europe created the agricultural surplus that enabled the growth of towns and cities and the emergence of merchant class. These helped undermine feudal power and laid the basis for capitalism in modern democracies.

In our era, we observe a shrinking of the middle class accompanied by the growth of a class of great relative wealth, and the growth of a new poor. The latter is epitomized by a class of "contingent" labour working in full-time jobs that are increasingly becoming part-time where entry skills are the same as exit skills. In prosperous cities, this growing marginalized pool of persons does not have access to such amenities as affordable permanent housing.

Associated with this structural change is the division of human experience through the staccato character of the media and the technologizing of home and kitchen—a division of experience that deters reflection on and relaxed enjoyment of the deeper meanings of human relations. Indeed, we are confronted again with the implications of the eating of the apple in the Garden of Eden. In a profound way, a serially divided process dominates the expression of purpose.

The System of Corporate Power and Property

At the centre of the power structure of our society is the interplay between the power of corporations driven by the sacred of money and the power of governments divided by the secular pluralism of our times. Law treats the corporation as an abstract person, protects it with limited liability and empowers it to hold and control property and to delegate the expression of that power of control to management. The ownership of the property of corporations is in the hands of shareholders and is contingent only with regard to corporate debt. Workers and their communities and the institutions of society are stakeholders without property rights. Governments, in relation to the efficacy and power of corporations, characteristically provide infrastructure of water, roads, energy and communications. They tax to provide subsidies and incentives to corporations. In Canada, they fund the basic structures for education and health care.

Governments and the Sociopolitical Conscience

The regret that corporations express as a consequence of labour displacement and plant closures associated with the technological dynamic of our time is reflected socially in the design of the safety net of unemployment insurance and pensions. However, their lack of portability and cumulative vesting is an affront to natural justice and fairness. Unemployment insurance, unsupported by inoperative and humane means for "labour adjustment," is a dispiriting bin into which the displaced and unemployed are consigned just as we institutionalize the old.

The hazards and abuses of work are given social attention through health and safety legislation, workers' compensation, and labour legislation delimiting working hours, minimum wages and severance pay. No labour codes that bear openly upon the ethical dimensions of the consequences of technological change to workers and communities exist. To create such codes of social ethics is perceived by corporations to intrude upon the freedom of the corporate person.

Workers and Communities as Stakeholders

The basic human issue is that of creating means for workers and communities to be recognized and empowered to be the stakeholders that they are in the corporate system for the production of goods and the delivery of services. The issue is the same whether the corporation is private or public in character. There is a need for a communitarian approach to living in a transformatively technological era, a communitarian reality that puts technology in the service of persons rather than persons in the service of technology.

There is a profound need for critical awareness of the consequences of technological change in the lives of workers, communities and society. There is also a need to create a basis for the undoubted stakeholders to participate in and negotiate the processes and practices of such change.

The Role of Education and Training

Education derives from the Latin word *educo* which means to "lead out"—out of ignorance into critical understanding of context and history. Training concerns the acquiring of concrete skills.

There are five key elements of enablement for a person. These are:

- Innate ability
- Experience
- Skills
- Contextual awareness
- Conceptual understanding

There is a pressing need to infuse teaching at all levels of education and training leading to an open and critical contextual awareness of how each of us is embedded in an interdependent system. Contextual awareness is essential for empowering the expression of initiative and dissent for both the worker and the community.

Policy Directions

For governments the focus should be on empowering all stakeholders to participate and negotiate in the processes of technological change that create, destroy and always transform.

For the educational system the focus should be on the achievement of critical contextual awareness.

WORKSHOP 12: Technology and Society: Law Reform

Coordinators: Dr. Frederick Vaughan, Department of Political Studies, University of Guelph; M.A. Prabhu, Department of Justice, Ottawa; Lorna-Lee Snowie, Barrister and Solicitor, Guelph

Chair: Dr. Martha Bailey, Faculty of Law, Queen's University, Kingston, Ontario

Rapporteurs: The Editors

Most sectors of human behaviour are directly affected by the dual factors of ethics and technology, such as in work, leisure, health or the national economy. Yet the interaction in all these areas and others, are little understood, and even less appreciated.

Similarly, most areas of human activity—personal, commercial or corporate—are subjects of the law. The law—civil or criminal—guides, moderates, judges and/or regulates behaviour. Conceptually, the law, that is, justice, stands above society. Public perceptions of the law focus on the law as written or legislated, on lawyers and judges, on argumentation and judicial decisions, and upon those profound and troublesome issues where the law, rightly or wrongly, is expected to reveal wisdom and to arbitrate. As life in the contemporary and future world becomes more complex, with the corresponding generation of perplexing and troublesome situations, the law is increasingly called upon to enter into newer and, as yet, unchartered fields of jurisdiction. As a result the law, to a greater extent than ever before, is required to respond to process and the ramifications of how ethics and technology are intricately and critically enmeshed, both in cause and in effect.

Two areas, which were the primary subjects of discussion at the workshop, and where the law must consider the effects of ethics and technology, were abortion and aviation safety.

In the conference as a whole, as in many of the other workshops such as health, industry or the environment, questions of the law were inescapable. Ultimately, as the introduction of new technologies increases the complexity of life and raises new regulatory and juridical issues, the law, in train of the political system or at times in advance of it, is thrust into fields where legislation or legal principles may not be complete or serve as a sufficient guide. New and troublesome moral questions arise when the general public and special interests—whether or not they are adequately informed—plunge into controversy fuelled by differing or opposing social values.

It was not, therefore, the purpose of the conference organizers that workshop participants would necessarily resolve any particular issue; though fully anticipating the propensity of many to propound particular positions. The editors, in preparing this report, have focused their attention primarily upon the manner and questions in which the law approaches these issues, knowing full well that the controversies generated by the issues themselves penetrate every level of deliberation.

Abortion

The abortion issue stimulated by the paper presented by George Anastaplo [Loyola University, Chicago], "Ethics and Technology: The Problem of Abortion and the Law," revealed most of the moral and legal implications of changing lifestyles brought about by technologically induced transformation of societal systems. Not all implications were fully developed at the workshop. Indeed many would/might argue that the interaction between ethics and technology is obscure, claiming only the obligation of the law to define the generic/common conditions of a particular phenomenon and determine the parameters of permissible and impermissible behaviour.

The practice and moral implications of abortion are undoubtedly age old, varying in time and place. But the fact that abortion has become a very intense and highly polarized public issue is not an historical accident. The transformation of the economy, concentrated urbanization, and women in the workplace in greater numbers than ever before have generated a powerful movement for women's liberation. The media carry the issues of women's liberation and of abortion in every home and every school. At the same time technological medical advances make it possible for abortion to be carried out with little danger to the mother. Similarly other factors, the nuclear family, single parent families and singles lifestyles for both men and women, have greatly increased the demand for abortion as a matter of decision for individual women.

By the same token, where these radical changes in lifestyles of industrial countries, such as Canada, have brought the issue to the forefront of the national moral, political and legal agenda, new health and nutritional technologies have greatly increased the birth rate in the developing part of the world raising enormous problems as consequences of the exponential growth of the world's population.

In a global sense the first has assertively affirmed the individual rights of women, as contrasted with the implied rights of the fetus—the right to life—whereas the second signals deleterious national and global consequences through unrestrained population growth which in turn has generated large-scale programs of birth control. The social and moral effects of new technologies are often unforeseen or ill considered. Legislators and the law are unfortunately called upon, after the fact, to make moral judgments of profound consequences and possible social disruption.

As acknowledged in the law workshop, the law itself is compelled to enunciate fundamental principles at a time when traditional values and practices are called in to question and where the principles themselves, once enunciated, will have profound, perhaps radical, moral and social consequences. The law is being called upon to determine the nature of womanhood; to define life and when life begins, to determine the rights, if any, of the father; to determine the nature and permissibility of certain technological practices of abortion; to anticipate the currents of changing social values and yet not ignore long-standing traditions; to mediate between individual and societal rights; to determine whether or not abortion is a criminal act and by whom; and, among other matters, to consider the social costs and consequences of all these areas of decision.

In his presentation, "Ethics and Technology: The Problem of Abortion and Law," George Anastaplo stated that "technological problems have helped create the problems we now have. Technology has provided safe ways of performing abortions, at least in the early months of pregnancy, which is when most of them are performed. Indeed, an abortion operation is now evidently a safer activity than childbirth for the woman patient." He went on to say that, "technological developments have helped make recourse to widespread abortion both 'needed' and acceptable, citing the likely possibility that abortion pills may become safe to use and inexpensive to manufacture."

What we have, he said, "is a question of the relationship between the law and nature. How can the law determine the nature of life, when life begins, and at the same time deny a woman the control of her own body?" Dr. Anastaplo, while favouring personal choice, also stated that unlimited access to abortion would be unconscionable. In fact, he argued that such a policy would be fundamentally exploitative of women.

Not surprisingly, the workshop was divided on what principles and role the law should adopt on the abortion issue. Some spoke of patriarchal bias and exclusive focus on the fetus at the expense of women. There was intense discussion on whether abortion should be the subject of criminal law. The issues are very profound with many ramifications. They are a matter of cultural contrast and grave controversy, challenging the law to be all wise on the one hand, but to lean heavily on one side or another of the controversy.

Biomedical Experimentation on the Human Fetus

Another related moral issue of great significance—the matter of bio-medical experimentation—was also discussed. Here again there is the question of where life begins. When does the fetus become a human person? Everyone agreed that there should be respect for all life, at whatever stage of development. But that moral position, however valid, does not resolve the issue.

Should embryos and fetuses be treated as objects? The workshop participants were opposed. Yet advanced medical technologies are developing the use of fetal tissue as treatment or cure for genetic and possibly other diseases. The interface of ethics and technology becomes inescapable. The need for ethical consideration before, not after, research is undertaken has become a paramount issue, an issue which was treated in greater depth in the workshop on Research Administration.

This brings the discussion back to one of the major issues raised at the conference, is technology neutral? Here the answer was no. There is intent in the development of technology and purpose in its use. Many in the scientific community, however, as well as in the general public, argue that technology is nonetheless neutral, only the ultimate user has intent.

The law workshop participants all held the view that embryo and fetus research should be regulated through peer review, though without stipulation of guiding ethical principles and related operational criteria. Under the circumstances, which certainly took into consideration the then Canadian parliamentary debate on the matter of abortion, the workshop decided not to attempt development of an agreed set of recommendations.

Technology and Aviation Safety

In the ever growing complexity of the modern world the law reaches more deeply into new areas of activity created by advancing technologies. The second workshop panel focused on aviation technology and the law, based on a presentation by Dionigi M. Fiorita, barrister and former representative of Canada on the Council of the International Civil Aviation Organization. The three issues raised were aviation safety, advances in aviation technology, and government policies and laws.

Where does responsibility lie for aviation safety? What criteria should be both morally and practically adequate? Is it with the design and operation of an aircraft, with the enforcement of laws and regulations, or as determined by an accident investigation authority? There arise many ethical questions. Among them are the confidentiality of information attained from a voice recorder or other sources; the confidentiality of the physician/patient relationship of those who operate an aircraft, the codes of conduct of medical associations; and, the quality of independence and the related political, industrial and/or legal obligation and responsibility of an investigatory authority. Who is liable for what?

Advancing technologies, such as microwave landing systems and future air navigation systems, greatly enhance air safety. But can Third World countries afford microwave landing systems? Who should pay for and maintain them? And since future air navigation systems require an international satellite monitoring and communication infrastructure, who will be internationally managed and regulated? Another seemingly innocuous matter was raised by Mr. Fiorito, namely, the efficiency and convenience of computer reservation systems. But when they are owned by a particular airline, does the computer software first favour bookings on its own flights? The answer to that question is yes—this time raising the moral question of unfair advantage through a general service technology.

Each of these questions is one where the development and use of a technological artifact induces practical questions which almost invariably lead to ethical consequences. But few are simple questions where the law is readily clear and unequivocal. The law is an active participant in these processes, with each new development in aviation bringing forth political and economic issues as well as matters of efficiency, safety and privacy.

The main aviation issues raised, without attempts at resolution, were the imposition of high cost technologies on the Third World, the independence of accident investigators from regulations to ensure unbiased investigations, confidentiality of doctor/pilot-patient relationship, whether governments should regulate the use of computer reservation systems, and ultimately, what ethical levels of safety should a government require and how should they be implemented?

Conclusions

Clearly, many questions were raised. Few, if any, answered. But the law workshop, though it dealt fundamentally with only two issues, raised questions which are correspondingly relevant to many issues discussed in most other workshops, such as environment, research policy, industry and Third World development. The ethical implications of new technologies raise new political, economic, social and juridical questions, ultimately demanding a reconsideration of traditional values. Where these are lacking, the development of new ethical norms are necessary to guide society and individuals through the maze of current and future technological innovations.

Since the applications of these technologies are worldwide, we must recognize that in many cases legal norms will have to be universal, not solely derivative of one society, nation or culture. Whether we like it or not, technologies are bringing people together from all parts of the world. Will they and we be willing to accommodate national cultures to the requirements of a transnational world? Perhaps we may be pushed to cross the threshold for the ultimate discovery of natural law, or the creation of a universal substitute. In any case, the law—national, international or transnational—will be playing an even greater role in the shaping of the contemporary and the future world. Public consideration of these matters has only begun.

WORKSHOP 13: Technology and Ethical Choice in the Field of International Peace and Security

Coordinators: Dr. Terry Gardner, University College, University of Toronto; Dr. Alan Weatherley, Department of Zoology, University of Toronto; Dr. Janet Wood, Department of Chemistry and Biochemistry, University of Guelph

Chair: Dr. Seymour Melman, Department of Industrial Engineering and Operations Research, Columbia University

Rapporteur: Metta Spencer, Department of Sociology, University of Toronto

Ethical Problems Related to Peace and Security

Seymour Melman, who chaired the first session, proposed some definitions. Technology, he suggested, is "the application of the knowledge of nature to serve a social requirement." Security he defined as "circumstances that enable the continuance of human life and that ensure the self-governance of a community." And, while peace can (commonsensically) be defined as "the absence of war," that does not take us far in a period when war preparations have become the largest industry in the industrialized countries. Melman suggests, therefore, that peace is better seen as "the diminished power of the war-making institutions."

Conrad G. Brunk (Associate Professor of Philosophy, University of Waterloo) in his paper, "Nuclear Deterrence and Risk Assessment: The Hidden Values in Strategy," maintains that technology has values implicit within it that tend to shape it. It is not a value-neutral tool that has effects which depend on the "goodness" or "badness" of the user. Rather, the combination of science and tool-making create a special world view that contains implicit values that drive technology and are biased against other types of decisions. For example, Star Wars is a massive technological "fix" for problems of arms control and disarmament.

This means that the moral critique of foreign policy is not even taken seriously. Such a bias has even prompted peace groups to frame their own dissent in terms that conform to the same technological orientation. Occasionally peace groups do cast their arguments in moral terms, but more often they have argued that nuclear weapons are dangerous, that current nuclear policy is bad *risk-management*. This is a consideration that technologists can address.

Brunk has been examining the way scientific risk assessments are reviewed, such as in determining whether a certain chemical should be banned in Canada. He says that technological values (especially military ones) are hidden; they masquerade under the guise of being scientific, not ethical.

Lynn Trainer (Professor of Physics, University of Toronto), elaborating on Brunk's point, mentioned Jacques Ellul's conclusion that technology's internally driving force means that anyone with a more efficient technology will come to dominate.

Professor Dietrich Schroerer (Department of Physics, University of North Carolina at Chapel Hill) took exception to Brunk's position, mentioning that in fact, the Strategic Defense Initiative was developed precisely on ethical grounds, since Reagan objected to threatening innocent civilians. Brunk replied that, while Reagan had seemed to be taking the moral high road, this must be seen as a cynical piece of rhetoric, since it was based on portraying SDI as a defensive weapons system, whereas it is actually better described as an offensive system.

Anatol Rapoport (Professor of Peace and Conflict Studies, University of Toronto) expanded on Brunk's discussion of the risk assessment approach to decision-making. It is an approach that pretends to be objective. The fact remains, however, that every risk assessment not only calculates the probability of an event (and the alternatives to it) but also the utility of the event and the alternatives. Thus one must appraise, not only the risk of accepting Gorbachev's proposals, but also the risk of failing to accept them while he is in power. Assigning probabilities is generally subjective; certainly assigning a probability to nuclear war is subjective while the assessment of utility is always subjective. Brunk agreed, but said he had attended a conference of risk assessors, all of whom had denied that the process was subjective.

The question was raised as to whether it would be easier for us to understand the hidden values if we knew who was pushing the technology embodying them. Brunk, however, saw that approach as relying on a conspiracy theory, which is a mistake, since we are all part of the conspiracy. By participating in institutions (whether it be the Pentagon, universities, or the market for consumer goods), we participate in a system of rationality that is consistent with the manufacture, selling, and use of weapons. It does not suffice to pin the blame on powerful military interests, when the whole system is a seamless web.

Dr. Gardner, one of the workshop coordinators, pointed out a deficiency in considering military technology as a "seamless web": It doesn't give us any idea as to how to intervene in the problem. Brunk agreed that it is hard to know how to intervene but suggested that the answer must come from reaffirming such traditional values as seeing the quality of life as a value in itself, and in asking ourselves what we owe to future generations. Moral debates should be carried on explicitly as moral debates. Of course, there is no objection to assessing risks, so long as that is what one is actually doing; what is wrong is casting moral assessments in terms of risk-management.

Robert W. Malcolmson (Professor of History, Queen's University) in "The Great Deterrent: Nuclear Weapons and the Pursuit of Security" reviewed the historical development of the rationale for nuclear weaponry.

In 1957, Air Marshall Sir John Slessor called nuclear weapons a crucial counterweight to aggressive communism. The hydrogen bomb, Slessor wrote, "brings hope that no one will ever resort to war again." This provided an ethical endorsement of the technology.

However, the U.S. Air Force held that it should and did have a disarming first strike capability. General Nathan Twining, Chairman of the Joint Chiefs of Staff, insisted that nuclear bombs were not built for deterrence, but for use. That being so, the number of bombs really mattered; the nation's well-being depended on keeping ahead in the race.

Atomic warfare, Malcolmson suggested, should be viewed in its true light—as harmonious with American tradition: the use of machines. America needed to be on the cutting edge of military science. Americans historically have trusted in their superior capacity for rapid development of new technology; they had no fear of an arms race. Instead, the military services concluded that they had better learn to ride the wave of that technology and get a piece of the action. Soon, the plans for war included detailed scenarios for the use of nuclear weapons.

Malcolmson attributes the arms race largely to the American technological culture. Lately the Soviet Union has tried to emulate this process. Nuclear weapons have been treated as tokens of political determination—as ways of sending a message that America stands ready to take whatever steps are necessary. A buildup of nuclear weapons enhances the credibility of this posturing. The weapons makers are part of a self-sustaining system of weapons production. If a new weapon could be built, the odds were that it would be built, regardless of the implications for national security. MIRVs (Multiple Independently Targetable Re-entry Vehicle) were one example. SLCMs (submarine-based strategic ballistic missile) are another upcoming example. When the Soviets follow the U.S. lead and deploy their own SLCMS, the U.S. will be the loser, because it has more coastline. Eventually, the initial possessors of advanced weapons have usually become their victims.

The production of weaponry has not been rooted in the requirements that are perceived now, but in the requirements of the next decade and beyond. Planners imagine what the other side might do in the future and justify new weapons systems on the basis of their conservative assumptions. To move toward a safer future, it is necessary to adopt policies of minimum nuclear deterrence, and more creative diplomatic approaches.

In remarking on Malcolmson's paper, Dietrich Shroerer picked up an issue that had been raised during the preceding session: Reagan's motives for promoting the Strategic Defense Initiative. All U.S. presidents go through the same experience: they say that mutually-assured destruction is morally unacceptable, and they ask for an alternative. The military advisors then say that they need alternatives in terms of war-fighting. The war-fighting plan is the consequence of raising the question: "What else can you do?"

Malcolmson agreed with Schroerer's opinion that Reagan did personally have a strong moral view of the matter. It was a small group that put the SDI proposal together, horrifying most of his bureaucracy. The civilian hawks in the Pentagon came to accept it, however, as soon as they recognized it as a means of blocking arms control. That is, they saw that SDI would be perceived by the Soviets as an impediment to arms control and therefore they promoted it. There was no consistently pro-arms control group in Reagan's Washington.

Malcolmson cited Herbert York, who had pointed out that the structure of the nuclear age was determined before 1960. In the 1950s, this emphasis on war-fighting developed. It became part of a system that has been difficult to wind down. However, there is a lack of money and an erosion of the Soviet threat, so SDI will probably not be sustained in the 1990s. The hardware could not have been used any way. It was being built and displayed for symbolic purposes.

Professor Gardner asked about the genesis of America's "technological exuberance." Malcolmson replied that it goes back several generations. Right after World War II, the U.S. did not immediately commit itself to an arms race. Two years after Hiroshima, it only had twelve nuclear bombs. Stalin's tyranny and the Korean War fuelled the arms race.

Brunk suggested that there may have been a mundane consideration in the SDI decision: a desire to recover the technological edge that was being lost to the Japanese and others. He recalls having talked to European NATO politicians and military people in the heady days of SDI, who said that SDI probably wouldn't work, but who supported it any way because it is "the leading edge." They believed that the spinoffs were the real thing.

Professor Melman, the workshop chair, mentioned Tom Gervasi's research, which itemized the principal identifiable technological innovations in nuclear weaponry. Of some 35 such innovations, the U.S. was the innovator in all but one.

Professor John Valleau (Department of Chemistry, University of Toronto) emphasized Malcolmson's point about nuclear weapons as a declaration:

> This is the crux of the problem. A declaration of superness is being made by this superpower. This removes any conflict with other major powers, such as the USSR, who cannot interact with the U.S. and therefore cannot interfere with American purposes. The superpower conflict is removed from the arena of economic competition. All kinds of actions can be taken (Grenada, etc.) because no one has to fear that the superpowers will confront each other.

Feasible Strategies for Change

Dietrich Schroerer presented a paper entitled: "Who Controls Arms Control?"

Schroerer admitted having once laid a bet that the INF Treaty would never happen. His own thinking is based more on technical feasibility than on ethics. He asks: What kind of criteria do we need to have for control? To approach the question, it is useful to compare it to the moon shot. What criteria were required for it to take place?

(1) It must be seen as feasible.

(2) The objective must have been part of the debate over the project.

(3) There must be leaders whose philosophies support long-term payoffs.

(4) There must be a dramatic occasion for the decision that creates an environment in which the objective seems politically feasible.

There is another set of criteria for arms control:

(1) Consensus must exist on the feasibility and desirability of the goal. (For example, it must be verifiable, and the cost-benefit calculations must have been analyzed.)

(2) There needs to have taken place a political debate, so the political climate favours the goal.

(3) The President has to be actively in favour of it.

(4) A dramatic occasion must arise to promote it; most likely this will come when the other side is ready to cooperate or even push us.

All four of these criteria are controlled by experts with different sets of technical expertise and with values that differ from those of ordinary people.

Past attempts show the necessity of the criteria. The CTBT proposal of 1958–63 failed, despite the approval of the public, of Eisenhower, and of the USSR, for technical reasons. There was no consensus that such a treaty could be monitored.

The INF Treaty achieved technical feasibility when the Soviets accepted verification. The political consensus had been achieved by 1979. This was a case where, purely by accident, the bargaining chips worked. The existence of the cruise and Pershing missiles gave the Soviets reason to accept the INF treaty. If a less amenable Soviet leader had been there, we would be facing a continued arms race.

What about the START Treaty? There is no strong U.S. leadership and no political clamour for it. The Soviets want it, but Schroerer is not optimistic about it until its objective is better defined. A conventional weapons treaty is also questionable, though the public and the Soviets favour it; political leaders in the U.S. do not. The current enthusiasm for arms control comes from the fact that Soviet cooperation has improved. But leadership has not improved. Not everything is under our control. We cannot force arms control when the time is not ripe, but we can get ready for it. When the opportunity comes, we won't have to debate it extensively. We can mobilize public opinion—on a long-term, but not on a short-term basis.

Seymour Melman pointed out that the term "arms control" was invented by the to-be advisors to President Kennedy. The idea of disarmament—reversal of the arms race—was swept out of the public discussion. It became unprintable. Not a single research grant was given by the foundations to study disarmament.

Technology and Public Perceptions of National Security

Brigadiers General W.R. Dobson and now-retired L.T. Rowbottom (National Defence, Canada) have attempted to predict the kind of military structure that will be needed 25 years from now. They consulted military professionals, political leaders, academics, institutes, and organizations. Many services will have to change in view of the aging population. The younger generation no longer vote according to their grandfathers' platform, but in terms of the party.

For the Air Force to remain at its present level, it needs more than a 3 per cent growth. To improve its capability it will require a 20 per cent increment. However, the same can be said for every institution in Canada. (Everyone is going bankrupt; it isn't just Gorbachev.)

Every nation in the world is going to have an army—either its own or somebody else's. The Canadian forces are going to have to do more with less. However, Dobson and Rowbottom reject the proposition that we live in an age of pervasive technology that is directed toward human beings. The individual is re-emerging on his or her own account, rather than as a slave to technology. People are coming to the fore. The age of the nation-state is passing, and this invites us to think of ethics in a different form, not a positivist notion. Our people are not enslaved to their technologies. The absence of justice still brings war.

The Profession of Arms will be working in a time of reduced budget and environmental crisis.

Dobson and Rowbottom predict that government will thin out. The insolvent jurisdictions of nation-states are causing changes. Societies have difficulty keeping hospital wards open; they will find it hard to keep their militaries going. There are no new ethical problems raised by these new technologies. The Third World War is likely to be more moral than ideological. Wars are taking place in the streets right now. We have to evaluate the kind of equipment that we need to do what the people of Canada want us to do. As Anatol Rapoport suggested, we should look at the military as we look at the tobacco industry. We are going to have to find other things for those people to do—such as disaster patrol, perhaps.

Anthony Di Filippo (Department of Sociology, Lincoln University) presented a paper dealing with "The Social Consequences of Military Expenditures." He noted that a nation is secure only if its economy is growing. Productivity growth in manufacturing has been extremely healthy in both Japan and West Germany, but sluggish in the United States. Basic to productivity growth is the use to which a nation puts its capital resources. Another important factor is international trade positions. In the past ten years, the U.S. has been losing out in markets—including hi-tech markets—where Japan has come to dominate. The manufacturers' trade deficit has grown in the U.S. from $5 billion in 1978 to $22 billion in a decade. In Japan and West Germany, emphasis is placed on the civilian use of technology, not military. In the U.S. about one third of the technical talent is being used for the military. Both Japan and West Germany devote a higher ratio to research and development, as a proportion of GNP, without even taking out the military portion.

The U.S. electronics industry is nearly nonexistent. Most of the consumer electronics market is held by Japan and part of it is held by West Germany. An emerging hi-tech area is superconductivity. U.S. manufacturers are reluctant to touch it because profits are not to be made in the short-term. Both the Japanese and West Germans have invested heavily in superconductivity, despite the fact that the profits will be in the future. In those two countries, there are civilian efforts combined with government policy.

What is the solution? A planned conversion from military to civilian economy. A questioner pointed out that before the U.S. can consider that, there has to be more trust between the superpowers. Japan and West Germany do not have that kind of rivalry with another superpower. Di Filippo replied, "Conversion could be planned before the disarmament agreement is reached."

Conrad Brunk noted that the point is usually made in the U.S. by saying that Japan and West Germany are getting a free ride, and that they should share the burden that the U.S. has been bearing.

DI Filippo said that the military expenditure will in any case harm the economies.

John Valleau expressed uneasiness about Di Fillippo's paper being so focused on national economies. That is not where the problems lie. We have to redesign our economies to take care of disparities between the South and the North. The U.S. has had two main strands to its strategy: global containment and global entertainment. How can the U.S. add a new strand to its strategy?

Another participant criticized the paper for "mixing wishful thinking with reality." It would be nice if we could simply decide that we want peace. You cannot say that war is caused by the instruments of war. In the future, there will be many small, self-contained, inexpensive weapons that are likely to be more available on world markets. The demands for these devices conflict with the established powers. Factions with very limited resources are going to have more military influence than ever before.

William Klassen (Principal, St. Pauls United College, University of Waterloo) observed that there has been very little talk about ethics here—just technology. Will the ethical questions be addressed?

Applications of Technology in the Furtherance of Peace and Security

Alan Weatherley (Professor, Department of Zoology, University of Toronto) presented a paper, "Use and Deployment of the 'Military-Industrial Complex' in Improved Times for Peace and Security." Professor Weatherley began by stating his conviction that, however it happens, disarmament will occur. The continued existence of large military classes is inimical to furtherance of peace and security. To convert them will demand great efforts. One aspect of achieving this goal is to frame appropriate oaths to military personnel. The Canadian Forces pledge to bear full allegiance to Queen Elizabeth. We should have oaths swearing service to society's interests and not follow illegal orders. In such a case, the military will become a sort of police force, with the task of defending the state from sabotage and from external attack.

All countries will profit from conversion in the long-run, but governments have to cooperate during the transition period, or there will be hardship. Peace groups need to develop scenarios as to how to disarm industries and military units. During the transition, surveillance systems are needed, and the military are good at that. Technologies of remote sensing, submarine detection, seismic system will come more fully into use. Teams of experts in arms disposal will have to be deployed in every part of the globe. The technologies that will increase are: better health standards; agriculture and land use strategies; waste disposal; production methods that create minimal noxious wastes; public transit systems; communications systems; computerized information systems; safe and automated mining techniques; and building techniques. The savings from military technology will be channelled into these things.

Dr. Schroerer took exception to this conclusion. "Are the sources of those problems," he asked, "really to be solved by what you get out of the military? Take health, for example. The problem with health in the U.S. is the poor distribution of services."

Mr. Lavoie (teacher, Notre Dame Secretarial College, La Prairie, Quebec) also expressed concern about the list, but primarily because conversion will affect many people's jobs. "One of the main oppositions to conversion," he said, "is the fear of losing jobs."

Professor Gardner called attention to the Tiananmen Square massacre. "This is part of the problem that Alan is trying to address by designing the appropriate oath. The military people who made the decision had to decide who—the students or the government—really represented the people to whom their loyalty was given." General Rowbottom said, "The militia soldiers had only live ammunition to fire, because they had no rubber bullets. They had only one choice: to fire on them or not. In Canada, we would have had another option." Seymour Melman made mention that "Four days ago, there was a dispatch to the N.Y. Times about the formation of a union of Soviet military. One was a General who had been cashiered out of the army and the Communist Party for refusing to fire on the people in a disorder a few years ago."

Anatol Rapoport's paper was about "Knowledge of Technology as an Aid in the Struggle for Peace." Professor Rapoport decided to enlarge upon the ethical side by speaking about addiction—a state where one has certain needs and the fulfilment of them only creates a greater need. The satiation never comes. We have certain non-addictive needs, which are typically cyclic; they are allayed for a while and then again increase until the next satisfaction. With addictive needs, this is not the case.

Not all addictions are harmful, but one type certainly is: the addiction to power. Technology is also addicting. Its success created an optimistic belief that it will go on and on, and that all problems will be solved. Americans may be especially prone to this addiction.

Technology has its own momentum. Weapons are designed without questioning how they are to be used. The scientist discovers something; the engineer says we can build it; the strategist then says we can use it. It is said that you can't disinvent nuclear weapons. But you can't disinvent the guillotine either. You can find another job for the hangman; you don't have to hang him.

Institutions are notoriously mortal: slavery, the inquisition, human sacrifice and so forth. There is no reason why war cannot be abolished.

The fetish of quantification is most prominent when it comes to arms control. The quantification of weapons is a fraud. It is like claiming you have to have a fair trial before you can burn a witch. All this is irrelevant, and serves only to keep the war system going. There is absolutely nothing that is worth going to war for. If the establishment is to be abolished, of course we have to take care of the people. But that is just the same as taking care of the hangman.

A questioner interjected: "War and strife will always be with us. You can't abolish them." Rapoport replied, "I didn't say strife. I said war." The questioner then asked, "How can you abolish war?" to which Rapoport said, "There is a technological solution for abolishing war. Abolish weapons. Without weapons you cannot have war. There are whole sections of the world where war has been abolished. I cannot imagine a circumstance under which the Danes would make war on the Swedes. I divorce hatred from war. They are not related ... But we might define peace as the absence of war, and security as the absence of threat. If you hold that definition, disarmament is an imperative. When do people feel secure? When they are not threatened. Therefore, in order to have security, you must have disarmament."

Seymour Melman spoke on "The Economics of Militarism." He began by describing the magnitude of the U.S. Defence Department, which is the largest entity in the world. Its powers gradually have been concentrated in one person, the President.

A misunderstanding of economics was created by the experience of World War II that casts a shadow to the present. In that war, the U.S. produced both guns and butter. Consumption increased. From this, economists inferred that the U.S. could have both guns and butter indefinitely. They also observed that the high level of employment induced by war production finally ended the mass unemployment of the Great Depression. Hence they were convinced that Keynesianism was a proper political strategy for the U.S. and that the government could be used to regulate market demand. Military Keynesianism is still believed in, from right to left, in the U.S.

The consequences of a permanent war economy differed from those anticipated. From 1947–87 the budgets of the Department of Defense amounted to $7620 billion (in 1982 dollars). Compare that to the national wealth of the U.S.—the money value of the plants and equipment of the U.S. industry—which amounted to $7292 billions.

The military cost had been more than sufficient to replace all that is man-made on the face of the United States. Moreover, the process of cost-minimalizing (which was standard inside U.S. industry) was displaced by cost maximizing. At the same time, there has been an avoidance of discussing the limits of military power. There is also an avoidance of discussing the alternatives to the arms race, so strong is the ideological fix. Yet now we are facing the idea of economic conversion. The idea is to plan to shift to civilian work, with the planning done in a decentralized way. House Resolution 101 was designated by the Speaker of the House, Jim Wright. It mandated that every base with 100 or more persons must set up a committee to plan for redesigning and re-using the facilities. Half of the members are named by the manager, half by the working people themselves. The law mandates occupational retraining for managers and engineers who have been in the military for a number of years. The bill provides relocation allowances, and links together the state employment computers. It envisages a considerable movement of people.

A key idea in disarmament is the cessation of military production. In the absence of a plan, this would put millions of people on the streets. Economic conversion planning is taking place in Germany. The Social Democratic part is headed by Gert Weisgierken, with members in principal trade unions. In Italy, Professor Amaldi heads it. In the Soviet Union, there was established in late September a national commission with a membership of 20 to promote economic conversion from military to civilian. They will be financed by the Academy of Sciences. In the U.S., a National Commission for Economic Conversion and Disarmament functions in Washington. It includes the presidents of the Machinists, Chemical Workers, Steelworkers Union, Clerical Workers, Mayor Andrew Young, J.K Galbraith, Lloyd Dumas, and Marcus Raskin. Melman chairs that commission. They are publishing a series of briefing papers and are trying to bring this to the attention of the public.

Christopher Trump (The Association of Colleges of Applied Arts and Technology of Ontario (ACAATO), formerly of Aerospace) spoke about the development of PAXSAT and the International Space University.

Mr. Trump said that he had attended a meeting of the Canadian Defence Industry in Ottawa during the previous week, and that the mood there had been mournful. The bold initiatives of Gorbachev have greatly reduced the prospective demand for arms.

Military people tend to plan their next wars on the basis of the experience of the preceding war. In World War II, the element of surprise played a major part in determining the success of an attack. Today, however, the technology of surveillance has been developed to such an extent that surprise attacks are no longer possible. This is largely because of the use of spy satellites in space.

Several years ago, Ron Cleminson, of External Affairs, visited SPAR Aerospace to discuss the possibility of developing such a satellite in Canada. His opinion was that the existence of such surveillance systems in space would create the conditions under which the superpowers could reasonably sign an agreement banning numerous categories of weapons. This program was adopted and so, for several years, Canada has been working on "PAXSAT."

PAXSAT is part of a growing industry—the technology of communications. Indeed, space communications is the only commercially viable use of space. It is the expansion of communications systems that have permitted Mr. Gorbachev to do many of the things that he has done that are reducing the risk of war.

Another effect of communications programs could be seen in the changes that went on in East Germany. The German Democratic Republic had been unable to block certain television programs, and for that reason they had decided to permit *all* TV programs from West Germany. They even put in cable so that towns that were situated in valleys could pick up Western programs. The spread of information resulting from this technology had political implications with which we are all now familiar.

Mr. Trump also described the development of the "Space University," since its inception at MIT three years ago. It was decided to raise about $1 million for the purpose of inviting young people of varied professional backgrounds from several different countries to meet for ten weeks in the summer. SPAR helped contribute to that fund. This past summer 125 students came together to discuss their special areas of expertise in relation to issues concerning outer space. Canada sent 10, the Soviet Union 12, the United States 28, and there were students from Brazil, Japan, Kenya, and other nations.

The Space University has become so successful that nations are now competing for the honour of hosting the next sessions. West Germany competed against Strasbourg, France. Canada will be the host in 1990, Moscow in 1991, and Japan in 1992. The Canadian sessions will be situated in Toronto for nine weeks and in Montreal for one week.

The chief value of this project is not technological, but moral. The participants come to view their own work from a more inclusive perspective, one in which their clientele comprises the whole of humankind.

The Formulation of Proposals for the Plenary

During the rest of this final session, the workshop turned toward the project of developing a set of proposals to be brought to the plenary. That effort was coordinated by Professor Metta Spencer, (Department of Sociology, University of Toronto) who prefaced the activity with some observations about what had, and what had not, emerged during the preceding discussions.

Ethics had not occupied a primary place in the conversations. She suggested that this may have been the case because of our individualistic conception of the nature of ethical problems. The term "ethics" usually refers to personal moral decisions. When we deal with the moral effects of technological innovations, on the other hand, we are not normally confronting personal moral decisions, but rather what has been called "structural evil"—societal, institutional arrangements that encourage certain kinds of outcomes and foreclose others. To deal with structures that produce decisions detrimental to human beings, we would do well to address the incentives and constraints that operate in existing social institutions. One popular slogan today is to "think globally and act locally." However, Spencer suggested that "local" action need not be regionally specific but may rather be devoted to those concerns in which one is already engaged.

In this workshop, the majority of participants were academics. Accordingly, for them "local" action might be devoted to improving the institutions in academic life that produce research that is not socially useful—research that addresses problems arising from previous studies, but which may not be problems for which humankind needs solutions. The institutions that encourage such misguided efforts are to be found in the mandates under which committees review research proposals for funding, or allocate rewards for meritorious academic work. Particular values are embodied in these social structures, but one would not normally think of the dilemmas of grant reviewing bodies as "ethical" in nature. Nevertheless, the most fateful good and evil choices involving technology are most often made in the context of such structures, and not in the context of private moral deliberations. Spencer suggested that, when we formulate our specific recommendations, we pay attention to the improvement of structures, such as the grant-review example she had cited, and not be led astray by the individualistic implications of the term "ethics."

When the group turned to the process of crystallizing specific proposals, what was remarkable was the exceptional consensus that emerged. The issues that were posed were evidently viewed in a similar way by all the participants.

Main Issues Raised

Malcolmson reviewed the historical development of nuclear weapons technology, which he said had to be explained largely in terms of the American exuberance about machines. The Americans' tradition led them to believe in their own ability to keep any technological lead. However, it was not long until such plans included scenarios for war-fighting. Nuclear weapons also became symbolic tokens for superpower "resolve," potent enhancers of credibility. Technology led; whatever weapons could be developed were developed. Also, planners work with anticipated requirements ten to fifteen years hence. There was a dispute as to whether Reagan's motives (moral aversion) toward nuclear war-fighting prompted the SDI decision. Were the hawks eager to use it because it would be an impediment to arms control?

Conclusion

We are still talking about disarmament and the arms race in technological, not moral, terms. The economic success of Japan and West Germany can be attributed to two factors: (a) the business leaders' willingness to invent for long-term profits, not short-term, and (b) the greater capital investment in the civilian sector, as compared to the U.S. expenditure on weapons production.

If one engages in risk-assessment as a criterion in decision-making (and, of course, that is one legitimate consideration), it is important to realize that this process is primarily subjective. Moreover, one should acknowledge the existence of risks and utilities involved in both options. Otherwise the reasoning is deceptive. Primarily, however, what is needed to approach the management of technology on humane grounds is to revive basic moral principles as considerations and criteria that are to have an important place in the decision-making process.

WORKSHOP 14: Ethical Choices in the Development and Support of Research and Research Administration"

Coordinators: Dean Larry Milligan, Office of Research, University of Guelph; Dr. George Renninger, Department of Physics, University of Guelph; Dr. Janet Wood, Department of Chemistry and Biochemistry, University of Guelph

Chair: Dr. Kenneth Davey, Vice President, Academic, York University

Rapporteur: Dr. Ursula M. Franklin, Professor Emeritus, Department of Metallurgy and Material Sciences, University of Toronto

Presenters: Dr. Henry Duckworth, Chancellor, University of Manitoba, "Physicists and Atomic Energy;" Drs. Edwin and Julia Levy, Quadra Logic Technologies and University of British Columbia, "A Research Priority: Science and Technology, Government and Ethical Choices;" Dr. Michael McDonald, Department of Philosophy, University of Waterloo, "Putting Ethics on the Research Agenda;" Justice T. David Marshall, Canadian Judicial Centre, "Biotechnological Advances and their Relation to Rules"

The request to summarize the events of the workshop and the outcome of the deliberations has turned out to be a very difficult task for me. It is equally hard to reflect on the experience of the workshop, as it was just one event in an extremely multi-faceted conference.

In part, the difficulty of summing up may also be due to the fact that the workshop was attended by participants of very divers background and experience. They never gelled into a coherent group in order to work together on a common task.

There was also no clarity regarding a common task, since the mandate and goals of the workshop appeared to be too large and complex for those gathered. The pre-conference material had made it clear that … " the workshop on Ethical Choices in the Development, Administration and Support of Scientific Research will address our need to apply ethical judgement within that research process." The workshop organizers had also indicated that … " our primary objective in the Research workshop will be to prepare a publication for use by future members of grant selection panels." It may not be surprising that a group of participants ranging from senior academicians and research administrators to graduate students, and spanning the realm of science from pharmacology and microbiology to nuclear physics and petroleum engineering—though fortified by two philosophers and one lawyer—found the workshop goal impossible to meet.

Despite the failure to meet the overall goal of the workshop, all participants were enriched by the views of colleagues they would not have encountered but for this workshop and conference.

It became clear to all just how complex funding and administration of research in Canada has become. Many considerations, not related to science or research, are today deeply embedded in the supporting mechanisms for science and technology.

The term "stakeholder"—not really common currency among research administrators even five years ago—was used quite frequently during the workshop discussions. Those responsible for the administration of large research budgets expressed the view that the mandate of the institution and the interests of the stakeholders (such as the industrial funders of research) had laid down—for better or worse—a binding frame of reference for their own decision-making.

Several young researchers were very concerned about the steering effects of funding on their own careers. To what extent, they asked, would their desire to be part of vigorous and novel research require from them the acceptance of research questions asked by others? What say would they have in the use or application of their research? How and from whom could they learn about the broader implications of research in their field, about stakeholders and their influence? Sadly, few of their elders had viable answers or practical suggestions.

Throughout these discussions on mandates, stakeholders, the steering effects of funding and the problems of researchers concerned with the use of their findings, the philosophers in the group were of great help. Their contributions made it clear that scientists could not hope for an "ethics doctor" who could give them detailed prescriptions for ethical conduct or who would make ethical decisions for them.

Only by means of ongoing interdisciplinary collaboration could ethical considerations become an integral part of research and research administration. In such collaborations, scientists and philosophers are at all times both teachers and learners.

The four C's of Professor MacDonald's paper—"CONTACT, COLLABORATION, CONSULTATION and COMMUNICATION"—found resonance in many of the workshop's discussions. The first of the workshop's concluding recommendations that ... "ethical considerations in scientific and technical research are not add-on items" ... reflects these discussions.

In general, the recommendations and the concluding questions are a fairly good summary of the discussions and bear repeating here:

(1) Ethical considerations in scientific and technical research are not add-on items. Time and resources must be allocated to the process of discerning ethical dimensions and integrating ethical decisions into scientific and technological research. It is both a personal and an institutional responsibility for all those involved to become informed about ethical issues in scientific and technological research. This group includes not only researchers, administrators and those who contribute funds from the public and private sector, but also the end users and those affected by the application of the reseach results. The input of the latter community should be actively solicited.

(2) Ethical issues must be integrated into research administration and practised at all levels. Since all citizens are competent to raise ethical concerns, all share that responsibility. For example, Canada's granting Councils should work with interested citizens to formulate questions that raise ethical issues. Those questions should be disseminated to all those whose research is supported, directly or indirectly, by public funds.

FIGURE 1: THE RESEARCH TERRITORY

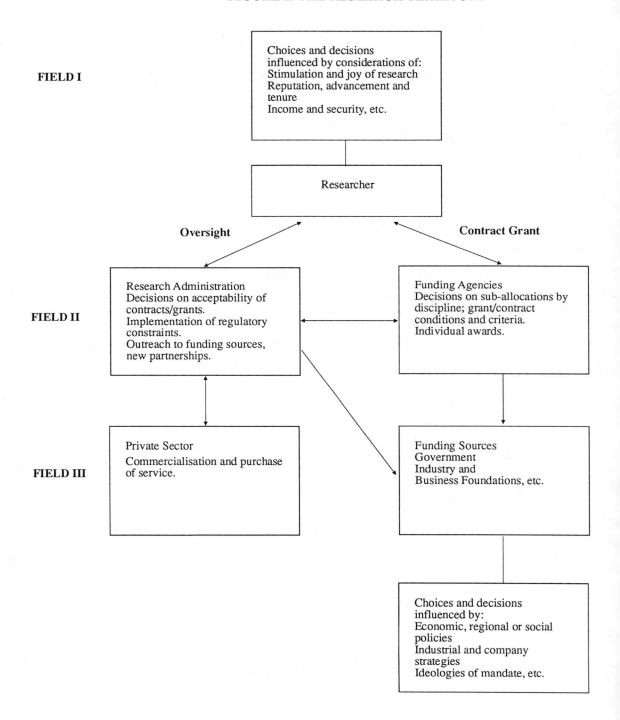

(3) Researchers and institutions in both the public and the private sector have a responsibility to make society aware of the ethical and societal impact of their research and to be sensitive to feedback from society on ethical matters. University researchers have a special responsibility both by example and possibly by more formal arrangements to demonstrate to their students the importance of ethical considerations in the planning and execution of research.

Much frustration for the workshop participants arose from their inability to visualize or agree on means to carry out the recommendations or to address the questions raised beyond abstract academic discourse. To the rapporteur it appeared that the only common ground that existed among most participants was the view that any ethical considerations were part of the decision-making **of others**. Such decisions could occur prior to their own research (i.e. via mandate or funding parameters) or after completion of their work (i.e. by the use of the research results).

Most participants, seeing themselves as unquestionably ethical, perceived the locus of ethical decision-making as being external to their own activities. There appeared to be considerable uncertainty as to who should exercise ethical judgements and at what point or points of the research process such judgements could be entertained.

In order to facilitate and focus the deliberations of the workshop, the rapporteur developed a schematic representation of the "research territory" and introduced it into the final workshop session. The scheme—illustrated in Figure 1—was not intended to be all inclusive or complete; it was only to serve as a map to locate areas of decision-making. Such a map can help to identify the different parties involved in research endeavors as well as their respective agendas.

Figure 1 consists basically of three interacting fields. Field I centres around INDIVIDUAL RESEARCHERS who may, though, be part of a group of researchers. Field II encompasses the FUNDING AGENCIES as well as the RESEARCH ADMINISTRATION of the institutions that receive grants and contracts. Field III represents the FUNDING SOURCES from whom the funding agencies receive allocation.

The personal decisions of the RESEARCHERS are influenced by the challenge and stimulation of the research *per se*; however, considerations of reputation, promotion, income and advancement are also part of the individual researcher's response to funding opportunities—or the lack thereof.

The choices before the Researchers, then, are related to the subject of their own research (i.e. do they wish to work on a particular problem, in a particular sub-discipline?) as well as to funding sources and grant or contract conditions. After all, no one *has* to do research if the subject matter or the conditions of a grant are on ethical grounds repugnant to the researcher.

Researchers are expected to assume personal responsibility for the conduct of their research and for the integrity and veracity of the results. Researchers are also expected to reflect and report on the research methodologies used, particularly on the problems of biases that may be embedded in their research designs.

By applying for grants or contracts, researchers interact directly with the FUNDING AGENCIES, although the research administration of their institution is charged with the oversight and enforcement of the grant/contract conditions. Funding Agencies have to make decisions as to the sub-allocation within their own budgets (i.e. what fraction of a budget should be allotted to specific tasks or areas of applications?) and on each particular request.

How and by whom the allocation decisions of the various funding agencies—public or private—are made, was one of the unresolved questions in the workshop. It was equally unclear how ethical decisions (not to speak of *what* ethical decisions) could enter into the allocation process. Within FIELD II of the map, the activities of RESEARCH ADMINISTRATION reach today beyond grant/contract supervision into active marketing of research facilities and research results.

Clearly, ethical questions for the institution will arise from such activities. Is every source of funds, every commercial partnership, equally acceptable to the institutions, even if it is acceptable to the researcher? Who can make these decisions? What are their guidelines and who will have input on such deliberations?

Finally, FIELD III illustrates the area of FUNDING SOURCES. Here the decision-makers are those who supply the funds that the funding agencies distribute. The levels of such funds, as well as any constraints accompanying them, affect many of the decisions in Field II.

The funding sources may be public (such as federal or provincial agencies, universities) or private (such as foundations or industries—sectorially or individually). Each funding source contributes money for research as a consequence of particular policies or priorities, not necessarily related directly to the pursuit of research. Governments may consider research funding as an aid to regional and economic development or as an instrument of social policy. Funding of further research may offer a welcome rationale for postponing political or regulatory action. Thus a series of fundamental questions arise within Field III, particularly with respect to the allocation of public funds—whether this occurs solely by governments or in partnership with industry.

Considering the proper use of public funds, one may ask how the levels of allotments and the constraints accompanying them were determined. Who is part of the decision-making process? How transparent and public is the process? Do the grant receiving institutions or their researchers have any role to play in the decisions within Field III? Is there a role for the public, their elected representatives or for special interest groups (for instance legal or professional associations, environmental groups, consumer or peace organizations)?

Using Figure 1 as a map, the workshop participants formulated the concluding recommendations and questions cited above.

In the opinion of this rapporteur any future workshop in the area of "Ethical Choices in the Development, Administration and Support of Scientific Research" should be preceded by a great deal more preparation of the participants and should be conducted in a much firmer structural framework.

FINAL PLENARY
DELIBERATION TO ACTION

Round-table: Common Purpose, Common Action, the Search for a Synthesis

Guests

William Winegard, *Minister of Industry, Science and Technology, Ottawa*

Francisco Sagasti, *Chief of Strategic Planning Division of The World Bank, Washington*

Lutz Baehr, *Management Team Director of the UN Centre of Science and Technology for Development, New York*

Ntombi Gata, *Assistant Director, Department of Research and Specialist Services, Ministry of Lands, Agriculture and Rural Resettlement, Zimbabwe*

Elaine Bernard, *Executive Director, Trade Union Program, Harvard University, Cambridge, Massachusetts*

Peter Hamel, *Anglican Church of Canada, Toronto*

Alan Thomas, *Ontario Institute for Studies in Higher Education, Toronto*

Ursula Franklin, *Professor Emeritus, Department of Metallurgy and Material Sciences, University of Toronto*

Kevin Hays, *Senior Researcher, Technical Services, Canadian Labour Congress, Ottawa*

Eugene Critoph, *Vice-President, Strategic Technology Management, Atomic Energy of Canada, Ottawa*

William Winegard

I am pleased to be here for two reasons. First because I think the results of this Conference will be of some significance to the Government of Canada and I am quite prepared to help you take those recommendations to the government. Secondly, I am pleased to be here because obviously you all thought the Conference was important enough to be held in my riding.

The issues and the recommendations before you, as well as the things you have been discussing, really comprise a pretty basic and, I think, complex set of questions. Perhaps it boils down to what is the place of ethics on our agenda. I use the word "our" here to include both us as individuals—which I think often gets lost in the discussion—and, in my particular instance, the role of government; that is the collective agenda that we all face.

To my mind, the question that conjures up is, "What is the role of government in a reasonably complex modern state?" That is a question with which you here will also have to grapple. Most of my life has been spent in academia *per se* or in the scientific and educational communities of Canada. But now in my current role as a member of cabinet I find that I and my colleagues have to make the kinds of decisions that you are really talking about, the kinds of things that are highlighted by this Conference. The interface of "Ethics and Technology" has a particular political dimension especially when my opinion on a matter differs from my constituents. That brings you right up against a difficult, ethical decision that every political figure has to make. Are you going to go with your constituents or are you going to go entirely with your own conscience? But political life is always compromise. The endless considerations that lie behind every problem guarantee that a solution, no matter what it is, is going to displease someone. And what I try to do, and I think what most political people try to do, is to make any decision with the best advice possible and in full knowledge of what those issues are. One cannot expect any more than that from political figures. You have talked a lot in this Conference about quality of life and how it should be maintained and enhanced. Nowadays, the political agenda almost always focuses on that issue. We would all like to see a better quality of life but often you cannot have that kind of quality of life unless you also have some economic prosperity. It must be remembered that the relationship between the latter was the focus of the Brundtland Commission Report. In paraphrasing, economic development does not preclude a global ethic.

Another major issue underlying much of what you have discussed here is the rapid change of technology and where this is leading us. This is an issue with which we will have to struggle all the time. You cannot turn off science and technology. You have to move it forward but it needs to be controlled and used for the good of us all.

In Canada I think we have a particular problem because we have a society that has been brought up on the belief that we could always cut it down or dig it up thus generating all the wealth we would need to promote our well-being. That is no longer true. Because there are many, especially in the developing countries, who can dig it out of the ground and cut it down, certainly more cheaply than we can, and they have more of it. And so Canada, in my opinion, faces a future where science and technology become even more important. Canadians have to start using their brains. And that thrusts you into all of the issues that are so important in the Conference.

It also thrusts you into an issue which for so long has plagued me, namely the three *solitudes* that we all recognize, exist in Canada—academia, government, and industry. When I say industry I mean, of course, labour as well. It takes a conference for us all to talk to each other. We cannot go on like that. If you look at some of the people that we are competing with in the world you will find that is not what they do. They would never dream of having, literally, a conversation, a conference on anything without the presence of those three. That focus is necessary. Canadians have a lot to learn in terms of where we are going.

If science and technology is going to play an even greater role then that raises some questions about where the people are going to come from in this country because once again we do not have them. We do not have the same number of people in science and engineering as all of our major competitors. We are literally at the bottom of the list for people trained in science and engineering. Worst of all, we have always ignored, with a few notable exceptions, the tremendous power that women could bring to science and technology in this country. If the participation rate in Canada of women in science and technology was equal to that of men we would be half way to overcoming this deficiency. Moreover, other than it not being right, it does not make economic sense to exclude women. That is something to which we must turn our attention. That is why, for example, the Canada Scholars Program has been initiated with 10,000 young men and women being sponsored as Canadian scholars. Fifty per cent of those scholarships have been designated for women.

Let me finish by saying that I do not have any more qualms about ethics in Government than I had about ethics when I was President of this University. What bothers me—and I come back to what I said at the beginning—is the question whether we ever have enough information upon which to make those ethical choices?

Ursula Franklin

This is probably the only time that I will be on the "right" of Bill Winegard. That was a set up.

I do not find this an easy assignment just as I did not find this an easy conference. There are a number of things that I would like to say that I think are fundamental to what we are talking about. We are talking about technology and one of the aspects of technology is that it interposes itself between people. It is the nature of technology and more specifically of the way technology has developed or has in fact increased the circle in which it is felt. It is like a stone that is thrown into the water. The circle of the ripples get larger and larger. Technology transcends both time and space in a way as nothing else has ever done before. That also increases for all "ethical people," the circle of care and concern. That is the nature of technology and it is that part that may not have been as central in both the application and the consideration of decision-making as it should have been. We are here now because we can really see the evidence that this widening circle causes serious consequences related to the application of science and technology. However, it is very difficult to reflect this circle in the decision-making process if the mechanisms of decision-making are not geared to the concerns of those who, at the receiving end, are most negatively effected. One of the things that I found difficult in this conference is that issues of power were not addressed. These are issues that affect women, that affect native peoples, who are notably absent, and it was this that was particularly on the lips of all those women of the Third World who spoke. It was not that they didn't know what to say, but they didn't have a place to speak where what they said would be taken sufficiently seriously to be considered as an important contribution to the decision-making process rather than as a mere ritual of the consultative process.

One should also remember that it is the nature of science as science to separate knowledge from experience. That is what science is all about and for that reason, through the development of science, we have come to discount experience as a source of knowledge. Thus women and native peoples, whose knowledge is experienced based and do not wish to separate their knowledge from experience, are not considered as serious sources of knowledge.

I would like to address these comments in particular to Bill Winegard and other decision-makers whose task, I must add, I often do not envy. There are essentially different strategies of decision-making and we need to talk about the fact that many of the decisions made at different levels, particularly in the past, are decisions aimed at maximizing gain whichever way it is defined. On the other hand, the constituents that were not heard here, including the womens' constituency, not only have experience but also have alternative strategies. Theirs is a strategy of minimizing disaster. Every woman knows that her children always have measles when her mother-in-law comes and it is two weeks before Christmas. There is no way to maximize gain, just minimize disaster. All poor people know that the last week before a welfare cheque comes, or the month before the harvest is brought in, has to be considered in a strategy that minimizes a pending disaster because they are not in a position to affect let alone control outside forces to mitigate the disaster. And so I would say to those who are part of the decision-making process to consider the widened circle of effects and responsibility, whether we like it or not, that technology brings into our decision-making and to adopt a strategy of minimizing disaster rather than maximizing gain. This task, however, would be made much easier if those with experience and alternative strategies were empowered as decision-makers. To conclude, I would like to say that the strength of a community is not only what can be dug up and what can be cut down and what the brain thinks. The strength of a community is what is in the heart and in the end, we will rise or fall, survive or perish on nothing more than what is in our hearts.

Peter Hamel

Ursula Franklin is a hard act to follow. I think probably we could open it up to questions right now and leave it at that. Some of the remarks that I would like to make are simply in support of what Ursula has been saying. I think the reality in our world today is that we are not so much threatened by other nations as we are threatened by the earth itself—Mother Earth—and the powers to throw over the abuses which we have reaped upon her. It is within that context that I think we are struggling to seek a new vision for the biosphere in which we are living.

Part of our problem relates to the fact that technology has been part of a growing alienation from the natural world, from the biosphere. As a result, decisions today are not based upon personal relationships to non-human life or life forms but focus rather on the objective, on reality as perceived by the decision-maker without that kind of personal experience. It is those deeper, ethical choices which are lacking in our decision-making processes. I believe that the natural world is a source for ethical decisions but without the personal relationships humankind abuses the natural world in which it lives. What we need is what I would call a personal story. This is where I think the aboriginal peoples of this country can teach us a lot. When they talk about their identity, they talk about the personal relationships of the natural world. When an aboriginal person talks about his identity, he talks about certain mountains, he talks about certain streams, he talks about forests in which he grew up and has lived all his life. Without those personal connections, the natural world becomes something to dominate. This is part of our problem and today, the reality is that both government and industry are using technology not only to dominate nature but to dominate people. The end result is increasing social conflict and environmental degradation. One of the great biblical truths that we have forgotten is that the results of social injustice are environmental and human degradation and disaster. There needs to be a connection between human rights and environmental rights and action taken to develop the linkage.

The sharing of information has been a concern at this conference. Information is power. One of the great challenges that we face today is to provide information to the marginalized so that they can become empowered to participate in the decision-making process. The marginalized are the victims of our technology. Our pursuit of certain economic systems further disenfranchises those who are already oppressed and don't have a voice. And yet, I think we need to remember that one of the main reasons why aboriginal peoples and those aboriginal communities around the world which are still viable today have survived, in spite of horrendous oppression and genocide, is their relationship to the natural world. Theirs is based upon a land ethic which is so different from our own.

What we need to develop is a decision-making process that not only includes all peoples but shares information. Working contrary to those principles is the Canadian federal government's involvement in a federal environmental assessment review process. It is going nowhere and one of the problems is that the information that is available is not able to be shared. I am talking about the scientists who work in industry and government who risk their jobs should they disseminate too much information in a public inquiry. What is needed is the power of subpoena to protect those people who are willing to make public inquiries into something less than the charades which they are now. With many of the mega projects that exist, there is an inadequate data base on which to make ethical decisions. How can we make, for instance, decisions on whether to explore for oil and gas off the east or west coast, or talk about a cumulative impact if we are lacking in information and do not even have coastal zone management plans in place? Unfortunately, that is reality in Canada.

Let me give you an example. I am a bird watcher. In the west coast offshore oil and gas hearings, the oil companies said it really would not matter if there was an oil spill between October and March because there are no birds out there. The fact is they have not done recent studies to substantiate that view. Moreover, they based their opinions on studies that were carried out in the 70s with the use of low-level airplanes. Well it is mighty difficult to see shear waters and puffins and gulls on the water when you are flying 100 feet or so above them. Much of the base line data that were done for the MacKenzie Valley Pipeline in the mid-70s were also by air reconnaissance. This is just not adequate. We need to first develop an adequate data base in order to assess the ethical choices. In so doing, it is also imperative that we look at the personal relationships.

We intellectualize issues to death and although it is exciting that we have the academic world coming together here with other parts of society to discuss some of these issues, we must cut through all the baggage that each of us brings. As a priest, I too bring baggage. We all need to see things in a more simplified way so that we can understand each other because in the end, things are very basic and down to earth. In order to do that we must empower those people without a voice. They are part of the third parties that appear at public hearings. They are expert witnesses, who quite often are denigrated and talked down to as being too emotional. At least they have some passion. But in our society you are not supposed to have passion. Rather we are to objectify the natural world in which we live, dominate it and exploit its natural resources. Even when we talk about resource management, we are still talking about managing, objectifying, when what we really need to talk about are ethical and moral decisions; the growth of an ethic and morality which relates to the natural world in personal terms and not just as economics.

One of the real challenges we face is to articulate those personal relationships, to articulate a morality and to stand up for one's beliefs. But this must be accomplished without simply digressing into "ego pornography." That is, to a great extent, what government and industry do.

Today we have the Brundtland Commission. Today we also have vice-presidents of industry who are now in charge of the environment. They simply use the concerns that are raised by such a thing as a Brundtland Commission to their own advantage. For instance, the National Task Force on the Environment and the Economy put out a significant report bringing together recommendations to further the decision-making process including having more people involved in the process, and so forth. Yet, much of what they said, although appearing to be progressive and well thought out, is simply discounted with one sentence on page 3 where they say that "sustainable economic development does not require the preservation of the current stock of natural resources or any particular mix of human physical and natural assets." In other words, nothing is sacred. The same applies to the Temagami issue and the stand on pine in that area. It applies to the aboriginal communities that exist which are being forced off their land in order to make room for hydroelectric developments and so on.

We need to develop those personal relationships and articulate a new philosophy. Much as Ursula Franklin was saying, we have to be willing to stand up and be counted.

Lutz Baehr

I would like to make a personal remark to Ursula because I sit even more to the right than she does in this seating arrangement. It is important to see what the majority thinks about right and left and I think for the majority here, we are on the left. And this, at least, is a lesson which political scientists have learned.

After saying this I would like to restrict myself to the international global dimension of ethical considerations which we have discussed here. I know this is not easy but I will reflect on those statements which were presented yesterday at the workshops and at the plenaries. I am not really coming up with any new, sensational ideas. Nor am I trying to be very original. But when we look at the global dimensions of ethical values we have to at least try to translate these values into norms which can be binding for the international community. And I think this is possible. Despite our thinking that ethics are something very personal and cultural specific, there is also a dimension which can be internationalized. Here I speak for instance about considerations on international development. There is a need, and this was expressed by many yesterday, to introduce ethical considerations in development strategies.

At a recent meeting on development, one of the participants pointed out that regardless of what we say or decide, 800 million people will go to bed hungry tonight. I think that this is an ethical issue. Development has to reflect and act on the social injustices that exist in all countries, but specifically, in developing countries. Many of the poor there can be described as victims of development and for that reason I think we have to introduce ethical considerations in development strategies. As Peter Hamel remarked, there is a very close relationship between the environment and social issues. But so far, the parallel between the two lies more in the indifference and unconcern of policy-makers and governments towards the environment and social issues. It is high time that we focus on the environment as an ethical issue as well as on socially sound and ethical development strategies.

Another area which requires special attention and ethical considerations is that of technologies. We are all aware of the huge, complex machinery which serves military purposes. This should not be tolerated. Something has to be done about this machinery whether we convert it to peaceful uses or eliminate it. Either way, we can no longer afford such a waste of human and financial resources. These financial resources are necessary, among other things, to develop new energy technologies which are compatible with the environment. We need to address and solve the social problems that affect so many of today's nations, especially in the developing countries.

There are also those technologies which do not specifically serve military purposes but which can be used for ethical or unethical purposes. These technologies, whether they be gene manipulation, reproductive technologies or communications require special attention and are no less wanting of some ethical groundwork.

I come from a department in the United Nations which is the focal point of technology assessment. There is an international discussion on the methodology of technology assessment and I think it is important that ethical considerations also be introduced into this methodology. The primary aim of this technology assessment is to prepare political options. Well, these political options have to be guided by ethical principles. They cannot only be left to economic considerations or to purely techno-logical considerations.

With the little time I have left, I would like to come up with three suggestions on how to treat these issues which I have just mentioned. The first one is that we should make an attempt, and when I say we, I include everybody here, to introduce these ethical issues and implement them as part of the international strategy for development for the coming decade. The nineties are the fourth development strategy of the United Nations. Ethics and technologies need to be an incumbent part of that strategy. I think there is a good chance that we can get the UN to focus its fourth development decade on these issues because I know that there are a number of people in the United Nations who have been disgruntled with the results of past strategies and would be willing to look at a strategy which is more in tune with environmental and social aspects.

The second suggestion is one which was expressed at this panel meeting and which is of particular interest to developing countries. It was a suggestion that member states include in their human rights declaration, the right of access to technology for all people. The right of access to technology should be heralded on the same plane as the right of access to information. This brings me to the third suggestion, power. Much reference has been made to the concept and practice of power by many speakers at this conference. With regards to where do we go from here and who has the power to continue the struggle, we need a constituency. The honourable Winegard referred to *his* constituency, but I think we also need a constituency for the ethical considerations involving technologies. I would wish that this conference consider itself as a constit-uency for ethical considerations in development at national, as well as international levels.

Elaine Bernard

If there is one item that I suspect everyone in this room would agree upon it is that the time is ripe for ethical considerations to be laid on the table, first and foremost, in every institution, in every government and in every endeavour. It should form, if you like, the mission statement of the corporation, the institution, whatever!

There is one further assumption that I do not think we can make. Despite efforts to place ethical considerations in the forefront, we would still not all agree on what is indeed ethics. I think that it would be tremendous if we at least agreed on laying it on the table because then we could start the real debate, not the debate of this objectivity versus that objectivity. Jean-Paul Sartre said that objectivity is the subjectivity of those who are ashamed of their subjectivity. I would suspect that what we would discover is that in corporate greening ethics do indeed exist but, nonetheless, the bottom line remains profit.

If the bottom line is profit, from where does it come? Profit comes from how we set up our economic system. Therefore, we could change that system. We could argue that our tax system in Canada currently rewards companies with super benefits and super profits for displacing workers and bringing in machinery. That's the way the system works. If that is *not* our belief as a society, then fix the system. Don't turn around and say, "Well, you know, that's not the firm's problem, it's somebody else's problem." "Whose problem is it?" "Well, the firm is doing the proper thing, they have the right to do that." "No they don't, we have to fix and change the system!"

I think one of our problems is that we spend a lot of time chasing our tails. By this I mean that we separate ethics from what we perceive as the "real" world. In a forum such as this, we can gravely shake our heads in agreement and then return to the "real" world and merrily continue as before. Our morals and values are unreal. There's the world of Sundays which is ethics, and then Monday through Saturday, we sin like hell.

The system is discordant with our values, with our morality, and with our beliefs. Some of our powerlessness is built around the idea of who we feel should have the right to a voice, who we perceive as an expert, thus elevating them gratuitously into the realm of power. We have to broaden our concept of expertise. People talk about enfranchising the disenfranchised, the marginalized. Many of us think we want to do that because it's good, it makes sense, it's nice, it's better. I would argue that it is an absolute necessity because the knowledge they bring to what we are doing is absolutely essential.

To give two examples. Firstly, the disabled or physically challenged. When we construct buildings, we do not construct them with the disabled in mind. They usually have to sue us afterwards. Then we go through a very costly procedure of knocking out walls and asking ourselves if they are structurally sound. If on the other hand, they were included in the overall design and decision-making processes of the building, it would actually be quite inexpensive and would provide easier access to and use of buildings for the disabled. The disabled represent a segment of the population that should have the same rights as everyone else but which has so far been ignored or dismissed by the rest of us because they are in the minority and any alteration of plans were not deemed to be cost effective. It would liberate us, in fact, to think differently about our environment because then we would have included, if you like, the wealth of human experience in the design of our shelter and our environment.

The second example has a more comical flavour but is nonetheless profound in its relevance. It relates to the tendency to believe that people who do, that is the ones who are practice oriented as opposed to theory oriented, don't really know, but the people who study the *doers* are those with the knowledge base. That is a pretty bizarre concept. But academia is based on it. Most Canadians and visitors to Canada have run into our wonderful postal code. It's a wonderful story of the engineer and the secretary. The engineer who designed that postal code is supposedly a brilliant person. He designed an algorithm that would allow Canada Post to find you in any city in this country, on any side of the street, in any single block, through the use of six characters—letter, number, letter, number, letter, number. If the person who had designed that went up to someone who is considered to have one of the most common skills in our society—a typist—and said,—I have just invented Canada's postal code. It's a wonderful algorithm which will unravel automatically. It's got about 47 billion possibilities. Take it, give it a try, she would have typed it (and we know it would have been she) numerous times and said, "Oh excuse me, this is very difficult. You cannot upper case a letter, followed by a lower case number, then again upper case letter and so forth. That is extremely difficult to do on a keyboard. In fact, it's very slow, almost impossible to memorize and is a real problem. The engineer would respond, "You'll get used to it." That is always the answer. "You'll get used to it, try it, you'll like it eventually," without regard for the practical knowledge base of the *doer*. What it means is that the worker, the victim of our technology often, the victim of our economy, holds up major knowledge, holds up, if you like, half the world. It is only when they also have credibility and power and are involved with real power in decision-making, that we will get ethical, interesting and exciting decisions. In fact, the challenge before us is a challenge of power. It is a challenge of how to share power and, most importantly, how to empower the disenfranchised. This is not just important for them but for all of us. Their liberation is our liberation. Their inclusion will free us. It is that process which needs to be included in ethical choices and considerations.

Eugene Critoph

When I was leaving the plenary session, yesterday, a colleague of mine asked me whether I would go to another conference like this in a year or two? I didn't have the opportunity to respond at the time but later I had an opportunity to consider the question very seriously. I would like to share that consideration with you. Now basically, my position is that I would not have missed this conference for the world. More specifically, however, I would not encourage another conference of this particular structure and format. If there was one, I would desperately want to go but at the same time, I would forfeit the opportunity so that I could send someone else with my point of view and background who is much more skilled at communicating.

Let me explain what I mean. I agreed entirely with a comment that was made yesterday by Fred Knelman when he said that there is evidence here of two cultures. He didn't define those two cultures and perhaps my definition would be quite different from his had he. However, I do agree with the statement and I would like to tell you what I think the two cultures are.

Put in simple terms, it is industry on one side and academia on the other, or in other words, technologists on one side, and non-technologists on the other. Personally, I would prefer to be known, as a *technology driven person.* This is perhaps the difference between the two cultures. In our company, we have finally adopted *technology* as our driving force. At the time that was done, there was great rejoicing, we were now recognized corporately as the technology driven company. This schism has not been a big issue at this conference. Neither has it been very visible, mainly because the two groups here have been out of balance with the underrepresentation of industry. This is in spite of the dedicated efforts of the organizers of the conference to get more industrialists to come in order to provide that balance. Now my own personal feeling is that even if they had succeeded in bringing in a more balanced dialogue, this would not have guaranteed communication and understanding between the two cultures. The reason is that there is absolutely no channel of communication open between these two cultures. There has always been a failure to start dialoguing. This seems to be a simple fact. Why has there been this failure? To my mind, and I am probably biased, the scenario can be viewed as two squares. The non-technologist stands on a square that is labelled, or he perceives to be labelled, *balanced ethical choice; measured progress.* In the far distance, there is a technologist standing on another square, almost out of visible or audible range of the non-technologist. That square is labelled, or is perceived to be labelled by the technologist, *balanced ethical choice; measured progress.* The non-technologist, however, because of the great distance separating his square from the other, perceives the other square to read, *unbalanced choice due to insufficient non-technological information input, precipitous action.* He feels he should communicate with the other to straighten out this problem but because of the distance he has to shout. Meanwhile, the technologist perceives what is written on the non-technologist's square to read, *unbalanced choice due to insufficient technical input; interceptible motion or action.* He feels he should communicate with the other to straighten out this problem but because of the distance he too has to shout.

If we could stand above this and look at it, what we would see would be two people on squares. From above, they would appear to be quite close together. In reality, though, the squares are not that close. As neither the technologist nor the non-technologist can properly hear what the other is shouting, forgetting the distance factor, they feel that each is ignoring the other. Frustration sets in and the shouting becomes abusive. What was attempted communication becomes insult and ridicule.

This is essentially the way I see the situation. I am going to leave it there but first I would like to make three recommendations as to how we can start to dialogue. I make these with a great deal of trepidation. I take heart in the fact, though, that any recommendations I make will be modified by wiser heads than mine (I said wiser not necessarily more knowledgeable).

The first recommendation is that there should be more, yet smaller meetings than this with equal numbers of what I call industry—technically driven people, and university—non-technologists.

The second recommendation is that there should be another group of equal people made up of industry non-technologists and university technologists. My feeling with regard to this conference is that the university technologists did in fact play a very valuable role. They managed to run back and forth between the cultures fast enough, in fact, to come out with agreements even though there was no dialogue.

The final recommendation pertains to the topic for these particular meetings. I have some hesitation in voicing it because it will not likely sit well with everyone, and I am sure that other people could make other recommendations. Nonetheless, my final recommendation is two-fold. One is the democratization of decision-making. I would think that while there is interest on both sides, we are coming at it from different angles which results in confrontation rather than reconciliation. The second one is the disempowerment of academia—is it true, why has it happened, and how can it be changed? I am rather proud of that one because it is the first time I have used the word *disempowerment*, which I heard a lot yesterday. And don't tell me I've used it out of context!

Ntombi Gata

I will start off by appealing to the audience and say that my misery started when my husband decided that there had been enough of this thing about women's emancipation. But he decided, nonetheless, to give me an opportunity to come here so that I could chart my path for emancipation. Then, as if that was not enough, I came to Guelph to find that this is where Professor Wiseman is actually stationed. He happens to have been instrumental to the United Nations team in charting the steps for the independence of Zimbabwe. He is now providing yet another opportunity to chart the path of our development in the developing countries. This is a very difficult ethical situation to be placed in. However, this is an opportunity that needs to be two-sided. Women in the developing countries cannot emancipate themselves without your assistance nor can developing countries chart their own path to development without the assistance of the entire Western world. In fact, it is not only a question of assistance, but rather a question of mutuality. We all need each other to chart the ethical path which will sustain our living organisms in a biosphere to which we all belong.

If I take the issue of the universal versus locality specific ethics then this conference has indeed reinforced our belief that ethics must preface decision and human activities in general. Responsibility, where ethical values are concerned, has to be borne by both the developers and the users of technology. The prevailing situation in developing countries dictates that we do not have much capacity for choice of modern technologies. We, in developing countries, have to take or receive what we get. And so far what we have received has failed us on two important accounts.

One concerns a lack of ethical considerations towards the developing society they are to serve. Technologies have not been generated with due ethical consideration simply because most technologies have not been generated for problems specific to developing countries. They have been transferred to us either as a means of generating income for the developed and developing countries or to "speed-up" development. Therefore, since these technologies were generated without taking the "real" needs and values of developing countries into account, and without their input, they did not incorporate the ethical values that are inherent in those societies they are to serve.

The second factor is that technologies have been generated in another society—a first world society—with objectives and inbuilt values for those societies which are then transferred to us. Most are inappropriate, both in terms of operation, feasibility, affordability as well as in terms of other economic and social considerations. Therefore, this raises the issue of universal versus particular ethical values.

We find that if we ignore the influence of local culture, cultural values and traditions for the sole consideration of universal ethical values, this could lead to situations of inadequate ethical principles superimposed on local communities from universal levels. Moreover, technologies *per se* do not address the problems that exist in the equation of development and underdevelopment. This is especially true in the rural areas where poverty, underemployment, lack of education and training programmes will not be bettered through a technological fix. Nor does it recognize that women make up the majority of the people in the rural areas. Their cultures and day-to-day roles are incongruent with the technologies that are supposed to help them. In fact, these technologies actually disrupt rather than improve the running of the system.

However, we find ourselves in a dilemma. On the one hand, we need the West to develop but if we adopt universal ethical guidelines as opposed to more particular ethical values, we could also be found guilty of harming the biosphere as the West has done in its process of development. Without a concerted effort by all countries to coordinate a more effective and interdependent development process, the end result could be the actual destruction of the planet. Signs of this are already evident. Therefore, it is important that we adhere to universal ethical guidelines or norms without excluding local applications and operations of ethical considerations. In other words, we need a common reference which encompasses the higher global level as well as the lower local level, while at the same time, taking account of the local specific considerations of our own cultures, our own ethics, norms and other social requirements.

I would like to add that my goal for this meeting or rather my plight is to convey and make understood that although the developed countries have a capacity for science and technology which we do not have, I feel that from my own perspective of development, it is the economic, social and political environment rather than the technological that actually impacts on humans. It is stability and equality in this milieu which enhances education and training, technological knowhow, and social capacity and will in any society. These, in turn, give people the capacity or incapacity to exploit or conserve our physical environment and biosphere.

What we need from you is not merely a transfer of technology. We have already seen that this approach has failed because our cultures, educational base, economies, social and other factors are not the same as the ones in which the technologies were generated. Therefore, what we are calling for now is for you to use your scientific and technological knowhow to help us generate or develop technologies appropriate to our own social and cultural environments. In doing so, I again reflect back on what I said yesterday, that we have dual systems—developed and developing. Investment by the former in the latter should only occur if development is not imposed according to the values of the first system. One cannot live without the other. Each has the capacity to destroy the biosphere. Although development is essential in order for the whole of the global system to sustain itself, this cannot be done unless you in the West are willing to give your assistance to help us develop appropriate technologies not only to enhance our own development and self-determination but to help create a global environment for sustainable development.

William Winegard

Having only arrived at the conference just before I spoke earlier at this plenary session, I would like to take this opportunity now to say a few words again after having heard some of the other speakers and to answer some questions from the floor.

I want to spend this time on the International Development question because it is one that has been at the front of this university for a great many years and one that I have spent much of my time in parliament being concerned about. I suspect that if we in the developed world do not handle this properly, we will not resolve the international problems that face all of us and certainly, we will not resolve the environmental problems with which we are faced. During the first development decade, we in the West went in with that marvellous arrogance and said, "We know best." We quickly learned, I suppose in ten to fifteen years that we really didn't know best. Then, as so often happens, the pendulum swung completely the other way and we said that the developing countries knew best, we will do whatever they wish. In my opinion that was equally a disaster. And now, maybe now, we have learned that if, perhaps, we sit around the table and talk about what is best, and listen to them, and supply the kind of expertise that is appropriate, we might get this international development thing right after all. This is a question of ethics. It is a question of discussing whether you want large projects or not and what the effects of those projects would be. But let us not be misled. Because a project may have some negative effects, that does not mean that it should not proceed especially if that is what the country wishes and that is considered to be a good thing to do. I often refer to Niagara. We might never have had the Niagara power system if we had looked at all of the ramifications down the road. Again, it is a form of arrogance for us in the West to try to make all the decisions. It is up to the developing country itself to make the decision and for us to support them as long as they know what they really want.

Question: Does the country have the accurate information?

Answer: I think that is part of the responsibility that we bear. It is incumbent upon us to provide whatever information we can through all of the organizations at our disposal. There is no question of that. But I also think that in terms of international development, one of the things that we surely have learned is that the smaller projects, particularly those run by non-governmental organizations, have so much to contribute to international development.

One of the things that our parliamentary committee recommended was that we put far more funding into the NGO community because they can do things, particularly with women in the Third World that are very exciting. In fact, some of the most exciting projects that I have ever seen in the Third World are now being run by women. I think this emphasizes the concern that most of us should have for the development. If you insist on centralizing all of your decision-making, you are going to slow down the whole pace of development. Thus you must decentralize, you must let people on the spot make the decisions, that includes the Canadian International Development Agency as well. You cannot make proper decisions about what should happen in Third World countries from Ottawa. These decisions have to be made by the Third World countries themselves. That does not mean to say that we cannot be involved. So we need to help them without imposing our decisions. We must have discussions and reach some common solutions concerning the environment, for instance, and the nature of projects that are taking place as well as the overall economic development of those countries.

I would like to say just a little bit more about discussion and consultation being a necessary part of the decision-making process because that has been the major theme here this morning. No one can possibly argue with that concept. I think before you make decisions, you should, if at all possible, hear all points of view. But at the same time, decisions ultimately have to be made and at times, no decision is in fact a decision. That can be equally as bad. Let me say, before I have to leave, that I am grateful for the opportunity to be here and to hear the concerns and points of view expressed around the table. I do look forward to the summary and the specific recommendations from the conference about what happens now so that this doesn't drop into the kind of vacuum that most conferences do after it ends.

Floor statement: It seems to me that one of the difficulties with this type of conference is that we are trying to solve very basic problems in an extremely short time entrenched as we are by modern technology and the speed of communication. It has not improved our speed of decision or discussion and maybe we simply cannot do it in such a short time. Dr. Winegard, in spite of what you say, you belong to a government which encourages the sale of military production to the Third World through DPSA, DDSA and DIPP in Canada. I cannot imagine that you believe that represents the ethical views of the Canadian people. If you believe it does, I urge you to make this a public debate and let us have a referendum on the subject because it seems extraordinarily unethical.

Minister: We do not promote the sale of military equipment to Third World countries. In fact, we as a nation probably export, with the exception of the United States and our NATO allies, fewer arms than any other OECD country.

Statement: This is simply untrue.

Minister: No it isn't. If you want to talk about trucks and things like that, but if you are talking about offensive military equipment, we do not.

Question: Why was overseas aid cut? What can we do about it? It does create havoc, it not only creates havoc in CIDA and in IDRC, it creates havoc in the world.

Minister: ODA was cut for the same reason everything else is cut in the government of Canada. That is namely that we have a thirty billion dollar a year annual deficit and we must get it under control. In terms of what can be done about the ODA cuts, I think you will find that what the Minister for External Affairs is after is fewer larger projects, fewer capital projects, and the shifting again of more of that funding into smaller NGO type projects. I know support for NGOs has been held fairly constant. The largest cuts will affect the big capital-intensive projects. Now, as most of you would know, I don't have any quarrel with that. I think we could afford to cut some of those projects. What I am concerned about is that we do not have the cuts in areas that I think—and I would gather this group would think—are much more important.

Question: I believe that from this conference, there are perhaps two imperatives that, for me, have emerged as the most important. The first is our great care and consideration toward the natural environment. The second is the importance of international development as described in the Brundtland Report and reiterated here. Would you, as the Minister for Science and Technology, state that for you and for the government of Canada these two issues, identified at this conference, are to be given priority by our government leaders and decision-makers?

Minister: I think I can guarantee that. As the Minister for Science and Technology, I am also on the Cabinet Committee on the Environment and I can tell you that we have been wrestling and continue to wrestle with a long range plan for the environment for the country. It is not easy because you do have conflicting things coming at you from all directions. Again, one of the things we have to do is to find out what is the proper role for the federal government. This is a complex country. Ottawa cannot just go ahead and do things on its own. We have provincial jurisdiction and municipal jurisdiction.

On the development side, there is no question that this government is dedicated to international development and always has been.

Henry Wiseman

I deeply appreciate the sense, the fervour and the issues which are being raised. The organization of this conference began two years ago as a conceptual, intellectual inquiry. We have tried desperately to put forward the central issues and to represent the various viewpoints. We have learned here of the difficulty in doing that. Just a few moments ago, one of our speakers, who occasionally feels himself to be in a minority, came forth quite willingly and very frankly to say how essential it is to have this form of dialogue. He said he would recommend to his colleagues in business, industry and finance to come forward in small groups and enter into the kind of dialogue with each other, with labour and with academe that could provide us all with a better mutual understanding of the issues, problems and constraints, however difficult that may be and whatever the contradictions. If indeed we here on the platform and others who have been so deeply and devotedly involved in setting up this conference are to pursue that again, we would like to have that opportunity for direct personal discussion between the various communities. However, I as chair, were I to know in advance that the conversations, the dialogue, the exchange and the fruition of that would simply turn into political confrontation then it would not be worth the two years that have gone into putting this before you and the people of Canada.

Kevin Hayes

This meeting is turning into a form with which I am more familiar. I was going to honour a few pieties about technological change, but I think I want to go to the heart of the matter of what we discussed in our workshop and, what was discussed here so well yesterday. I am glad that the conference was not just called—ethics and technology—and that it was called—ethical choices because "choices" is one of the key words, and the question is, "Who makes the choice?"

For the labour movement and for workers generally the choice is not made by workers with respect to the kind of technology they are going to use. The choice is, as most of us know, a corporate choice and one which is increasingly in complicity with government in the sense of government increasingly executing a corporate agenda. A word that has been used here quite frequently is "empowerment," that is empowering people. There was even the suggestion that decision-making in our institutions be democratized. Some of our institutions provide for worker input and it is called—collective bargaining. There are also labour standards and social programs which, to some extent, empower workers. However, we are increasingly seeing major cut-backs in those programs that empower workers—including a decline in labour standards.

At the present time, there is a bill before the House of Commons, which will probably become an Act, to amend the Unemployment Insurance Act. The government has actually described it more accurately as a "labour force development strategy." It is a strategy designed for the technological age but it is designed in such a way that the powers of workers will be severely weakened. They will not have the kind of empowerment that I think we have all been talking about here. There will be mandatory training which will be financed from cutbacks in unemployment payments. Workers have little choice but to acquiesce to large-scale layoffs so it is an interesting ethical choice that the benefits will be taken away from those who have no jobs, no income and no say. It is a very curious ethical choice too that the amount of money being pirated from workers runs between two and a half to three billion dollars. That amount could finance Via Rail three times over, and it is that kind of "power" that is being taken away from workers. I would have liked the Minister to stay longer to comment on some of these kinds of ethical choices.

There are also other issues with which we have been very concerned and again, it goes back to who makes the choice and how is the choice made.

There is the issue of increased deregulation in the economy. We are all, believe it or not, workers and any lessening of regulation, not only in the workplace, but of the economy, thus allowing the full play of market forces, only increases the power of those who already have vast powers to determine how much capital should be invested or divested and what kind of technology is to be created and used.

I just want to leave you with one thought. This concerns how we can use existing democratic institutions so that the users of technology and those that are affected by technology, not only in the workplace but as consumers and communities, can acquire more control. Firstly, an increasing concern is how we participate in the global economy. The Minister referred to it this morning. This takes the form of a vast expansion in international trade and so forth. Workers in Europe have already suggested (and believe it or not the European Community has agreed to it), a social charter. This means, for instance, that there would no longer be social dumping, massive closures of plants or moving to a lower-cost wage area. We, in the international labour movement want a similar multilateral social clause to be inserted in the trade agreements under the GATT. It is this type of instrument that is necessary to help us deal with worker displacements resulting from technology.

We have to keep in mind that technology is not value-free. Technology is not simply hardware. Technology is all about the organization of decision-making. It includes the mergers, down-sizing, take-overs, and so forth. I think we all agree, therefore, that in any decisions made pertaining to technologies—whether it be hard or software technologies—industry and labour must include a statement of ethics. It is particularly the software technologies—organization and management—that are the most difficult to change and deal with and it is here that technology is its most pervasive and can also be the most destructive. Consequently, ethical choices can only become a reality if workers are able to participate in those choices.

Francisco Sagasti

I would like to start by making one observation. I have been associated with Canada and the IDRC for about 20 years and what I have seen yesterday and today is one of the reasons why I have faith in your country. This capacity to discuss issues in an open way, to confront each other, yet still have the willingness, tolerance and patience to accept divergent opinions is something which I have very seldom seen, especially in Latin American countries, and particularly, at present, the country I come from, Peru.

My comments can be divided into two parts. The first part will be simply some ideas that I wanted to share with you before I came to this meeting. These consist of some concepts and views that came to mind after reading the conference material and program. In the second part, I will offer some general and personal reflections about what I have observed yesterday and today and the sense I got from many of the participants at this particular meeting.

The first point I want to make is that, for the first time in a very, very long time, not only in Canada, the U.S., or in Europe, but certainly in most of the Third World, ideas are behind events, concepts are behind facts. In political, economic, social and technological terms, events occurring in the real world are moving very fast. Those of us who have had the task of thinking concepts, explanation and theory have fallen behind. What we need now is a very urgent program of trying to adapt the whole conceptual and intellectual arsenal at our disposal. We must first be able to apprehend correctly, and secondly begin to understand, then explain and hopefully correct some of the things that we see at present. We have a great deal of catching up to do. In this sense, the famous saying that "there is nothing more practical than a good theory" is very applicable. I think we need more theories, more concepts at present. I will go even further. It is at moments like this when the power of ideas is greatest. I would argue that the conceptual building blocks and the frameworks with which to apprehend reality and alter one's perceptions of what is happening, is much more powerful and important than any practice or technique. To those who wield powers as intellectuals I say that there is a need to move from action to rethinking. Take the time to think without acting too quickly.

The second point I would like to make is that ethics and values evolve over time. Therefore, one of the most urgent tasks before us at present is that of creating, inventing and putting into practice new values, new concepts and ideas. For example, the issue of environmental preservation is a new value that is emerging and being shared by a host of nations and peoples. We just finished a review with one of my students at Penn State University on the revolution of paradigms and the relation between environment and development. Until very recently—20 to 30 years ago at the most—there was no conception at all of any responsibility towards the physical ecosystem in which we live. We need more new values. Solidarity with other people is an important one. Can we invent, develop, create and disseminate new values? That is also a task of the utmost importance at present. In speaking about the importance of ideas and thought, that does not mean that all we have to do is to sit down in isolation, splendid isolation, and invent concepts and values. That is only one part of the task. We also need to bring about those values, concepts and ideas to the practical world in our day to day decision-making. The statement "praise the Lord and pass the ammunition" is quite valid here. We have to do the two things simultaneously.

The third point I would like to stress is that there are at least two or three concepts which I think are essential for us to grasp. One has been brought forth quite strongly here. It is the concept of "empowerment." It is a very crucial one. If you take a look at the history of thought regarding the notion of progress, we have moved in the last 60 or 70 years from the concept of progress to the concept of development, and now we may be moving to a third phase: the concept of empowerment. It is very naive to believe in a linear and mechanical progression of humanity. The same way that progress was replaced several decades ago, I think we are replacing our naive conceptions of development with the much more powerful concept of empowerment. Let me highlight one important point. Development as we knew it is no longer possible. It is no longer possible not only because of environmental reasons but because of moral or ethical reasons. The development of the industrialized North was based on the exploitation of child labour and women. Who doesn't remember the sweat shops, the photographs of New York in the garment district at the beginning of the turn of the century. Who doesn't remember the pictures and photographs of children working in coal mines. It was this type of exploitation, along with the process of colonization, over decades and even centuries, which built the prosperity of the industrialized nations. Today, none of this is morally or ethically acceptable. We have lost, if you wish, an unethical way of generating surplus.

The task of development as we conceive it today, is to bring about in two or three decades or less, without environmental and social costs, the same type of prosperity and development that exists in the industrialized nations. However, that is no longer possible. It won't happen. So therefore, what we need to do is to think new theories, to reconceptualize what development is all about. It is here that I grasp for the concept of empowerment. Let's try to give each and every human being the capacity, the knowledge to decide for him or herself and then carry out these decisions efficiently and effectively.

The second concept that I think is important is that we have made a transition from sialogism, to the dialectics, to paradox. Let me explain that a little bit. We used to believe that there was a very logical, one and only one way of proceeding with regards to ideas, concepts and explaining things. Then we were able to argue different ideas and through extrapolation of the past, predict the future. Now, what is required in a rapidly changing, uncertain, difficult, messy and complex world is the capacity to think in paradoxical terms—to be able to understand that there are simultaneous and equally valid and good alternatives. We need to learn to incorporate more than one perspective without being paralysed. This requires a different level of thinking. A different set of logic from the one we are most accustomed to dealing with.

Finally, the third concept I would like to refer to is the change in the concept of leadership. I think we have to move away from the concept of a leader as a martyr, as a saviour or as a hero. We no longer need martyrs, heros or saviours any more. What we need, I believe, are people who *enable* others. We need a style of enabling leadership—people who can guide with a light touch; leaders who are prepared to restrain their personal ambition to advance collectively; men and women with practical vision, with practical imagination. That is probably one of the most difficult things to put forward. Let me relate a statement made by Eric Trist, professor of Management Studies at York University and someone who had a great deal of influence in the Canadian Labour Movement. "The type of leader that we need at present is someone with more conventional views of management. This person must be flexible, resourceful, resilient, able to tolerate emotionally both surprise and ambiguity while continuing to work on complex issues intellectually and practically."

Floor Statement: Mr. Sagasti spoke about how the Western, or the Northern world had been able to industrialize and become quite affluent because we exploited child labour, women labour which we will no longer tolerate. I find that a little hard to believe because we do tolerate these abuses. The only thing we do not do is to export them to other countries where there are economic zones in which women and children are working for dismal wages in terrible working conditions. These economic zones in the South, owned by transnational corporations, seem to be exempt from environmental laws such as they may exist, and they do not pay much in the way of taxes. My understanding is that often these countries get loans from the World Bank to build the infrastructure which makes it easier for the transnationals to exploit the resources of those countries. Once the transnationals have depleted the resources and the profits, they move on to more profitable ground leaving behind a debt-ridden country. It is the poor people who are left with the debt. We still do tolerate exploitation.

Sagasti: There is no question in that, I deplore that. The question is what to do about it? Do you have any suggestions?

Speaker: I thought you'd never ask. I suppose that before anything is considered, ethics should be considered and when money is lent for any project, the ethical considerations have to be taken into account. That is one thing. As individuals, we could refuse to buy products that are produced in these terrible conditions. We should hold our government accountable, to the extent that they facilitate this sort of thing.

Sagasti: I agree with that and I think that a corollary to your suggestion is for all of us, individually and collectively, to try to convince those who are in power in our own constituents and areas to take the same position. An agenda each and every one of us must set for ourselves is to take on the responsibility of effecting change in our own milieu.

Speaker: I first want to say that I agree with all you have said but then knowing that you work for the World Bank, I have a few questions. One is, to what extent your thinking about empowerment is accepted within the World Bank? How is that concept built into their development programs which seem very directed? Also, how much do you or the World Bank, in general, worry about the structural adjustment imposed on the South by the IMF (International Monetary Fund)? I would add that the IMF does not seem to take into account any concept of empowerment.

Sagasti: At a personal level I worry about the concerns you have raised. In terms of the institution, we have to be very careful and realistic and this is why I said earlier—praise the Lord and pass the ammunition. You have to do the two things in that regard and the fact is that institutions like the World Bank are not grant making institutions. They are not the IDRC (International Development Research Center). It is a bank and what it does as a bank is to borrow money from the capital markets (at very favourable interest rates because the bonds that the World Bank emits are held in very high esteem by borrowers). Out of the 90 countries that are actually borrowers from the World Bank, I would say that at least 80 could not go and borrow the same amount of money on their own. So we play, what is called in the financial system, an intermediary function. This is the harsh and hard reality. Now, when you go and try to sell bonds to someone who manages pension funds in New York or someone who manages a lot of money in Saudi Arabia or Japan and so on, the reality of the world is that they do not care about poverty or inequality. They are interested in getting a secure return for their money. Therefore, the Bank has to live between two different and conflicting realities. One is the reality of the financial market place while the other is development. What we are trying to do is to mix and match those two realities together in a more sensible and pragmatic way.

What is beginning to happen now more and more in the relations of the Bank with non-governmental institutions, is the acceptance by the former of the concept of empowerment, the concept of participation. These are really taking hold where it matters—at the project level. This takes a very long time. It is an extremely difficult process because the Bank is and has to be a very conservative institution because of the imperatives of being an intermediary between capital markets and developing countries. As I said, it will take a lot of time but there is a clear sign that the Bank is moving in that direction.

As for your question on structural adjustment, I will return to it in a moment and now allow Lutz Baehr to comment on your first question.

Lutz Baehr: I think there are two dimensions to empowerment which can also be applied to the operations of the Bank. One is at the government level. Institutions such as the World Bank and other regional development banks, represent governments, and at least theoretically, respond to the people of these governments. If the public knew more about how these institutions operate, they and the NGOs (non-governmental organizations) would have more influence over how these institutions work.

The second dimension lies in the Third World countries. Without changing very dramatically the way these international institutions operate, a certain degree of empowerment can be introduced. There are models of this bargaining process in the United Nations such as the "stakeholder" approach or the "national dialogue" through which the various groups which are involved in the development process can have a voice. So we can move things in this direction. I must agree, however, that there is a dilemma between operational performance and financial performance. The financial performance is always very important for a bank, but maybe governments can also be influenced to reconcile this dilemma. We must introduce more qualitative objectives to balance the financial perspective.

Sagasti: Let me respond very briefly to the question on structural adjustment. Structural adjustment lending is basically when the World Bank provides a loan to a country in exchange for the implementation of certain policies which are supposed to improve the climate of macroeconomic management in the country. When the bank first initiated it, it thought it was going to be a temporary operation for just two or three years until the debt crisis was over. Therefore at its inception in 1980, 1981, social concerns were not associated with structural adjustment because it was thought that these would disappear once the macroeconomic situation improved. As the operations took longer and the programs became more entrenched, we could not help but realize that social concerns and poverty had to be taken into consideration.Consequently, a special forum has now been set up called the Social Dimensions of Adjustment. It is specifically designed so that every single structural adjustment loan that is made must pay attention to social issues and include explicitly the consideration of how we can minimize the negative effects on the poor and those who suffer most during the period of adjustment.

Hans Bakker: (Associate Professor of Sociology and Anthropology at the University of Guelph) I would like to make a very concrete proposal not only for the members of the panel but also for members of the audience, that deals with dialogue. Despite many newsletters which bring people and ideas together, there is no newsletter that represents the voice of the Third World people working in rural development. I'm wondering if the representative to the World Bank, the Atomic Energy Commission or any other international body would be willing to support, in a relatively small way, both financially and in terms of institutional support, this rural development newsletter. It would allow people from Third World countries to present to us research notes of specific problems and difficulties that they are having at the community level with integrated rural development. This would enable them to let us know what they need rather than the reverse which is what has always been the trend.

I would like to add a brief ideological comment. We have talked a great deal about the pervasiveness of technology, yet we have not really talked about one theorist who I think should be mentioned much more in this context. When John Kenneth Galbraith said that many people in the West are reading Adam Smith and many people in Japan are reading Karl Marx, had he thought about it, I think he would have added that many people in the Third World have been reading, and I hope will continue to read, Mahatma Ghandi.

The works of M.K. Ghandi are often stereotyped and simplified but the concept of *Swadeshi*, *Servodia* and *Ahimsa* are central to ethical choices in this age of technology. I think we need to seriously consider Ghandi in an academic sense and take his ideas and concepts to their logical and intellectual conclusion.

Question: What is the relationship between the World Bank and the IMF?

Sagasti: They are two sister institutions that were created at the Bretton Woods Conference in 1944. Right from the constitution of the two organizations, there has been a certain pattern of consultation built-in between them. There are many areas, especially when we deal with macroeconomic policies in borrowing countries, in which the Bank and the Fund have to work together to some extent. There is no way that the Bank can operate independently of the IMF although there is some flexibility in the relations. These two institutions were created at the same time to fulfil different purposes under specific charters but were intertwined in their operations.

Speaker: (Earl Wrinkler from the Philosophy Department at the University of British Columbia) I want to try to highlight a certain tension that I sense coming out of the deliberations of the last couple of days and invite the panellists to briefly respond to it. For my first point, I think it is undeniable that given the magnitude of planetary problems we need a relatively swift and uniform response, at least at the global level. The second part concerns democratic pluralism. There has been an emphasis on the need to extend the franchise, to extend participation, etc. Now, it has also been mentioned repeatedly in the conference that certain problems arise as a result of the dominance of process over purpose. There is no clearer example of this, I'm afraid, than what often happens with procedures of democratic pluralism. These procedures have the effect of frequently co-opting, watering down and eviscerating purposes that were noble in the beginning. This was experienced in the 60s from within the so-called "movements" as one attempted to include more and more participants, and more and more perspectives and voices. The result was divisive rather than unifying. So, I just want to open this up as a problem. It is one that concerns me and I don't have any solutions to it.

Response by Peter Hamel: When you talk about watering down and democratic pluralism, one of the exciting things that I have found in terms of participating in environmental assessment review panels across this country dealing with issues on forestry, mining and so on, is that it is the marginalized, and in many cases the aboriginal people, who are the only ones coming up with viable alternatives to the industrial proposals by government and industry. However, they are never recognized or listened to. Aboriginal people sit at the table but they do not participate in co-management whether it be in fisheries, forestry or otherwise. Democratic pluralism is important but it doesn't necessarily have to be watered down. One of the biggest problems we have not yet faced here is racism. It is a dominant factor in the decisions made around resource development whether it is taking place in Canada or elsewhere. The co-management proposals of the aboriginal peoples are really powerful in terms of not only protecting resources but also in allowing for harvesting at a level where jobs are available.

Ursula Franklin: I just wanted to add something to the first part of that question in terms of the sense of urgency. I think that it is not so difficult to use, for instance, as Ernie Rehger and the Environmental Studies people at the University of Toronto have done, the concept of stress. As somebody very sick, you need to take two steps. First of all, you have to remove any stress that is removable. Then comes the consultation and diagnosis in tandem. Just as with a dying patient, you give a blood transfusion and use other life saving techniques before you consult everybody about what to do next. We can't think in either/or terms. We must do both. I feel that some of the needed measures are quite evident and are readily available. It simply requires political will and power. Then we can go on with the diagnosis, the consultation and the healing in parallel and do immediately whatever can be done to help the dying patient.

In spite of the complexity of the issues that face humankind, we must have a more pluralistic decision-making process. Although this will probably create additional, if not different problems, we have to nonetheless come to terms with the urgency involving the resolution of these issues and take a serious look at how to deal with them. There is always a risk if certain decisions are not taken now—and when I say now—I mean also in the next 10 years. Otherwise, there may be no more room for any ethical considerations. Then we could have an unmanageable crisis which would no longer afford us the time to consider and reflect. For instance, the Greenhouse effect is one of these very urgent problems. It cannot be tackled in 10 years time. It will be too late. There will be no more chance in about 10 years time to reverse or to stabilize the atmospheric pollution which exists at present. It is our lack of resolve to act conclusively that is, I fear, a very real problem.

Francisco Sagasti: I would like to make two final remarks before I leave. The first one is related to this question of action, power and politics. One of the things that we must be very realistic about concerns the opportunities as well as the limits that exist to influence political decision-making. One of the things that I have realized is that if we want to really do something effective, we have to take the route that Dr. Winegard took. After 20 years of being president of a university, he got into politics. If we really want to move one step beyond and get the attention of the politicians, then we must get involved. In fact, we have a responsibility to do so.

My last comment is that I think that events like this conference are absolutely essential. Having arrived towards the end of the conference and having had only a short time to interact with you, I nonetheless feel that this is a type of event that helps to crystallize the fact that ethical and moral choices and problems are now coming to the forefront of the political arena. Whether you want it or not—or whether you realize it or not—you are part of a phenomenon that is really moving and happening throughout the world. Even your own criticisms about the ethical and non-ethical conduct of this event is in itself a demonstration that those concerns have already begun to move in a forceful way to the front of the political arena.

Speaker: I would like to underline the fact that survival enhancement of the earth's ecosystem has to be the major concern for everyone. The existence of all species depends on the soundness of the world ecosystem, on appropriate technological development and on sustainable population growth. We are on the verge of going over an ecological precipice where vital ecosystems and cycles suddenly and irreversibly break-down. We can no longer do "business as usual." If the environment is to be sustained, everyone must become a dedicated environmental catalyst, at least from an advocacy position. As David Suzuki says, we must question everything we do and possess in regard to its environmental impact. Though we can make changes in our individual lifestyles, this will not be enough to bring about sufficient change. We must focus on institutional change.

It is with the institutions that our efforts as environmental catalysts can best be invested. We must prepare ourselves for institutional conversion to a broader environmental conception and a highly valued environmental ethic.

One can boost one's level of understanding of technology and environment by reading the works on technology of Lewis Mumford and Langdon Winner, and the writings of Bill Duval on deep ecology and those of Mary Butchican on social ecology. We can also seek out the reference books and articles of the Environment Health Association and the research papers of the American Association of Heating and Refrigeration, Air-conditioning Engineers (AAHRAE), which indicate the gross inefficiency of existing environmental health standards. Realize too, that our environmentally unfriendly way of life is sadly being forced on our minds especially by the foreground and background of television, film and other visual media. Writers arguing for the elimination of television such as Jerry Mander and James Cavell in *Subliminal Seduction* give one a better understanding of this anti-environmental value media conditioning process.

With this and other knowledge from one's own sources, one is in a better position to communicate and dialogue with decision-makers in their institutional positions and to influence them towards a more inclusive environmental conception and a more valued environmental ethic.

Speaker: Sometimes people have said that I am a Canadian Indian, or an Indian Canadian. In either case, native peoples are conspicuously absent from this conference.

During a conversation with another native Indian, he narrated a four-line poem which I would like to narrate here. The poem goes something like this:

The white man came to our land with the Bible in his hand.
Now we have the Bible and they have the land.

That pretty well sums up the history of the Americas from the native point of view. The question he asked me afterwards which I pose to you again is what do you think of the squatters? All the people who are squatting on Indian land.

Panel Response: This question is the oldest question in Canadian history since the Europeans arrived. Either we have never answered that question or if we have, we still perpetuate the injustices against aboriginal peoples. Until the squatters resolve the issues of aboriginal injustice through the recognition and honouring of treaties and the settlement of the comprehensive claims which are now being negotiated (and which may go on for another two hundred years), then there really isn't any opportunity for aboriginal peoples in this country to participate in their destiny and ours.

Speaker: What is happening is that nothing is happening. There are simply endless and fruitless debates on whether or not it is a federal or provincial responsibility. That is what I call mystification of the real ethical question by turning it into a so-called neutral technical-legal question. In other words, "the Third World ain't out there, it's right here among us" and it has various names, one of which is privatization.

Speaker: I would just like to make three very short statements. One is that the world must become more religious and ethical. Secondly, there should be a spiritual, ethical propaganda through the media, and thirdly, society must create a climate and a core of ethical conduct. In other words, instead of creating innumerable committees, let's have an ethical court or mechanism to ensure that those who are in positions of decision-making are ethical themselves and remain so.

Sydney Gata: Mr. Chairman, I felt a bit sorry that I did not have a chance to communicate earlier with the representative of the Canadian Government and that I no longer have the opportunity to speak with the representative of the World Bank since both had to leave. My comments would have borne directly on those two individuals.

I am from Zimbabwe where I am the head of the National Hydro Company. I am a representative of one of those sectors that have borrowed millions and millions of dollars from Western institutions and is consequently responsible for what is called the debt crisis in the Third World. As a matter of fact, at a conference in Montreal, this debt was estimated in the order of trillions and the revised statistics showed that about 50 per cent was due to the kind of energy infrastructure projects that I represent. I have lost the opportunity to talk to a representative from the Canadian government and the World Bank but I am still delighted that I can communicate with the Canadian people.

I would like to put across a perspective for you so that you can appreciate what is really happening with these massive loans and mega projects. I think Canadians might be led to feel that they are shouldering the burden of the poor world through development aid. You are not doing that; you are actually shouldering the financial burden of the extensive First World capital projects in the Third World. I know that in my own country, out of over a billion dollars of borrowings, my own organization has made only about 15 million of which less than 2 per cent has gone to the rural areas. Yet the rural areas represent over 80 per cent of our population. I was moved to say this because I think the Minister of Science and Technology intimated that it is the Third World nations themselves who have control of how these monies are distributed and spent. I don't buy that, I'm sorry. It is not the Third World; it is the extensions of an international system of capital in collaboration with Canadian authorities, Swedish authorities and others who determine where these investments are to be made and their decisions don't at all benefit or involve the vast majority of the poor people of this world. I feel extremely strongly about that.

The World Bank representative talked about structural adjustments. In terms of the energy sector, these adjustments actually amount to recreating an environment in which Western technologies can survive. We see it as a strategy that is destined to increase our capacity as a market for these technologies. So really, I feel so sorry when I see the aspirations of Canadians and I see the misery of my brothers. The general public in the West means well but unfortunately, there are governments and their representatives who have goals which are no different from the international capitalist system. This is the sad thing about it all.

Lutz Baehr: I think it is important to reformulate our priorities. The cake will not increase, will not become bigger, but we have to set the right priorities and I hope that this conference will help to reformulate priorities and get a bigger piece of this cake for the sake of those who have do not have the possibility to raise their voice.

The other message is that whatever we say here has also to be applicable to developing countries. So when we speak of development of technologies and so on, please think of ways and means of how we can incorporate them in developing countries. This is very essential.

We speak of empowerment, participation—please let developing countries participate in this process. One final suggestion: I think it would be a wonderful idea to have such a conference organized by the University of Guelph, and also supported by the Canadian government, in a developing country. That would show that there was a political will to view and address all of these ethical issues and considerations in a more urgent light. This would also be a wonderful learning process for all of us.

Henry Wiseman: There have been exciting and creative moments at this conference. When we planned this event, we knew that unless we created a sense of conviction and a dynamic during these four days, all we would be doing would be exchanging words; they would pass through ears and not touch anybody's heart. I never really expected that the intensity and the level of interaction would rise so high and continue so well despite the occasional problem that this creates. I am deeply grateful for how you participated and contributed to this very exciting day. Before I offer any of the other announcements, I would like first to express my gratitude to the personal friends who have worked together so valiantly for a long time in preparing this conference and particularly for the conduct of this day. Thank you.

Alan Thomas

Matching Social Values with Changing Technologies

Individual summaries of collective events, particularly when the event is an intensely experienced conference, can only be unsatisfactory. Offered usually towards the conclusion of the meetings, they invariably miss aspects and qualities of that experience that are of the greatest significance to other participants, especially when it is a large conference, divided for reasons of "democratic" efficiency into many—in this case 15—relatively large groups meeting concurrently. Even with more than usually efficient and inclusive reporting, as was possible in this case, a summarizer inevitably misses the quality and the flavour of the sub-group discussions. It is in the intensity of those sub-discussions that the individual summaries of each participant are formed, and those are the really important ones. It is those private summaries that are most likely to lead to action, once the drama of the conference has ended. With the reader of a conference report, it is the summarizer who has the advantage. Both parties have access to the same documentation, but the summarizer was there, with the great advantage of having experienced the flavour and quality of the "great" conference in its corporate reality. Nevertheless, a summary, something in the manner of the preamble to an international agreement, can only underline, remind, and emphasize. Action, if there is to be any, rests with the individual reader.

The impulse to act lay not far beneath the surface of the entire conference. It was referred to repeatedly in the sub-group discussions, and asserted itself in plenary on at least two occasions. What should we do?—an ethical question; and what can we do?—a technical question, informed the proceedings profoundly. The gulf between the two; how it occurs, and how it manifests itself in our public and private lives, and the consideration of both was important. This was what the conference was about.

Reflection on other recent conferences, such as the "Alternate Economic Summit Conference" held in Toronto, and the apparently spontaneous recourse of its participants to the streets in the manner of the nineteenth century "Chartists," prompts speculation over what would have provoked a comparable outburst on the part of this conference. If such a demonstration had occurred, who would have been the proper target? What signs and placards might have been displayed? Imagination suggests lines of posters saying "Ethics now!" Indeed there was a tinge of the "instant fix" in the discussions. Who would have paid attention? Who should?

The best place to begin, therefore, is with some elaboration of who "we" were; that is, whose attention had already been secured by virtue of attendance. There were approximately 735 persons, 534 male and 201 female in attendance. The preponderance of them stayed the course from Wednesday evening until Sunday afternoon. That in itself represents a considerable achievement, and reflects the significance of the subject. Few conferences these days extend beyond three days; and fewer still over a Saturday evening. Of the total, 665 participants came from 9 provinces; 41 from 21 American states; and 29 from 18 other countries, among them, the Netherlands,

France, the United Kingdom, Trinidad and Tobago, Zimbabwe, Bulgaria, the U.S.S.R., China, and Senegal, to name a few. The complaint that it was not truly an international conference had to be acknowledged, but it was open to the world, and a review of sub-group discussions reveals the very real presence of the Third World at every table. Finally, there were 354 individuals from universities, 103 from secondary schools, a matter of special note; 56 from various levels of government; 43 from private and public industry; 29 from the media, some as reporters, some as participants; 14 from the clergy; 6 from labour organizations. The range of ages was impressive. The younger group, who in this context might properly be designated as "Brundtland's children" was strengthened in numbers by the actions of some imaginative secondary school teachers. Clearly this was an establishment conference, where the presence of sub-components—universities, industry, labour, government; medicine, law, the clergy, education—were critical to the purposes of the undertaking. One is entitled to remark on the absence of the military.

The design of the conference itself demanded and received proper comment. Familiar in its initial emphasis on key-notes and plenaries moving towards increasing use of sub-groups based on specialized interests, the procedures were designed to make the best use of the impressive human resources, and to move towards some increasingly generalized understandings, if not agreements. Obviously, there was high dependence upon sophisticated reporting procedures, including a mid-term newspaper intended to share the specialized discussions.

Most criticism was directed to the use and composition of the sub-groups, which undoubtedly contributed to technical specialization, itself the most frequently identified "villain" in the considerations. The presentation of key-note papers in most of the sub-groups, a true embarrassment of riches, meant that, at their best, each of the workshop groups was a genuine reflection of the conference as a whole. While the representative mix was not true in every case, it was sufficiently present to prompt cross-over discussions. Education talked passionately about the implications of computers; Environment dealt extensively with education; the concern with technical problems of increased "interactivity" prominent in Computers was indirectly reflected by concerns for increased participation by all stakeholders in most of the groups, particularly in Food Systems and Animal Husbandry. The tentative agenda of Computers—integrity, privacy, and access—might easily have served the direction of discussions in most other groups. Nevertheless, the villain did not go away. While technical languages seem to have been less of a barrier than one might have anticipated, distrust of motive and of the inescapable demands of specialized environments—profit-making in industry for example—was articulated, but for many, remained unresolved.

All conferences have their ethical and technical dimensions. This one was no exception. The subject stimulated more than the usual reflection on these issues, and for the most part, though not totally, a reasonable balance was achieved. Because so much of our public business is accomplished by conferences, particularly when the stakes are high, and the specialized expertise is predominant, reflection in this area could be one of the important outcomes.

The initial presentations were largely and usefully an attempt to place participants in some comprehensible common time and space. Taken as a whole, they make stimulating, if disturbing reading. Has humankind faced a comparable situation or situations before? Is the impact of gunpowder, the press, and the compass—those functional symbols of the growth of the West in the beginning of the world's second millennium—to be compared with the impact of the atom, the chip, and the pill on its final years? Or are there no precedents, as at least one speaker insisted? Are we simply on our own, with so little time that previous experience cannot be depended upon? The passion and determination of the environmentalists, not confined to that particular sub-group, with their occasional impatience with "due-process," underlined the significance of these early concerns. The terse, and austere report from the Law workshop formed a quiet counterpoint.

The composition of the conference takes on a new dimension in the light of William McNeill's reference to the "clerisy," and the previous attempts by that body, in previous societies, to assert its power. Without doubt the conference body represented a contemporary "clerisy," and without doubt, it was interested in re-inserting the power of "ethics" into the predominant scientific and technical concerns of contemporary society.

What were the ethical problems? How can one get a grip on them? Are they the same for everyone? Are they specific to the different intellectual and technical domains in which we operate? Lists of problems were presented by different speakers, each one an attempt to locate the discourse, if not to preempt the agenda—a legitimate enterprise. Some were lists of horrors, particularly those concentrating on the environment, a preoccupation that dominated the conference throughout. In contrast to basing the concerns on nightmares, the Computer group, with the help of W.B. Yeats, preferred to start with dreams. But the fears for the environment prevailed, perhaps because they involve all special perspectives in the world and represent the limits of specialization.

Despite that latter claim, a second theme to emerge was whether ethics itself represents a specialized, technical approach in need of new emphasis and support. Galbraith, again indirectly, subscribed to the notion of special expertise by recommending the creation of a kind of super-commission.

In contrast, there was a more pervasive argument, found in all of the groups, that ethics is something else entirely. The most complete expression, perhaps, is to be found in the report of Research Administration workshop—"ethical issues must be integrated in research administration and practice at all levels," like the goods and services tax. There were many references to "new ways of thinking:" "holism," a term that defies precise definition, along with "earth literacy" and the abandonment of the "technological imperative" and its accompanying "technological trance." But there were few, if any, clear examples of what those new ways might be. One exception was the argument for a return to genuine dialogue in teaching, as distinct from the transmission of fact that can be accomplished more efficiently by computers. To the credit of the participants, and perhaps to the conference structure, little time was wasted on the conventional scapegoats of contemporary life: the politicians, the press, and the teachers.

For a brief moment, during one presentation, the participants were reminded of a lost innocence, of some of the satisfactions of the technological trance. What was evoked was the 1950s, and the wonder and optimism associated with the spectacles of successive technological rabbits emerging from scientific hats.

Nevertheless, those same presentations also reminded the participants that their attention to ethical problems seems, and is, somewhat uneven. Why are some areas high on the agenda, and some not? How should we deal with the tempered optimism of Computers and Food Systems in contrast to the nearly unrelieved apprehension and gloom of Environment? Is it possible that there are some areas of ethical concern and technological development that have been, or are being successfully coped with? Are there examples from which, with some patience and deliberation, hope and success can be reasonably drawn? Are the dreams as productive as the nightmares?

What of technology itself? Throughout the major presentations, and more particularly the discussions of the sub-groups, that concern asserts itself. There seems to be general consensus among the participants that technology, like science, is not ethically neutral. Some ethical characteristics inescapably adhere to its presence. But the consequences of that conclusion are not so clear. What are those inescapable ethical consequences? Is there only one ethical position to be identified? Is it possible to have ethical and unethical technologies? Is it simply a matter of better management? It would, of course, be unreasonable to expect such a conference to provide much in the way of satisfying answers to these problems. But is it reasonable to ask if they are the right problems? Are they the subjects of immediate further deliberations? They are very likely the ideas in terms of which the participants will pursue further action. Perhaps, therefore, Galbraith's proposed agency makes more sense. Maybe it can be designed so as to give us some necessary breathing space and so, at future conferences of this kind, it will be clearer where to march and what the placards should say.

The competition for the agenda, a proper competition in this context, included invocations to the "feelings" of the participants. There were frequent invitations to despair. Recitations of environmental destruction, of failed or aborted development programs—many of which were already familiar—provoked the notion that there is no alternative but to apologize. At the very least, there was general recognition that Ben Johnson, a banquet speaker, was not the only person obliged to do so because he got ethical behaviour and technical promise confused.

Yet a reader of the reports of sub-group discussions detects some toughness and resilience. There is no example of a sub-group giving up or dissolving in frustration and despair. Each addressed itself to the difficult task of accurately defining and agreeing upon the problem, and each volunteered possible solutions, for the most part alternative ways in which we now must live. And yet there remains a great deal of reticence, if not dissidence, in advocating specific ethical behaviour. As in other areas of Canadian life, participants were not especially slow to "scorn" some proposed examples of ethical behaviour. It is possible that the reticence and ridicule are part of a more profound diffidence about the "inner-most environment" referred to by King. Perhaps the second agenda item of Computers—privacy—comes to the point, for in addressing ethical questions about the public behaviour of institutions like science, technology, education, government, etc., we are in fact struggling to make public what Canadians at least have been raised to believe are profoundly private matters. The shift of realities from one of those categories to the other, particularly from private to public, is perhaps one of the most fundamental changes contemporary humans have to confront.

A thread that runs throughout the conference itself and the workshop records is that both can be set in a not entirely hostile or even friendless environment. Speaker after speaker referred to other groups, and other occasions, where these concerns are growing in intensity. In other words, there is a constituency, or constituencies, for participants to carry their concerns to, beyond the brief environment of this conference. The "clerisy" is not alone in these preoccupations. In addition it seems, they are comparatively late arrivals, perhaps the last major group. One of the functions of such conferences is often to legitimize and highlight what have been generally unrecognized as marginal concerns among the members of a particular group for some period of time. What we may, in fact, be witnessing in this event is less the beginning of the articulation of a concern, and more the end of the beginning of a world movement that has been underway in a fragmented form for some time.

Linked with the previous emphasis on other sources of interest in ethics and technology is the repeated commitment to increased collaboration. The term "stakeholder" appears repeatedly in the discussions of the sub-groups, along with the need to identify who they are on every occasion. There is some unique experience in Canada, fragile at the moment, but undeniable, with the extension of public consultation. In this case, there is a technology involved, but it is the exercise of will—political will—that makes it significant. Who can forget the pictures of Thomas Berger, Chair of the Royal Commission on the MacKenzie Valley Pipeline, in his small outboard boat, his peaked cap, hurrying across a wilderness lake to a meeting with a small band of Native Canadians, who in the past, would have been sacrificed to the technological imperative? Who can forget his words; "You may not represent the public interest, but it is in the public interest that your opinions be heard." None of us should forget, none of us can afford to.

The recurring message of the conference is unmistakeable. We can no longer afford to do things simply because we have the technical capacity to do them. Other considerations, considerations of living beings have to take precedence. What they should be exactly, how they should be applied, remains unclear, but the basic premise has been established.

It is impossible to conclude these observations without some reflection on the appearance and presentation of Ben Johnson, and his associate, Carol Anne Letheren. In some respects the event, and it was clearly an event, provides a summary in itself, contradictions included. The evocation of the life of the athlete and its context of world sport was compelling. At the same time it is tempting to wish, however wistfully, that the same attention might be paid to young artists, musicians, and others whose dedication and fitness seems no less admirable and important to our well-being. However, more sober thoughts prevail. Is it not precisely the worship, the glorification of technique and technique alone that dominates world athletics? Is it not that obsession that lay at the root of the conflict of ethic and technology? Are there therefore examples of a meaningful response to that conflict, from within athletics, or even on our part, that may serve us as examples of solutions to the problems the conference embodied and confronted?

Since the conference concluded, the world has changed. The political geography of Europe has been dramatically altered. Certainly, the participation of stakeholders has increased everywhere. It may be that with the apparent collapse of these ideologies, there is a real opportunity to depend upon human thought, as Galbraith argued. An example of such thought, indeed, the result of both thought and deliberation, can be found in the following highlights of the conference:

- There is a larger constituency for the conference's concerns than was apparent before it took place. Environmental issues insist that inclusion in that constituency is total and irrevocable. Other voices argue that such inclusion must be the result of an act of will if anything is to be done.

- To be able to bring something about technically is no longer an imperative or even sufficient reason to do so.

- Specialization has been and remains the problem. A common concern for ethics, whatever the specific ethical position, will reduce and temper the effects of specialization.

- Ethical concern is not an additional specialization, but a state of mind that is sharable and discussable.
- The threat of specialized, technical language is not so great as once thought, provided there is a will to understand and to be understood.
- It is apparent that a major problem lies in shifting ethical concerns from the private to the public domain.
- The concern for ethical behaviour in the realm of technological development is world wide.

Dr. Alan Thomas is Professor of Adult Education, Ontario Institute for Studies in Education, Toronto.